SLEEPING DOGS

Quebec and the Stabilization of Canadian
Federalism after 1995

What happened to the Quebec sovereignty movement after 1995? In
Sleeping Dogs, Andrew McDougall reveals how a change in federalist
strategy, combined with an improving political context, helped Canada
stabilize its federal system and bury the "Quebec question" for the foreseeable future.

The book identifies five potential reasons the Quebec sovereignty
movement lost momentum and argues that all contributed to a political environment that benefited federalists. McDougall explores topics of
elite accommodation, generational change, changing identity politics,
economic globalization, and constitutional fatigue. He argues that Canada's federalist political elites have capitalized on these developments to
stabilize the country by dropping the national question – even when they
might still hold very different visions of the Constitution. Building on
"constitutional abeyance" theory, the author conceives of this strategic
change as the restoration of a constitutional abeyance among federalist
actors. Considering recent history in light of subsequent developments,
Sleeping Dogs is a timely and important attempt to understand the evolving situation in Quebec and Canadian federalism.

(Political Development: Comparative Perspectives)

ANDREW McDOUGALL is an assistant professor of Canadian politics at
the University of Toronto Scarborough.

Political Development: Comparative Perspectives

Editors: JACK LUCAS (University of Calgary) and
ROBERT C. VIPOND (University of Toronto)

Political Development: Comparative Perspectives publishes books that explore political development with a comparative lens, with a particular focus on studies of Canadian, American, or British political development. Books in this series use historical data and narratives to explain long-term patterns of institutional change, public policy, social movement politics, elections and party systems, and other key aspects of political authority and state power. They employ cross-country comparison, within-country comparison, or single-case analysis to illuminate important debates in comparative political science and history.

Editorial Advisory Board

Books Published in This Series

Sleeping Dogs

Quebec and the Stabilization of Canadian Federalism after 1995

ANDREW McDOUGALL

UNIVERSITY OF TORONTO PRESS
Toronto Buffalo London

ISBN 978-1-4875-0298-0 (cloth)   ISBN 978-1-4875-1638-3 (EPUB)
ISBN 978-1-4875-2221-6 (paper)   ISBN 978-1-4875-1637-6 (PDF)

Political Development: Comparative Perspectives

Library and Archives Canada Cataloguing in Publication

Title: Sleeping dogs : Quebec and the stabilization of Canadian federalism
    after 1995 / Andrew McDougall.
Names: McDougall, Andrew W., author.
Series: Political development: comparative perspectives.
Description: Series statement: Political development: comparative perspectives |
    Includes bibliographical references and index.
Identifiers: Canadiana (print) 20230208509 | Canadiana (ebook) 20230208541 |
    ISBN 9781487502980 (cloth) | ISBN 9781487522216 (paper) |
    ISBN 9781487516383 (EPUB) | ISBN 9781487516376 (PDF)
Subjects: LCSH: Federal government – Québec (Province) | LCSH: Federal government –
    Canada. | LCSH: Québec (Province) – History – Autonomy and independence
    movements.
Classification: LCC JL246.S8 M33 2023 | DDC 320.971 – dc23

Cover design and photo composite: Matthew Jubb, Em Dash Design; (scale) optimarc/
Shutterstock.com

We wish to acknowledge the land on which the University of Toronto Press
operates. This land is the traditional territory of the Wendat, the Anishnaabeg, the
Haudenosaunee, the Métis, and the Mississaugas of the Credit First Nation.

This project was carried out thanks to the financial support received from the
Government of Quebec, under the financial Research Support Program in matters of
Québec Studies.

This book has been published with the help of a grant from the Federation for the
Humanities and Social Sciences, through the Awards to Scholarly Publications Program,
using funds provided by the Social Sciences and Humanities Research Council of Canada.

University of Toronto Press acknowledges the financial support of the Government of
Canada, the Canada Council for the Arts, and the Ontario Arts Council, an agency of
the Government of Ontario, for its publishing activities.

Canada Council   Conseil des Arts
for the Arts   du Canada

ONTARIO ARTS COUNCIL
CONSEIL DES ARTS DE L'ONTARIO
an Ontario government agency
un organisme du gouvernement de l'Ontario

Funded by the   Financé par le
Government   gouvernement
of Canada   du Canada

Canada

Secrétariat aux
relations canadiennes
Québec

Contents

Acknowledgments

No sole-authored book is ever really written alone, and there are too many people to thank for their help in bringing this project to the finish line. Regardless, an imperfect count has to start with my doctoral committee, who oversaw my project to a successful end and upon which this book is based. Grace Skogstad remains the best supervisor and professional mentor anyone could have, who along with David Cameron, Graham White, Robert Schertzer, and my external committee member Michael Keating gave me the best education in political science anyone could receive. I would also like to thank all the people who agreed to be interviewed for the book and who otherwise assisted with the research, whether anonymously or for the record. I very much appreciate your help.

While this research began coming together as a book, a new and very different process began, as anyone who has undertaken that challenge will understand. In addition to the ongoing support of Grace, Robert, David, and Graham, I want to thank Professor Robert Vipond in particular for taking an interest in this book and bringing the project to the next level. As someone who understands the publication process nose to tail, Rob was instrumental at every step in getting the project into a publishable format. This included suggesting and organizing a book workshop, helping me refine my thinking on several substantive points related to Canadian federalism and politics, and offering advice on timelines and funding. He also listened to my endless complaining throughout the writing process when he really had better things to do, and he was very important in helping me avoid the various pitfalls that can trap a scholarly work. Despite the crushing schedule he had as an interim chair, he really went above and beyond. While my committee members have been doing this for quite some time and very much continue to do so, it was nice of Rob to take some of the burden.

I also want to extend my sincere thanks to Éric Montpetit of the Université de Montréal and Daniel Salée of Concordia University, whose attendance and input at my book workshop fundamentally affected my thinking about Quebec. As a non-Quebecer who thinks and writes a lot about Quebec, I rely deeply on my Quebec colleagues to offer perspective and reflections on my work and to tell me when I am off base. Both Éric and Daniel gave critical, honest, and important feedback on my ideas, and the final manuscript is much stronger for it. I also thank François Rocher of the University of Ottawa for sharing relevant work and experience on contemporary Quebec nationalism. In the same vein, I thank my pals from graduate school Alexandre Paquin-Pelletier (now at Université Laval), Gabriel Arsenault (now at Université de Moncton), and P.O. Bonin (currently at Employment and Social Development Canada) for always listening to my thoughts and telling me exactly where they thought I was wrong about Quebec. And while I doubt he remembers, I want to thank the kindness and generosity of Alain-G. Gagnon for having me at Université du Québec à Montréal as a graduate student years ago (helpfully organized through Alex Pelletier), where I could present these ideas at an early stage to a group of his students. The feedback was enormously helpful, and it is surprising the impact that such invitations and experiences can have.

I want to thank the many people in the Department of Political Science at the University of Toronto who have helped me along the way, both during and after my doctorate. In particular I thank Christopher Cochrane, Ran Hirschl, Peggy Kohn, Elizabeth Acorn, Stefan Renckens, Peter Loewen, Michael Donnelly, Andrea Olive, Alison Smith, Randy Besco, Linda White, Phil Triadafilopoulos, Torrey Shanks, Filiz Kahraman, Erin Tolley (now at Carleton University), Julie Moreau, Connor Ewing, Heather Millar (now at the University of New Brunswick), Evan Rosevear (currently at Hong Kong University), Marion Lawrence (currently with the Canadian Forces College), Matt Wilder (now at Employment and Social Development Canada), Adrienne Davidson (now at McMaster University), Matt Lesch (currently with the University of York), Jessica Soedirgo (now at the University of Amsterdam), Renan Levine, Aisha Ahmad, and Matt Hoffman. I also thank the late Richard Simeon, whose work continues to have an impact on me.

I would like to thank my endlessly helpful editor, Daniel Quinlan at the University of Toronto Press, who genuinely was everything that a new book author could want in an editor: kind, available, understanding, and always encouraging. Special thanks go as well to Angela Wingfield and Janice Evans at UTP, whose help during the production phase was extraordinary. I also thank the anonymous reviewers of the manuscript who really did far more than I could ever ask when reviewing my manuscript multiple times, and it was improved enormously as a result. Marcus Closen also played a key role as my research assistant.

This project was carried out thanks to the financial support received from the Government of Quebec, under the Research Support Program in matters of Québec Studies. I am also grateful for the generous support of the Connaught Fund's New Researcher Award program, the Awards to Scholarly Publications Program (ASPP), and the financial support of the Department of Political Science at the University of Toronto, and of the University of Toronto Scarborough.

On a personal note, I thank my family – my parents, Rowena and John McDougall; my sister, Kelly; my brother, David; his wife, Sundeep; and my nephew Wolf. On the other side of the family, I thank Tom and Shirley McKay; my brother and sister-in-law, Arran and Olga; and my nephew Anton. Special thanks go to my non-academic friends Abouzar Nasirzadeh, Graham F. Scott, Carol Kim, Mike Clark, Adam Wakefield, Devin Glowinski, and Kfir Gluzberg.

Finally, above all others, I thank my partner, Jonathan McKay, for everything.

SLEEPING DOGS

Quebec and the Stabilization of Canadian
Federalism after 1995

1 Introduction

On the night of the Quebec sovereignty referendum in 1995, after coming within a whisker of victory, former Parti Québécois (PQ) premier of Quebec Jacques Parizeau told a large crowd of supporters that they would not have to wait another fifteen years for another chance to vote for independence. In light of the very close result, he assured them their next chance was only just around the corner and they would very soon have another opportunity to take Quebec out of Canada. Now, almost thirty years later, that "next chance" has yet to come and it is nowhere in sight. The Quebec sovereignty movement has found itself increasingly leaderless and rudderless and searching for a new basis to justify its mission. What happened between 1995 and now? That question is the central puzzle of this book.

The answer is twofold. The first involves a change in federalist strategy: federalist Canadians and Quebecers chose a course of action that became an imperative after 1995 but would have been unthinkable in the middle of the twentieth century – drop the subject. They did not solve the "Quebec question," and federalists continue to hold deeply conflicted views on what the country is really about. Even to this day Quebec has never "signed" the constitutional package of 1982.[1] But, recognizing that any attempt to resolve the problem of Quebec's place in Canada would lead to almost certain disaster, federalists of every stripe decided to leave the question alone. They successfully depoliticized the subject and changed the political agenda to other, less existential topics.

That alone was not enough, however. Fortuitous political, social, and cultural currents that changed in Canada enabled them to pick this course of action, and this is the other side of the story. Five different explanations have been proposed for why the momentum went out of the sovereignty movement in Quebec, which gave federalists their chance to change the subject. This book dedicates a chapter to each one: constitutional fatigue, non-constitutional accommodation for Quebec, Quebec's changing identity politics, generational change, and finally economic globalization. What is important to understand at the outset is that there is no one explanation. This phenomenon is multicausal. Taken together, they help us understand better the evolving situation in Quebec and Canadian federalism. Conceptually, the book argues that the country's federalist political elites have capitalized on these developments to stabilize the country by simply dropping the national question – even when they might still hold very different visions of the Constitution. Alongside these greater forces, much of the momentum that the secessionist movement had in the late twentieth century has not carried over into the twenty-first.

In focusing on the conduct of elites managing the country, alongside these otherwise fortuitous political currents, the book contributes the constitutional theory of abeyances. This concept refers to situations in which political leaders refuse to engage in political conflicts that are so existential that, once politicized, can only be resolved with one of those visions "losing" to the other in a constitutional crisis (Foley 2013; Thomas 1997; Cameron 2015; see also McRoberts 1991; Webber 2021 for a similar argument). To that extent, this book connects the abeyance literature to that of agenda-setting – federalists have taken advantage of improving political conditions to focus on other things as much as they can. Sovereigntists who support Quebec independence have struggled to justify their project and to generate the political support they need to elect parties like the PQ and to find the "winning conditions" required to hold and win a vote on independence. Federalists have done nothing to upset the status quo, refusing to be drawn into significant constitutional fights with Quebec or to do anything that might stir up a sense of outrage against the rest of the country. Recognizing the morass that constitutional politics have been over the course of Canada's history, federalists, whether they be from Quebec or the rest of Canada, have refused to engage. The decision to play up or play down a political issue rests in particular with political leaders; they are policy entrepreneurs who can decide what they want their governments to focus on (see Kingdon 1984). Over the past twenty-five years, no Canadian prime minister, and no Quebec premier who was not otherwise leading a PQ government, has suggested any interest in reopening the national question. Leaders like Jean Chrétien, Paul Martin, Stephen Harper, and Justin Trudeau have been loath to engage in constitutional fights with Quebec. But this has been matched by a similar reluctance on the part of Quebec premiers Jean Charest, Phillipe Couillard, or François Legault. The attitude of these leaders stands in contrast to the priority that was given to the Constitution by an earlier generation of leaders like Brian Mulroney, Quebec premier Robert Bourassa, and above all Pierre Trudeau, who felt there was an urgency to resolve constitutional disputes in order to preserve national unity.

The conflict at the root of the Quebec-Canada debate will be familiar to students of Canadian politics as the so-called contract-compact debate between Quebec and Canada. In Quebec, federalists and sovereigntists alike tend see the country as a union of peoples, equal in status and powers, which has important implications for the powers that the province thinks it should have under the Constitution. The rest of the country generally does not accept this argument, viewing Canada as closer to a contract of provinces, of which all are equal in status and powers. The failure to reconcile these positions has driven the national unity crises from the patriation debate in 1980 through to the Meech Lake and the Charlottetown Accords, as well as the two referendums on sovereignty association in 1980 and 1995.[2]

No longer. While the secessionist leaders contend with the decline of their movement, federalists, even those who disagree, have tried to move on and avoid becoming drawn into yet another debate over Quebec's place in the country. This unwillingness can be seen, for example, in the shared reluctance of the Quebec Liberal Party (QLP) and the federal Conservative Party to be pulled into a discussion about constitutional issues. The QLP, which views Canada as a compact of nations, has a very different view of Quebec's place in the federation than does the federal Conservative Party, which historically has adhered to a more contractual view of provincial equality since it combined with the Canadian Alliance in 2003. Neither has expressed as much interest in squarely tackling the subject over the last two and a half decades as they did in the last two decades of the twentieth century. In doing so, they show that the proverbial genie *can* be put back in the bottle, at least for now. To put it differently, the national question is in abeyance until something, or someone, upsets the status quo.

Decline of the Sovereignty Movement

Five explanations for the decline of the sovereignty issue in Quebec are commonly cited. Each has arguably helped those national and provincial political leaders who are interested in Canadian unity to adopt the abeyance-restoring strategy:

- *Constitutional fatigue.* This is perhaps the least coherent argument and may be the one most in need of study. The argument is that people grew exhausted of the debate and simply moved away from it. If so, why is everyone in Quebec still so tired almost thirty years after the referendum? Nonetheless, it gave space to federalist elites to change the topic to other subjects.
- *Non-constitutional renewal.* This argument attributes the decline in interest around solving the national question in Quebec to the growth of Quebecers' "institutional security" within Canada; essentially, the problems that confronted Quebecers prior to the Quiet Revolution have now been addressed and hence removed any need for Quebec to pursue independence. A subset of this claim is that the "open federalism" practised by the federal Conservatives since 2006 has helped them keep a lid on the sovereigntist political project by respecting the traditional division of power. This might also help explain why the supporters of the sovereignty project have started to go so grey: fewer people remember a time when there were legitimate reasons to vote yes.
- *Identity politics.* Here, the argument is that after 1995, Quebecers entered an inward-looking period in which there was a loss of consensus on who counted as a Quebecer and what sort of accommodations could be considered reasonable for new immigrants and outsiders.[3] This could have resulted from a weakening of secessionist support, which gave way to other issues, or from the independent growth in interest around minority accommodation. This new focus on accommodation resulted in a delegitimizing of the sovereignty movement, at least partially, as Quebecers embraced a more tailored view of citizenship that called into question the extent to which a Quebec homeland was really needed. Whether or not the identity of ordinary Quebecers really changed is an open question, but, without doubt, political elites turned their attention to this discussion at the expense of pushing for constitutional change. The inward turn to focus on accommodations effectively left the rest of the country off the hook for solving the national question, and Canada has refused to be drawn into an internal Quebec matter. There has been no time, as a result, to have a fight about federalism.
- *Generational change.* The argument here is that the sovereignty movement was really the project of a single generation, and succeeding generations are less engaged with the project than their parents were. This argument is particularly associated with Vincent Lemieux and his work on generational parties (see, e.g.,

Lemieux 2011, 1986). Whether or not the young are really more federalist, or they just have different priorities, is an open debate. Perhaps if young people were given a chance to vote in a referendum on sovereignty, they would vote yes. Nonetheless, there seems to be a lack of interest among young people to push for that chance, and this has assisted federalist elites to focus on non-constitutional issues.

- *Economic globalization*. Writ large, the argument is that Quebecers have lost interest in the narrow aims of the national project and have become more involved with global questions regarding the economy, the environment, education, social justice, and the rise of neoliberalism. The relationship between globalization and nationalism is not clear, and the story has played out differently in different countries. Consistent with recent research, however, chapter 7 argues that globalization need not be "good" or "bad" for nationalists; what often matters more is how effectively nationalist leaders take advantage of the opportunities it offers them to advance their project. In the case of Canada, the chapter will show that federalists have simply been more effective in arguing that economically Quebec is better inside than outside of the country of Canada.

The constitutional-fatigue argument has been among the most popular of the explanations offered. It was an easy argument for the federal Liberals to make after they took power in 1993. Roger Gibbins wrote at the time that "to the extent that a country had 'burnt out,' Canada had" (1999, 273). To be fair, there never was any evidence that the Constitution was a priority for the Liberals when they came into power, and when he was running for office, Jean Chrétien had made much of the new priorities with the famous slogan of "Jobs, Jobs, Jobs" to capture the mood of the country. Certainly after the near-death experience in 1995, there were those who could justifiably point out that there was a legitimate weariness of the crisis, and with Quebec itself, in the rest of the country (e.g., Mahler 1995, 465). The idea of a malaise in Quebec is not new; the idea has been around since at least the 1960s (e.g., Aquin 1962). Still, it remains an important part of modern discussions about Quebec's identity (J. Pelletier 2007, 49; Jacques 2008; Laforest 2010, 11; Robitaille 2014). In the world of practical politics, this sentiment is perhaps best phrased by Stephen Harper's insistence on avoiding the "*vieilles chicanes*" of the constitutional era, instead suggesting, perhaps with reason, that the public has moved on to other issues. While this made sense in the 1990s, why the fatigue has persisted is still very much an open question.

To the second explanation, there are those who feel that sufficient progress has now been made by way of non-constitutional accommodations in the Canadian federation to render the sovereignty movement a more or less out-of-date project. Indeed, of the reforms that the PQ and the Quebec Liberals introduced in the 1970s *inside* Quebec, those on language, culture, and the economy would be the most important, far more than accommodations to Canadian federalism generally. But the importance of institutional factors, and the role they play in reassuring minorities in the Western context, has been stressed by a number of scholars who study secessionism (e.g., S. Dion 1996; Kelemen 2004; Sorens 2012). There has been work connecting the "open federalism" approach of the Harper government to that of the government of Jean Chrétien; Éric Montpetit (2008) is perhaps the best known among these authors. There are many, however, who feel that the reforms undertaken over time have had an important effect in diminishing support for sovereignty (Guindon 1978; Pratte 2008). In his recent work André Lecours has drawn a distinction between dynamic and static autonomy in political systems and has shown that nationalist movements that are more constrained by static arrangements are more likely to turn secessionist, while those under a more dynamic framework will often remain more autonomist in outlook. Quebec, he argues, has become more autonomist over time given the flexibility of the Canadian system and the level of decentralization (Lecours 2021, 173). This flexibility of the system has been cited as a driver of non-constitutional change in other contexts as well. Martin Papillon (2012) has cited a similar dynamic when examining the evolution of Indigenous-settler relations over time.

As part of the institutional argument, some argue that the decline in interest around the national question in Quebec is connected to the refusal of the premiers and prime ministers to engage with constitutional grievances, for example, which can enflame the politics. The role that grievances have played in supporting the sovereignty movement is something that has been long recognized by those studying Quebec (Pinard and Hamilton 1986; Mendelsohn 2003, 512). Secessionist support may have been sapped by the style of government that Stephen Harper brought in with his concept of open federalism. His willingness to recognize Quebec as a nation and give it additional latitude on the international scene, and his refusal to meddle in provincial jurisdictions, are among the features of this approach. Critically, he avoided meeting with the premiers as much as he could. But, importantly, while making these small concessions, he never repudiated his own view of the country as one that is better understood as a national "contract," a point that was important for his supporters. His style reflects a more classical conception of federalism, one also demonstrated by Harper's willingness to work to address the fiscal imbalance and by his refusal to be drawn into interprovincial fighting (Fox 2007, 45; Norquay 2012, 46–7; Harmes 2007, 418–22). His successor, Justin Trudeau, has broadly copied this approach with success, although he has never had to face a PQ government in Quebec City.

Of the work that has been done on the federal tactics and strategy used in managing the unity question, the material tends to be event specific and with little sense of the overall historic arc. The only serious exception to this is Russell's *Constitutional Odyssey*, an account that starts with 1867 and, in its third edition, ends in 2004. In general, the questions posed are more like, What really happened at Meech Lake? or, How could Canada almost lose the 1995 referendum? (e.g., Monahan 1991; McRoberts and Monahan 1993; Argyle 2004). Within these pieces the narrative tends to resemble that of a boxing match, focusing on who won a particular "round" or who did what to whom. Much is made of the emotions and betrayals of different people or the competing versions of events. Little attempt has been made to unify and explain the commonalties of tactics across governments. Furthermore, the assessment of tactics is usually bound up with certain individuals and their judgments, like the debate over the possible duplicity of Pierre Trudeau (Laforest 1995). This is important because it touches on a key tension that rests in the study of federalism: whether federalism is best studied as a synthetic, elite-driven response to the problem of governing a divided society or whether it must be seen as a product of the underlying populations within it, as a way of maintaining community distinctions within a greater whole. The first tradition has been associated in particular with the work of K.C. Wheare, and the latter with that of William S. Livingstone (Smith 2010, 4).

The latter line of thought has been revitalized by new-institutionalist or neo-structuralists such as Jan Erk and Jörg Broschek, both of whom look at how the social context governs and limits what elites can do (e.g., Erk 2008; Broschek 2014). Recent years have also seen explosive growth in the study of how multinational and "plurinational" states accommodate subnational groups through recognizing different concepts of justice and identity – especially groups like the Groupe de recherche sur les sociétés plurinationales (e.g., A.-G. Gagnon and Tully 2001; Rocher, Gagnon, and Guibernau 2003; A.-G. Gagnon 2010, 2014, 2021). An examination of why politicians push into abeyances reveals that changes in the underlying society have an impact on the types of reforms that are possible or politically desirable. Work by Erk, Broschek, Gagnon, Tully, and others helps explain the motivations of constitutional reform efforts. The debate over whether federalism is studied best as reflective of a protean underlying social context or through the top-down design and shifting ambitions of political leaders will not be resolved here, but both lines of work can be drawn upon to explain what is and is not possible when it comes to pushing into abeyances. Depending on the issue, each factor will have a role to play. Suffice it to say, however, that actor agency will always be constrained and shaped by the social context in which both they and their political institutions are embedded.

Looking at the more limited scope of the formal political arena, one can see that significant work has been done on executive federalism (the process through which federal-provincial issues are negotiated through their respective executive branches) and its institutions. The massive output of the Institute of Intergovernmental Relations at Queen's University alone leaps to mind. However, while there have been boatloads written on executive federalism, much of it is from the perspective of its ongoing activities and output and of the potential opportunities for intergovernmental relations (IGR) to create better national policies (e.g., Bakvis and Skogstad 2012; Inwood, Johns, and O'Reilly 2011). Most are quite forgiving of the system, treating it as an inevitable reality whose shortcomings must be acknowledged but indulged. A leading exception is Donald Smiley, who warned in a 1979 article that executive federalism can serve to generate intergovernmental conflicts with little meaning for those not actually involved (Smiley 1979). Picking up from Alan Cairns (1977), Smiley worried about the growth of provincial governments and the implications for intergovernmental conflict. Even so, the creation of instability is only one of the six charges he raises against the system, and he does not anticipate that it could be used strategically for this purpose. Along with Smiley, the work of J. Stefan Dupré, as someone who wrote about the problems surrounding the system's workability, is also widely cited. Dupré was doubtful of the potential of executive federalism to resolve constitutional questions, seeing it as unlikely to succeed given the emotions, personalities, and scope of the issues (1988, 247–8). R. Kent Weaver thought that executive federalism certainly had the potential for destabilizing effects, although he still counted it as one of the more important institutions for reconciling conflict in Canada (1992, 48–50). The ability of these conflicts to inflame sovereigntist sentiment has also been discussed

(R. Pelletier 1998; Howse 1998), but the role of these structures in the contemporary ebb of the sovereigntist cause has not been looked at seriously (with É. Montpetit 2008 as a possible exception). And much of this work is old, predating even the first referendum, in Smiley's case.

The next two explanations, generational change and the evolving debate on Quebec's identity, share a singular focus on the social forces acting inside Quebec. The extent to which these forces are actually changing political conditions in Quebec is widely debated, of course, but federalist elites have done their best to leverage these forces, real or imagined, to move the subject away from the Constitution. The former explanation on generational change has a very long vintage in Quebec, and given the age of the PQ membership and the recent divisions that the party has faced over age, it is an explanation to which people commonly turn. The quest for independence was always driven by those who came of age in the Quiet Revolution, the moment when Quebec truly developed its modern political identity. As that group has aged, it has contributed to the latter explanation, that perhaps Quebec nationalism no longer needs independence to fulfil itself. But that is only part of the story, as many currents combine to contribute to a wide literature on Quebec identity and how it has evolved over the years away from constitutional questions. Indeed, few issues have as overtly framed the political discourse in Quebec in recent years as who "counts" in Quebec society (e.g., Turgeon 2014; Rocher 2023). It is an open question whether the focus on identity reflects real change among ordinary Quebecers, but it has become a real focus among the political elites and party leaders. The focus on this issue has overshadowed the debate over federalism, as Quebec has taken a fundamentally inward turn. Spurred on by incidents such as Jacques Parizeau's blaming of ethnic minorities for the 1995 referendum defeat, and the Hérouxville debacle, much of the past two decades in Quebec have been spent trying to nail down who is really a Quebecer and how to accommodate newcomers.[4] The clearest expression of this endeavour was probably the Bouchard-Taylor Commission, with its work on "interculturalism" and reasonable accommodation. The commission's recommendations reflected an urge on the part of many Quebecers to adopt a more cosmopolitan view of their community without losing their cultural distinctiveness. Arguably, this process has not been kind to the sovereignty movement because to a large extent any nationalistic project depends on a narrower conception of membership for the project to make sense:

> Therein lies the crux of the problem for sovereigntists. The unity of the political subject and the paradigm of citizenship and belonging that it entails are fast becoming targets of reprobation in modern-day politics. Quebec sovereigntists are operating on the basis of a universalist, consensus-driven, Enlightenment discourse at a time when this kind of political narrative, the institutional arrangements it favours and the social hierarchies it justifies are facing enormous resistance throughout the western world. Quebec sovereignty is being challenged not simply because it implies the dismantling of the Canadian state, an unacceptable option for many obviously, but also because insofar as it rests on the fundamental will to create an all-inclusive, universalistic and rationalist civic space, its conceptual underpinnings are under siege. (Salée 2001, 173)

The challenge posed to sovereigntists of creating an inclusive and universalistic civic space has not gone unnoticed by sovereigntist thinkers themselves. The philosopher Serge Cantin, for example, has decried this trend as contributing to a slow loss of focus on the compelling, underlying reasons behind national liberation, an erosion of the dream of an independent Quebec (2005, 60). More recently, Mathieu Bock-Côté attributes the decline in the sovereignty movement to the abandonment of traditional nationalist ideals (2007, 2012). Although he is a committed sovereigntist, both his books are premised on the claim that the nationalist movement has more or less run its course and will not regain momentum until it has re-embraced a more nationalist dialogue. Bock-Côté argues that there is nothing fundamentally racist or intolerant about the need for the people of Quebec to maintain their own cultural identity. Quebec can be open and accommodating while maintaining a strong stance in favour of secularism, the defence of the French language, and the requirement that newcomers accept the limits of Quebec culture. He argues that the sovereignty movement will remain stuck until it re-embraces a clearer form of nationalism, which is needed to both ground it and give it direction.

The final argument, economic globalization, was among one of the first to appear and is tied to both economic and ideological changes that have occurred in the province in recent years. Unlike the prior two arguments, however, it also looks at forces outside of the province as forces for change. Here again, modern literature on nationalism suggests that globalization does not necessarily help or hurt the nation state, but it creates conditions that can be leveraged by political leaders to pursue their particular objectives (e.g., Kaldor 2004;

Hutchinson 2004; Mann 2012). Federalists have been more successful in using globalization to change the subject from federalism to social and economic issues in Canada. The Quebec left, in particular, is described as having become increasingly interested in questions surrounding education, global inequality, and the environment. Daniel Salée made this argument as early as 2001, pointing to the intense opposition in Quebec to the Multilateral Agreement on Investment, and the protests surrounding the Summit of the Americas in Quebec City, as examples of the shifted discourse. He argues that people are transcending the national debate and becoming more engaged in contesting global economic and political structures in which Canada is largely irrelevant (2001, 185). Pascale Dufour echoes this theme and has argued that the commitment of the PQ to free trade has pulled it away from its traditional supporters in the years since the 1995 referendum. This has opened up globalization as a "political space" on which traditional sovereigntist actors have now focused their attention, apart from the national question (Dufour 2007, 145). "Sovereignty is no longer a 'hot' subject, even for groups who were very engaged in the debate in 1995. Today, they are reasoning in terms of social justice, redistribution of wealth, and for some, radical political change. The development of globalization as a political space in Quebec has influenced the reappearance of the division between left and right and the delegitimization (at least partially) of the federalist/ sovereigntist debate" (Dufour 2007, 145).

This line of thinking would seem to ring true, particularly in relation to the more recent emergence of the socialist Québec solidaire in 2006 and the student strikes that rocked the province in the spring of 2012. In this context, Canada is a bit player, neither really loved nor hated, but seen more as an anodyne bystander, given the scope of some of these issues. The argument that globalization is damaging to the sovereigntist cause is not uncontroversial, however. Daniel Béland and André Lecours have written extensively about the supposed death of substate nationalism over the years and its subsequent rebirth, and the importance of social policy in constructing the modern national identity (2008).

Furthermore, there are those who feel that globalization is also a powerful check on sovereignty for those on the political *right* (although they tend to be more federalist anyway). This side of the debate was also summarized by Daniel Salée, who argued that once francophone Quebecers controlled the economy, politically and for economic and financial reasons they began looking outside of the province, and neither the destruction of the Canadian state nor a narrow conception of Quebec citizenship served those purposes (2001, 169). A similar argument was advanced in the forthrightly titled article "Why Is Quebec Separatism Off the Agenda? Reducing National Unity Crisis in the Neoliberal Era" (Changfoot and Cullen 2011). In it, authors Nadine Changfoot and Blair Cullen argue that neoliberal ideologies have increasingly formed the basis for intergovernmental cooperation with Ottawa. This neoliberalism has created just enough asymmetry in Canada to allow the sidelining of the sovereignty movement, as the governments of Quebec and Canada join in a common commitment to pursue economic well-being based on common economic assumptions.

The argument that globalization has eroded the sovereignty movement is interesting, and convincing in many ways, but there is nothing guaranteeing that globalization would have such an effect on Quebec sovereignty. Other subnational regions have seen a rise in separatism over the same post-1995 period (Scotland, Catalonia, and Flanders, for example; see Lecours 2021 for an important work on how secessionism can vary in time and space). Indeed, even if Quebec were increasingly economically and politically integrated with its neighbours, this does not necessarily mean that a decline in nationalism would be expected. This point was made in the aftermath of the 1995 referendum by Michael Keating, who wrote in *Nations Against the State: The New Politics of Nationalism in Quebec, Catalonia and Scotland*: "In many ways, Quebec is thus becoming like the rest of North America. But this has not stilled nationalism. Quite the contrary. As a global society, it does not need to justify nationalism by pointing out differences with the wider society. The reference point for values becomes internalized and the society provides its own legitimacy. This is consistent with de Tocqueville's paradoxical finding that nationalism can become stronger even as cultural distinctiveness diminishes" (1996, 106–7). Furthermore, there is something unconvincing about the argument that Quebec really has taken a neoliberal turn, even if several prominent Quebec thinkers (e.g., *les lucides*) have urged it to do so. The Quebec welfare state has not seriously diminished in size and remains an aberration when compared to the rest of the Canadian federation (Marotte 2013). If neoliberalism is the explanation, it is an incomplete one.[5]

Given the competing explanations that exist for the decline of the sovereignty movement, it is important to recognize that many forces are at play. Ultimately this is a question of causation, something that is extremely hard to grapple with in the social sciences. All of these explanations have at least some level of truth to them. People in Quebec *were* tired of the debate after the referendum in 1995 and had little appetite to have another referendum. Quebec is a more open economy than it was before and is more exposed to the effects of globalization. It has gone on an inward-looking journey in recent years to define better who is a Quebecer and how to reconcile minorities within its society. But are these complete explanations? Do they matter for the sovereignty movement?

Each of the mentioned developments likely assisted the federal government, to some extent, in accomplishing its goals, as they did the QLP. The identity debate proved highly fractious for the PQ, for example, and probably gave the federal government some traction among cultural and linguistic minorities in Quebec. Globalization may have challenged conventional understandings of the nation state. Obviously, institutional reforms that reinforced French Canada would have counted in federalism's favour, and reluctance in the aftermath of 1995 to return immediately to the debate clearly gave Ottawa some breathing room. This has to be recognized. It is clearly important to examine the different explanations, even if it is hard to pin down which factor is doing what.

Outside of the natural evolution of Quebec's political society, however, it would be wrong not to acknowledge that federalists learned a great deal over the last several decades about the inflammatory nature of constitutional questions in Canada, and that those experiences would affect how they approached the national question in Quebec. Those experiences would shape their political strategies and the way in which they addressed constitutional questions after 1995. Most critically, they have tried to avoid talking about it at all.

Quebec and the Theory of Abeyances

This book argues that the end result of these forces has been to create the conditions under which the national question can be set aside without actually being resolved. Put differently, what happens when two sides realize they are never going to agree, or agree to disagree, or even agree to drop the subject? In Canada's case the answer is simple: you simply refuse to engage with the question further, and it becomes a political taboo. That is the current attitude towards the national question, and towards the Constitution in Canada generally, among the political class today.

This change in behaviour also needs to be accounted for theoretically. At root there are two clashing visions of Canada that history has shown to be flatly in conflict, and yet there is little appetite to engage with the matter. In this regard Canada is unusual by comparison to other countries that are struggling with disaffected national minorities. No adequate solution has ever been found, and the level of support for sovereignty among the Quebec public has not disappeared: around 40 per cent of people still say that they would vote yes to separation in the event of another referendum. That leaves the obvious puzzle: why has the politics of crisis disappeared, even when a significant level of support for separation remains?

This book accounts for the answer by developing the idea of a constitutional abeyance. In brief, while the issue is unresolved, presently there is a refusal to deal with the question at the elite level among federalists; it has become a taboo subject. This explanation is separate from the previously mentioned arguments that attempt to explain the decline in the sovereignty movement. I do not attempt to account for the decline of the sovereignty movement per se, in the sense that it is a dependent variable. That is a causal question requiring far more study than a single book can provide. Rather, this is a study of elite behaviour and what is possible under the improving political conditions faced by the Canadian and Quebec political elites. Once again, it explains the continuing stability among *federalists* who disagree, and their decision to deprioritize the Constitution. The biggest fights over the last fifty years have often been not between the "rest of Canada" and Quebec, but among people who want to remain a part of Canada and have competing views of what the country should be. Faced with a lack of solutions, the disagreement would appear to have been simply set aside.

Chapter 2 is devoted to exploring why this is so. Fundamentally, the choice was driven by electoral considerations of federalist parties, and their individual leaders, to refuse to discuss the Constitution any longer. There might have been some public interest in having additional constitutional talks in the aftermath of 1995, especially in Quebec, but this interest was nowhere near high enough to convince political leaders to take the risk of reopening the Constitution. An abeyance is therefore related to the concept of agenda setting: federalists did not want to make the question of Quebec's place in Canada a political priority. After the end of the mega-constitutional era, and the near-death experience of the 1995 referendum, there was no appetite to rock the boat among the federalist base, and there was an expectation that however much the problems in federalism had yet to be resolved, it was better to move on to other issues. This meant that the issue would be kept back for another day, a day that is almost certain to come at some point.

Instead of the tackling of the national question, other priorities have taken its place, with the economy and health care being the most prominent. Where it becomes impossible to avoid talking about the Constitution and Quebec's place in it, we have seen the politics of deferral and disengagement on the one hand, and one of compromise or minor admissions on the other. We saw the Harper government in 2008 willing to recognize Quebec as a "nation," as demanded by the Bloc Québécois (BQ), but only as part of a "united Canada," an elegant way to square the circle. We saw the Quebec Liberal Party willing to join the annual premiers' meetings after taking office in 2003, but only once the province had been recognized for its "unique character" in the Calgary Declaration of 1997. Otherwise, there is careful avoidance of anything to do with mega-constitutional politics.

Outline and Approach

As discussed, chapter 2 reviews the theory of constitutional abeyances and the process through which the question of Quebec's place in Canada has been moved off the political agenda without being effectively resolved. Today Quebec's constitutional agenda no longer dominates either Canadian or Quebec politics; nor does the question of any possible referendums on sovereignty. This depoliticization of the issue among Canada's political leaders was only possible because the sovereignty movement declined in importance in Quebec and throughout Canada. Against this backdrop, federalists were able to set aside their differences in the interests of restoring constitutional stability.

From that point, the book devotes a chapter to each of the explanations that has been offered for the decline, with a view to examining the evidence either supporting or undermining that explanation. It is this decline that made the restoration of the constitutional abeyance possible, however it came about. Chapter 3 examines the concept of "constitutional fatigue," or the argument that the people of Quebec simply became tired of fighting over the national question. This argument had considerable appeal in the years soon after 1995 but diminished over time. As the chapter makes clear, it is probably the least theoretically coherent explanation, and very little work has gone into developing the idea. In theoretical terms, I conceive of the constitutional-fatigue explanation as a drop in issue salience, meaning that it fell off the political agenda because there was no political incentive to pursue it. On its own, however, it only made the most sense in the immediate aftermath of 1995.

Chapter 4 is dedicated to the argument that it was Canada's process of non-constitutional accommodations, taken over many decades, that ultimately helped soothe many of the fears that people in Quebec had about being a minority language group in Canada. Chapter 5 addresses the identity question, arguing that Quebec's leaders have turned the discussion around Quebec's identity to one focused on reasonable accommodations, and as a result sovereignty became less of a political issue. In its place has come a wider discussion about who counts as a Quebecer and what is owed to minority populations. The final two chapters are dedicated to generational change and economic globalization. The discussion on generational change reviews the argument that the young are, if not more federalist, less interested in sovereignty, which has made managing the issue easier for federalists in Quebec. The final chapter argues that federalists have done a better job in managing the forces of economic globalization, effectively winning the argument that in an increasingly globalized Quebec separatism is a less appealing option. The book ends with some concluding thoughts.

In terms of sources and approach, I adopt a historical narrative style to canvas the competing explanations of why the national question fell off the political agenda. The book does not attempt a formal process-tracing method that seeks causal mechanisms to determine which of the forces at play may be most important, although the text does offer thoughts about the relative importance that each background force is playing. A wide variety of sources are used, reflecting the amount of material available. There is an enormous amount of archival content available for review. Good examples include the two-volume set of primary documents on constitutional change collected by Anne Bayefsky (1989), and the documents maintained by the federal Ministry of Intergovernmental Relations, the Canadian Intergovernmental Conference Secretariat, and the library system of the University of Toronto. Primary documents – such as major court decisions, legislation, parliamentary resolutions, Hansard, work done by royal and other government commissions, reports, studies and other official material written by institutions or actors or otherwise commissioned by them – are critically important. Media coverage and editorial content are also key. Both scripted and unscripted comments in the media from policymakers, officials, and other relevant participants can give a good glimpse into events. In addition, the tone and content of editorial and opinion pieces can offer clues as to what the "attentive public" is thinking at a particular time and how effective the actions of policymakers are proving to be. Polling data is also important in order to understand what the public is thinking about. Very extensive information is available in this regard; for example, the polling house CROP has conducted seasonal surveys on Quebec public opinion, and there is a wealth of data available in the secondary literature about public reactions before, during, and after major events. Significant use is also made of the vast amount of material available in the secondary literature, including the published memoirs of key actors.

Finally, thirty-eight people were interviewed for this project between 2012 and 2015. Under ideal circumstances, an interview-based project exhausts the population of involved people to gain their insights and, when that is not possible, succeeds in generating a representative sample until "saturation" is reached; this leads to a convergence on the truth, given the repetition of the different sources. Practitioners often advise a snowballing technique, in that one interview leads to others. However, the sample here is non-representative, given the time scale and the number of people potentially involved. Importantly, there is a significant oversampling of federalists. Nevertheless, a non-probability sample is useful when managed along with other evidence and is particularly important given the focus on government strategy and the fact that interviews are otherwise considered among the best types of evidence for process tracing (see Tansey 2007 for uses of non-probability sampling). There are a number of people with good first-hand knowledge of the events in question who have been interviewed for background knowledge, in particular for the way in which contemporary IGR is conducted. They are listed in the appendix at the end of this book.

What happened to the Quebec sovereignty movement has been a subject of growing scholarly interest among both anglophone and francophone scholars, in Canada and abroad (Rocher 2019; 2023, 281). In what follows, I do not seek to be triumphalist about Canadian federalism or to claim that Canada will always exist with Quebec as a part of it. Indeed, André Lecours in his excellent recent book (2021) has effectively demonstrated how nationalist movements can vary between being secessionist at some points in time while only being "autonomist" at others. Rather, I aim to explore the different explanations for the decline of the independence movement that are emerging and to present them to a politically attuned audience. The situation could change in a heartbeat, of course; crises between Quebec and the rest of Canada have been the natural hum of Canadian politics ever since 1759. But even if the independence movement were to see a resurgence in the coming years, understanding the period after 1995 and the constitutional quiescence of the era would still be a project worth doing. Even so, right now the mega-constitutional era appears to be over, and there is no interest among federalists to address the questions that drove that period of Canadian history, even though they have never been properly answered.

2 An Abeyance Restored: The "Quebec Question" as the New Taboo

In looking at why the "Quebec question" that dominated the constitutional politics of Canada in the 1980s and 1990s has fallen off the political agenda for federalists across the country, this chapter argues that the issue has reverted to constitutional abeyance, its condition for much of Canada's history before it exploded onto the political agenda during the Quiet Revolution of the 1960s. At the height of the mega-constitutional era, the theory of abeyances was used to make sense of why the issue of Quebec's place in Canada was suddenly so charged. This book argues that at the present time federalists of all stripes have returned this question to a state of dormancy. The process for restoring an abeyance in the form of a taboo is the central contribution of this book to the theory of abeyances.

An abeyance is an unsettled, constitutive matter at the heart of a constitution. It is constitutive because it concerns what the political community is and how different institutions and actors relate to one another at the most basic of levels. Competing interpretations on abeyances are therefore more serious than ordinary run-of-the-mill disagreements; they lead to existential questions for political communities about how they should be governed and by whom. When a stakeholder with an interest in resolving an abeyance tries to supply a definitive answer, it will almost always set up an existential clash with those who hold a competing view, and a constitutional crisis will emerge as the two visions collide. The crisis arises because to "lose" on the point would leave the vanquished party with a constitution it cannot accept. Thus, abeyances are subjective in nature; they require actors to define them as constitutive from their perspective. As a result, the specific content matters less than the perception of the importance of what is at stake. Furthermore, because they are constitutional questions fundamentally, they get at deep issues of identity and governance that are reserved for constitutions.

Abeyances are ultimately a question of agenda setting by elites and have to be studied in relation to elite behaviour and elite accommodation (Kingdon 1984; Birkland 1998; Jones and Baumgartner 2005; Baumgartner and Jones 2009). They reflect decisions, taken independently by policymakers and political leaders, to keep a problem from becoming a political priority. Among those who disagree about the subject matter at the heart of an abeyance, the refusal to address it is not an agreement to disagree; rather it reflects an awareness of the trouble that lies ahead if an argument is pushed. Seeking to avoid that argument, elites will try to push a troublesome subject at the heart of an abeyance off the political agenda. If other leaders also come to the conclusion that they do not want to force a problem to the surface, it can be effectively suppressed in favour of other topics. But the ground on which they are standing is never solid; it requires a mutual willingness by those involved to downplay and delay a conflict. Moreover, it is not a strategy that will always be available. Political conditions, new actors, or other factors may force the topic at the heart of an abeyance to the surface. The literature on agenda setting covers well the reasons some issues rise to the surface, and others do not (e.g., Kingdon 1984; Baumgartner and Jones 2009). In some situations there is nothing that a leader can do. In our story about the constitutional position of Quebec, it is not sufficient to simply say that federalists chose to keep the national question in abeyance, and that was it; they could do so because other factors after 1995 created the conditions in which the adoption of this strategy was possible. However, it would not have been possible in 1976, just after the PQ came to power, to have addressed Quebec nationalism as a taboo subject or to have refused to acknowledge it. Similarly, one cannot look at a country like Spain and say to those who favour national unity, "Just drop the subject of Catalonia," and expect that to work. But in Canada there are many different background forces that have emerged that have led federalist elites to view Quebec's constitutional status as an irresolvable problem, and they are operating in a political space that is amenable to this interpretation. As it has become possible to restore the question of Quebec's status in Canada as an abeyance, federalists have done so.

The sources of abeyances can vary. An abeyance might arise out of a logical tension in a constitution that had been overlooked at the time of drafting, for example. This may be especially so if the constitution is formed under pressure, leading drafters to gloss over matters of disagreement in the interests of getting a deal. Abeyances may also develop over time as a constitution evolves and only come to light when the actions of a political leader lay bare a problem that had not been fully realized. This can happen as different institutions change, others are added or dropped, or the political culture of a community evolves. Abeyances may lurk unresolved in the constitution over a long period of time, doing little damage to an otherwise perfectly functional constitution. As the actors may be otherwise quite content with the constitutional order, there may be little interest in addressing the subject.

More often, however, actors have a sense, even if it is unstated, of the trouble that awaits them if they start to push into the matter too deeply. They will try to avoid doing so, and from this, one can discern a typical pattern of behaviour surrounding the management of an abeyance. While not talking about abeyances per se, Kenneth McRoberts described this type of conduct perfectly in his 1991 essay *English Canada and Quebec: Avoiding the Issue* (1991). Writing between the Meech Lake and Charlottetown disasters, he understood the observable desire by political leaders not to discuss the constitutional issue while nevertheless being forced to do so. Webber (2021) has described something similar with his concept of "agnostic constitutionalism" in the years since, and how the lack of clarity around constitutional visions can be important for letting the Constitution operate effectively (see also Walters, 2023, 179). In the ordinary course, one expects actors to hold a matter in abeyance, in a sense showing a common willingness to avoid getting into a morass they would rather avoid. During these times of stability one recognizes a mutual pattern of issue avoidance or of attempts to depoliticize a matter being held in abeyance into a discrete, technical, unimportant or uninteresting question. At all times, however, when the matter must be addressed head-on for whatever reason (perhaps on account of an external shock), one often finds a willingness among actors to resort to half measures in an effort to keep the problem camouflaged. This will entail appearing to entertain multiple visions of the question at once, acknowledging different positions without agreeing with them, or offering modest or superficial concessions without conceding what they see as the "true" interpretation on a deeper level.

The concept of a constitutional abeyance is particularly associated with the work of Michael Foley, who developed it in the British and American contexts in his book *The Silence of Constitutions: Gaps, "Abeyances" and Political Temperament in the Maintenance of Government* (2013). Foley's central argument is that constitutions are important not just for what they say but also for the things they leave out. The material that is left out is often more than omissions or points that need clarification, but can actually have beneficial, ameliorative effects. In fact, confronting an abeyance can have a catastrophic effect if it is not handled correctly. Foley initially defined abeyances in this way:

> Abeyances should not be thought of as empty constitutional "gaps" to be filled in through the normal course of legal interpretation and political development. Neither should they be seen as constitutional "deals" by which particular issues are attended to through a conscious form of mutual accommodation between contending parties, nor as "conventions" demarcating expected behavior through informal but generally obligatory agreements. On the contrary, abeyances should be seen as akin to barely sensed disjunctions lodged so deeply within constitutions that, far from being susceptible to orderly compromise, they can only be assimilated by an intuitive social acquiescence in the incompleteness of a constitution, by a common reluctance to press the logic of arguments on political authority to conclusive positions, and by an instinctive inhibition to objecting to what is persistently omitted from the constitutional agenda. (Foley 2013, 10)

He goes on to state that abeyances are valuable "not in spite of their obscurity but because of it" (2013, 10). Abeyances are gaps that "remain vacuous for positive and constructive purposes. They are not, in any sense, truces between two defined positions, but rather a set of implicit agreements to collude in keeping fundamental questions of political authority in a state of irresolution" (10).

Foley initially gives examples like the fight of the Stuart monarchs with Parliament in the lead up to the English civil war and the expansion of the powers of the US president under Richard Nixon's "imperial presidency." The abeyances in these two cases reveal that there is less of a distinction between a written and unwritten constitution than one might think. Both share essential "unsettlements" that help to make it work, in that those who hold competing visions of how the state works slide past one another while ensuring that the broader whole functions. However subtle abeyances may be, though, they are also tremendously important, and in the event that they are politicized, they can lead to a major constitutional crisis. In the example of the early Stuart constitution, the direct confrontation arose out of the ambiguity that surrounded the power of parliament in a monarchial context – the idea of the "king" versus that of the "king-in-parliament." The unlimited sovereignty implied by the first institution, and the limits implied by the other, were left unresolved, a point never seriously pushed and left to the complicity of the different parties involved. The constitution survived precisely because the matter was never addressed. "The constitution, therefore, did not just rest upon the feasibility of unanswered questions; it also survived by proceeding on the basis of the question remaining unasked" (Foley 2013, 31). It was only after Charles I began to assert his technical authority as he saw it that the abeyance was revealed and necessitated a response.

Something similar occurred in the American case under President Nixon. The Constitution never specified exactly what the president's powers were, and under Nixon the office began to reveal the extent to which it had not been clearly hindered by traditional checks and balances (Foley 2013, 64). As exemplified by the famous exchanges with David Frost, Nixon thought of the office as being able to take whatever actions it had to in order to defend the nation, including illegal ones. It would not be practicable to seek the consent of Congress. The office of the president could do it "by definition" (68). Foley points out that, for most of the American public, the actions of Congress and the subsequent resignation of the president in the face of almost certain impeachment gave the illusion that the Constitution was working as it should. Nevertheless, the point of the illustration is that Nixon was only able to take the actions he did because the range of the office, and its relationship to the other branches, had not been made clear, and as in the case of Charles I, the crisis only emerged once the ambiguity had been pressed to the office's advantage (72).[1]

Why Do Abeyances Become Politicized?

Abeyances help us understand voids in a constitution that are void for a reason, specifically because they represent zones of conceptual tension that cannot be reconciled in a way that would keep the rest of the constitution – as otherwise understood – satisfactorily intact. They also differ from other ideas because their existence is betrayed by a specific type of observable behaviour, one that exists when different political actors collectively avoid an intractable issue for fear of doing damage to the greater constitutional whole. When an abeyance emerges and becomes the subject of political conflict, it can be said to have developed into a political issue because the avoiding behaviour is no longer present. Turning a constitutional abeyance into a political issue nearly always results in a constitutional crisis.

Abeyances can become politicized or "collapse" for many different reasons, but whether they do is ultimately dependent on one or more political actors making the calculation that they want to push into an area that has been kept off-limits, in order to assert their particular vision over another. In other words, they rely on policy entrepreneurs (see generally Kingdon 1984; Jones and Baumgartner 2005; Baumgartner and Jones 2009 for the origins and use of the concept). The motivation of political actors to make this calculation can vary, but in Canada it has almost always been electoral considerations on the part of political party leaders. Political leaders who see an advantage in making an abeyance an issue can distinguish themselves from their opponents or offer a vision that is compelling to followers. Conversely, electoral considerations often dictate that abeyances be maintained, creating a willingness by leaders to offer vague concessions on key points or political fig leaves or to ignore the questions altogether. Of course, at this point the sociological literature on federalism becomes important, and one inevitably must consider the social context of abeyances. They speak to different groups at different times. They will predate the careers of most politicians. The success of their efforts will therefore depend on more than their innate skills or degree of planning in their designs. Furthermore, it will depend on which section of the electorate they wish to speak to – some abeyances can be quite technical. Thus the politicization of abeyances by elites and the success of that effort in public opinion are related phenomenon but not exactly the same. Indeed, traditionally, more than anything, abeyances have been an intra-elite struggle among political leaders and institutions. In Foley's examples, public opinion played a back-seat role to a struggle among constitutionalized actors (king versus Parliament; president versus Congress). However, in Canada, an advanced liberal democracy where the public is attuned to political debates and their place in them, electoral considerations become the key consideration. The Quebec-Canada constitutional struggles started with debates among elites about the Constitution, federalism, and the true nature of the Canadian state, but perhaps inevitably public opinion became critically important in the resolution of abeyances and the way they were framed by political leaders.

This is not to detract from the authentic beliefs of the actors, however. For example, there was little public pressure on Pierre Trudeau to begin the patriation process in the late 1960s after he succeeded Lester Pearson. Trudeau arrived with a federal vision that was clearly at odds with many provinces, and whose dubious popularity led to its initial failure at the Victoria patriation round in 1971. But it was up to Trudeau whether to proceed, and he made the choice to make the Constitution a political priority notwithstanding public opinion. However, he only did so after successfully gambling that his actions would not prevent him from winning the next election. Similarly, the ardour that most *péquistes* (PQ members) feel for the independence project is beyond doubt; the commitment is solid and complete and, for many, utterly un-shakable – notwithstanding the polls. How to frame the matter (which issues to push and which to leave), though, and how to frame the narra-tive, is a tactical decision. Here abeyances can play in the overall strat-egy, although the purchase that one gets from exploiting them will vary depending on the time, the context, and the subject matter. As might be expected, in Canada their relevance and presence in the public debate has waxed and waned accordingly.

Electoral calculations are tricky. They are always rooted in the judg-ment a leader has of the mood of the society that he or she is governing or seeking to govern at a particular time. The cost-benefit of action or inaction is never clear and is usually only apparent in hindsight. The forces that change public opinion are themselves influenced by a wide variety of factors. Beyond the natural evolution of public opinion, out-side events and structural changes in society and its institutions can change the political calculus in myriad ways as well. For example, the addition of new provinces in Canada over the latter half of the nine-teenth century and in the early twentieth century likely made it more difficult for leaders to keep vague much of what had been kept vague in 1867 (such as an amending formula). At different times the provinces and territories have themselves been critical actors in the story, sup-porting different views of the country and occasionally playing the role of spoiler. Clyde Wells of Newfoundland, for example, took a strongly contractual view of the federation that contributed to the death of the Meech Lake Accord, while Ontario under David Peterson tried to play the role of an "honest broker" in Canada and was more sympathetic to a dualist vision. Thus, a theory of abeyances, and the one used here, attributes much to the agency, judgment, managerial skill, and political acumen of those charged with running a country that is often changing in front of their eyes.

To clarify, like other political issues, abeyances gain the greatest traction when the differences in vision are the widest. Members of the electorate will have an easier time understanding the problem if it is laid out before them and if critical differences in opinion are given suf-ficient attention by leaders. If an actor can bring clarity and salience to the abeyance, the increased understanding and sense of importance will lead to more polarization and galvanization of the electorate. Con-versely, if the issue is unclear, treated as unimportant by leaders or hidden from the public, interest in the abeyance under discussion will wane. This decline of public attention is critical to the restoration of the abeyance.

Abeyances as Distinct from Other Concepts

For the concept of abeyances to have descriptive and explanatory power, it is important to distinguish this particular aspect of constitutions from other ideas that are common in constitutional law. What do we get out of the idea of an abeyance? What explanatory purchase does it give us? And how do abeyances differ from similar concepts? For example, how are they different from simple *conventions*? Why are they not *omissions*? Could they not also be thought of as unconsidered *ambiguities*, the kind that courts are set up specifically to address?

Abeyances differ from conventions in that they are not overt political understandings, which conventions invariably represent. This point was made by Foley who differentiated abeyances from conventions in that the latter amounted to forms of "expected behaviour" that were overt, whereas the former were the behaviours to which people adhered *in spite* of the fact that there was no agreement. Foley stated:

> The point about abeyances is that they posit another layer of the "unwritten," another dimension to the written-unwritten distinction, but one which is not the same as attributing everything to convention, pragmatism, and the common law. To mistake it as such is to lose an important, indeed vital, perspective. A convention that becomes operative can usually be written down without disastrous results, even if it is open to dispute and the constitution does not have its source in a single document. But an abeyance is not only unwritten; the assumption is that it cannot and should not be written. (Quoted in Thomas 1997, 12)

Moreover, conventions are usually not reflective of a contradiction in quite the same way. There is nothing contradictory about the king's absolute theoretical right to withhold his assent from parliamentary action, on the one hand, and the convention that this will never occur, on the other. It is how the king, who "reigns but does not rule," maintains his legitimacy in a liberal democracy. Nor is an abeyance necessarily revealed by different conventions coming into conflict, any more than when different laws might conflict and necessitate the turning to an arbiter. For example, such a conflict arose during the prorogation crisis of 2008–9, where the issue was whether Governor General Michäelle Jean was required to grant Prime Minister Stephen Harper a prorogation when it appeared that the government was on the cusp of losing the confidence of the House of Commons. There were two important conventions here. One was the idea of responsible government, the idea that the executive has legitimacy only insofar as it can command the confidence of a majority of the sitting members. The other was the right of the head of the government to prorogue the House of Commons whenever he or she saw fit, based on the convention that the royal prerogatives are exercised by the king or queen on the advice of the prime minister. In the face of an almost certain loss of confidence, could the prime minister still prorogue the House of Commons in an effort to save his skin?

This question was up to the governor general to decide. In the end, she resolved the point by finding that, absent an actual loss of confidence, the sitting government was still entitled to ask for such a temporary measure, and the Crown granted it. The point was heavily debated, although most scholars concluded that the governor general was probably correct in this assessment, and that in any event she had the authority to interpret the contradiction as she wished (there is considerable literature on this point; see Franks 2009, 46; Cameron 2009, 192; but see Walters 2011, 135–7). The position she took was validated somewhat in the weeks that followed when it became clear that the united bloc of opposition parties could not survive the necessary six weeks to push the point again. Nevertheless, this did not amount to an abeyance, but merely to two conventions that were brought into conflict and which needed an arbiter to have them resolved.

Nor are abeyances merely *ambiguities*. Courts are routinely asked to supply clarity to conceptually vague constitutional ideas, some of which can be startlingly broad. Many parts of the Constitution are in fact left intentionally vague with the idea that they can be resolved on a case-by-case basis; the language rights in section 23 of the Canadian Charter of Rights and Freedoms provides an excellent example, guaranteeing minority-language education rights to French and English communities "where numbers warrant" (Canada 1982, sec. 23(3)). Section 15, the general equality provision, is similarly vague in that it specifically grants protection against discrimination to some groups, but it is phrased generally enough so that additional groups may be found to be included depending on court decisions. More often, the ambiguity arises in cases that were not foreseen at the time of writing. The so-called Person's Case was an instance in which the courts were called upon to decide on the right of women to be appointed to the Senate of Canada, and whether they fit into the legal definition of a "person" (*Edwards v. Canada (A.G.)*, [1930] AC 124). Notable for creating the "living tree" doctrine of constitutional interpretation in Canada, the Judicial Committee of the Privy Council found that the evolution of Canadian society had expanded the meaning of *person* to the extent that it now included women. This right was unclear before the ruling and only solved through litigation. But it was not on account of an abeyance that the matter was not litigated. The change came from the progressive evolution of views on women's political participation, an evolution that changed what had been a political consensus about the proper role of women in society into a political issue and eventually a legal disagreement, which was then clarified and resolved in the courts to reflect changing circumstances.

The unwillingness to confront abeyances means that they are more than simple omissions as well. Much can (and must) be left out of constitutions for the sake of economy or as a result of oversight, and the residual-powers clauses in many constitutions are a good example of a step that framers take to confront their inability to see what the future holds. An omission might be an abeyance if there is evidence that political actors are unwilling to solve it because doing so would bring competing or irreconcilable visions or values into tension. In and of itself, however, an omission does not count as an abeyance, which requires reluctance on the part of different actors to offer solutions they know will be unacceptable to actors with competing views.

Abeyances are related to constitutional fictions and myths. As Thomas notes, the former is usually sustained by the latter, but both are needed to maintain the credibility of a liberal democratic system (1997, 27). Fictions are usually overt and accepted parts of constitutions; they are not literally true but accepted anyway. A key fiction in the United States is the idea of popular sovereignty, which suggests that the people are really in charge and their rulers are only their delegates expressing that will. One does not have to poke too deeply to see the problem with this, but we accept it for what it is: a "constitutional truth," if not a scientific one. Such fictions are often taken to be self-evident and allow for the suspension of disbelief (Morgan 1988, cited in Thomas 1997, 26). A similar situation arises when a court makes a finding of fact, a ruling that a situation which may be empirically false is nevertheless considered true as far as the law is concerned. A good example is the laws surrounding parenting, in which people can be legally made into parents, regardless of any actual biological connection, by court orders. Fictions are usually sustained by more general constitutional myths, such as those surrounding the intents of the founders of a constitution, or the inherent nature and values of the people in a political community. They focus on stories and actors and "help our fictions survive" (Thomas 1997, 27). But neither alone is an abeyance. "[F]ictions may conflict or contain glaring contradictions, abeyances remain silent" (27).

Abeyances and the Crisis of Canadian Federalism

How does the abeyance concept apply to the Canadian case? Where did the abeyances implicated in the sovereignty movement in Quebec originate?

It is in the federal context that abeyances have received the most attention in the Canadian literature. This began with David Thomas, in his book *Whistling Past the Graveyard*. Thomas saw much to like in the theory of abeyances as it had been used in the British and American contexts. Writing in 1997, he used it as a useful framework for looking at the ongoing federal crisis between Quebec and the rest of the country. For Thomas, much of the crisis was rooted in the direct confrontation of Canadians' contrasting views, views that coexisted without ever being spoken about. The fact that so much could have been hidden for so long was the result less of the unwritten nature of the Constitution than of the practices that political leaders used to skirt the ambiguities, which Thomas closely identified with the beliefs of Edmund Burke. The Burkean tradition, with its emphasis on compromise, continuity, and organic evolution, as well as the goodwill of the different actors, had kept the British on track for hundreds of years and was a good lens through which to perceive the Canadian experiment. What Thomas admired most about Burke, however, was that he was explicitly *practical*, prepared to sacrifice nearly any principle in demonstrable service of a broader whole (Thomas 1997, 19). It was this attitude and practice that permitted the Constitution to be written with so many holes. Thomas (1997, 62) includes a list of abeyances that are relevant to that discussion:

- the future constitutional relationship with the United Kingdom;
- the status of French speakers and Catholics outside Quebec;
- the use to which certain key federal powers could be put;
- whether provinces were equal;
- the future process of constitutional amendment;
- the role of the upper house;
- the locus of sovereign powers;
- the question of judicial supremacy;
- the contradictions between parliamentary sovereignty and federalism;
- the special status of Quebec;
- the right of secession;
- constitutional equality between the centre and constituent units;
- provincial participation in central institutions; and
- the protection of rights.[2]

Combined, these points pretty much capture the dispute that Quebec has had with what has uncharitably been called the rest of Canada. Not all of these matters have remained abeyances over time, however. Arguably, some, like judicial supremacy, are no longer really unresolved but have become politically accepted by almost everyone over time, although the refusal of the Quebec government to participate in the *Secession Reference* (Reference re Secession of Quebec [1998] 2 S.C.R. 217) suggests even this may not be the case. (Some of these abeyances have been given a fuller treatment through the lens of abeyance theory. See for example Bateman 2000, 206, on constitutional interpretation; LeRoy 2004 on the *Secession Reference*; DiGiacomo 2010). Each of them is derivative of and implicated in a deeper constitutional ambiguity, however. This "mega-abeyance" is one identified by Thomas, and it is still very much alive, captured in the question of cultural duality in Canada: Is the country a union of French and English or a compact of the provinces?

This is the primary abeyance in Canadian French-English relations and is the root abeyance of this book. Coming down definitively on one side or the other will invariably prove to be extremely controversial, even constitutionally fatal, as Canadians have learned over the years. But the aforementioned additional questions are also part of the story because resolving them is contingent on the answer to the root abeyance. They are derived from this underlying problem. These sub-issues are held in abeyance not on their own accord but because any discussion of them will expose the primary abeyance that surrounds the question of duality versus provincial equality. To attempt to bring clarity to them is to immediately confront the contract-compact dispute and to immediately invite the crisis. Thus, this book may refer to any or all of the listed matters on their own, but their relevance arises from the fact that they are implicated in the deeper discussion about duality in Canada. Perhaps it can be said that the failure to settle the question of duality was the original sin of the Canadian constitution as it was developed in the 1860s, and that, had this been answered, we would have avoided a lot of trouble down the road. Whether this was any clearer then than it is now is doubtful, however. More charitably, it can be said that the refusal to address that question squarely in 1867 permitted the constitutional system to work, along Burkean lines, for nearly a century. The question remains very much open in Canada today.

While the contract-compact dispute is the simplest formulation of the dispute between Quebec and Canada, it can be seen as the avatar for wider disputes about the boundaries of political identity and belonging in Canada. We talk of the "mega-constitutional" era because it was through altering constitutional arrangements that federalists hoped to placate Quebec nationalists into staying in the country. But the disagreements between English and French Canada go well beyond the formal constitution or Quebec's role as a province; the political battles reflect the disagreements that arise out of living in a multinational state. It is inevitable that different political communities will never see eye to eye on questions surrounding the boundaries of their communities, on who belongs and who does not, and on how different nations should interact with each other (for a recent discussion of these issues in Canada and Europe, see A.-G. Gagnon 2021). There is always a certain naïveté about people who seek constitutional reform to "design out" issues that are inextricably bound up in culture and community. The Quebec-Canada relationship is similar in some ways to the Indigenous-settler quest to conceptualize their relationship and answer the question on how Indigenous rights fit into the Canadian mosaic. There is unlikely to be a time when it is solved; rather, it is a matter of finding common ground where both communities feel respected and empowered in their relations with each other. More often than not it is the concept of reconciliation that structures the debate surrounding the proper relationship between Indigenous and non-Indigenous peoples, but what that means has no fixed answer. At best it reflects the need to maintain trust and understanding between the two communities, and it is through constitutions that we try to elevate our understandings into tangible solutions.

Moreover, the contract-compact dispute channelled the energies of political leaders who each brought their own, idiosyncratic views on what the political community should be about. The individuals who star in this story are not so easy to pigeonhole on one side of the debate or the other. For his part, Pierre Trudeau did not see Canada as really either a contract or a compact; for him, Canada was a multicultural society that was based on individual rights. The importance of language led him to adopt elements of the dualist nature of Canada, and the equality of citizens wherever they lived led him to reject special status for Quebec. But for him, it was the *individual* – not the group or the province – which took overarching priority. Provincial leaders associated with the contractual viewpoint about the relationships between the provinces often had more fundamental beliefs about identity, democracy, and citizenship. Clyde Wells, closely associated with the contractual viewpoint, would likely say that the heart of his vision of the country is that it is the *people* who are sovereign. Special status for Quebec, or any province, is in conflict with that perspective. For leaders like Robert Bourassa, who held a "dualist" view of the state, their vision went beyond what Quebec "deserved." At the heart of Bourassa's perspective was the idea that it was the rights of the *community* that had to take priority over those of the individual in order to preserve a way of life, at least in some areas. We see this today in the support that all parties in Quebec give to the notion of interculturalism. Such a policy demands that there be an agreed definition of the *public sphere* and what is acceptable in it, which in Quebec is rooted in the prominence of the French language and the equality of men and women. That wearing a hijab or a kippah is ruled out when delivering public services to preserve this sphere is anathema to many classically liberal-minded Quebecers and in the rest of Canada, where the rights of the individual to express their religion as they wish take priority. While these disputes exist at a basic level, however, during the mega-constitutional era they flowed through the structures of federalism as proxies for deeper political clashes. The fathers of Confederation, in failing to resolve the contract-compact dispute, all but invited the eventual clash. But perhaps some crisis was inevitable when they failed, unlike the American founding fathers, to make any definitive statement on what Canada was actually about.

Thomas (1997, 62) argues that pure practicality was the most common and straightforward explanation for why the question of whether Canada was a union of French and English or a compact among provinces was left unanswered, and why so much else was left unresolved in 1867. Relying in particular on the leadership of Sir John A. Macdonald, as described by Rod Preece, Thomas argues that abeyances allowed Macdonald to come to agreements on a union with fellow fathers of Confederation from Canada East George Étienne Cartier and Étienne-Paschal Taché. They were too frightened of the possibility of annexation to the United States, and too unsure of the position of their community within anglophone North America, to go it alone. The pragmatic conception of Confederation was an empirical rather than ideological project led by Macdonald, who eschewed clarity in favour of compromise. It allowed both communities to cling to certain irreconcilable beliefs about the other – that Confederation was only an incremental step towards independence for the French Canadians, on the one hand, and that assimilation would actually come to pass in the rest of the country, on the other. This conception finds support in works by P.B. Waite, Edwin Black, and others, although it is rejected by Peter Smith (see Thomas 1997, 66, for an extended discussion on this point).

The overriding pressure to find a deal sets up conditions that are ideal for creating abeyances in constitutions. If drafters face an overwhelming political imperative to come to a constitutional agreement, there may be a strong incentive to ignore or gloss over comparatively smaller issues in favour of finding an overall workable solution. This incentive was clearly apparent in Canada, but as will be argued subsequently, the Spanish constitution is similar in this regard. In that case, the need to democratize after the dictatorship of General Francisco Franco allowed drafters to leave unresolved many issues that are now returning to menace the unity of the country. The crisis of Scottish nationalism that is currently confronting Great Britain cannot be traced to abeyances, but the solutions being contemplated do appear to hinge on them to some extent.

While political urgency goes some way to explaining where abeyances come from in the Canadian case, recent scholarship arrives at a more precise answer to why such pragmatism for managing them was even possible: in 1867, Canada was not supposed to be a sovereign country, at least not one with a completely independent existence outside the British Empire. Canada could live with a level of constitutional ambiguity because it could rely on the wider structures and practices of the empire's constitution to supply answers to uncomfortable questions. It was not until Canada truly decided to break away from the United Kingdom and forge its own constitutional trail that many of the ambiguities and contradictions came to light (DiGiacomo 2010). Furthermore, early Canadian federalism was far less developed and had far fewer provinces than it is and has today. One must ask what the effect of adding units has on the likelihood of an abeyance becoming politicized and emerging. In the Canadian case, additional provinces had two effects: first, their arrival diluted Quebec's place in Canada on questions such as constitutional reform, and exacerbated its claims to special status; second, none of the new provinces was francophone, and none, with the possible exception of Ontario, accepted a dualist conception of Canada. As a result, Quebec became increasingly outnumbered in its view of duality.

In both Ontario and Quebec, an *entente cordiale* between the English and French communities had existed since at least the time of the American Revolution and became increasingly formalized in the following decades. The political arrangements that emerged from the 1837 rebellions were designed, at least initially, to swamp the French Canadians and lead to their extinction (Cameron 1990, 6; McRoberts 1997, 6; but see Ajzenstat 1988 for her famous rebuttal, suggesting that Lord Durham was actually quite tolerant). Not only did Durham's plan for a united Canada leading to cultural homogeneity fail, but it actually backfired, with the populations of Canada East and Canada West seeking common objectives such as responsible government, better defence, and mutual protection of their respective religions. The agreements and practices that emerged among the local population during that period have been identified by Arend Lijphart as "consociational" and achieved without input from London (Lijphart 1977, 124–5). The legislature was split down the middle with forty-two seats for each half of the province, and the double-majority principle ensured that laws only passed if more than half on either side accepted them (Lijphart 1977, 125; McRoberts 1997, 6). In addition, separate administrations were maintained, with dual heads of government in both, which kept the colony working (Verney 1986, 197–9). The fact that there were even dual prime ministers may be the ultimate expression of consociationalism. Another indicator is the fact that the capital moved several times over the life of the province, eventually alternating between Toronto and Quebec City on a four-year cycle (see McRoberts 1997, 6–9, for a discussion of the different practices). French was more or less secured by the 1850s with the repeal of British legislation that records had to be in English only (McRoberts 1997, 7).

That this political arrangement eventually collapsed into a more federal structure did not derogate from the understandings that had been achieved up to this point. The choice of Ottawa as a capital, situated as it was on the border of the provinces, was an effective symbolic choice for everyone, and the preservation of both languages as being equally official for the federal and Quebec legislatures represented an important compromise for anglophones and francophones (Canada 2012, sec. 133). Moreover, the mirroring protections for minority religious school boards in Ontario and Quebec bolstered what many considered to be one of the most important aspects of cultural protection in Canada (sec. 93). Other dualist institutions followed, such as the alternating aspect of the leadership of the Liberal Party between anglophones and francophones, cementing an electoral coalition that kept the party in power for most of the twentieth century. Constitutional amendment was not a serious issue when the country was part of the empire and before the provinces had developed strong institutional identities.

The size of Ontario and Quebec preserved many of these understandings at the national level. Even when the Ontario premier Oliver Mowat began to assert provincial rights more aggressively, his behaviour reflected a muscular view of the powers for all provinces under section 92 of the Constitution Act, rather than a questioning of the deeper constitutional foundations on which the country rested. In this, all provinces could more or less agree with Mowat and otherwise offer their support (Cairns 1971, 320–5). This policy continued through much of the early twentieth century, with the two largest provinces working together, such as via the Drew-Duplessis axis, to keep Ottawa in check.

However, while these understandings worked east of the Manitoba border, they fell apart almost immediately as other provinces joined the country. It did not take long after Confederation for it to become apparent that while the French language was entitled to some deference in the east, it would not be entitled to the same treatment as one went further west. This story has been told many times before, such as when the regions were still territories and there were aggressive actions to stamp out French as an official language (Aunger 2001). The conflicts began relatively early, with the crises unleashed by Louis Riel and the admission of Manitoba and, later, the Manitoba schools' question. Thomas points to that experience as one of several in which the different visions of the country began to collide, along with the conscription crises that came later (1997, 121). Throughout this period, and well into the twentieth century, elites kept these issues off the agenda, but with each additional province it became harder and harder to keep the abeyances that had been created in 1867 from emerging. Thus, while the rise of nationalism in Quebec has much to do with the internal political development of the province, the evolving federal context made the preservation of abeyances, and also that of national unity, harder to achieve. A federation with ten strong, autonomous units existing outside of the British context was simply not something the framers of the British North America Act had anticipated and was a situation with which the Constitution was not prepared to deal. The gaps on questions such as constitutional amendment had not become political issues, due in part to the willingness of the different actors to largely ignore the problem – which was possible in earlier eras but had become more and more difficult to ignore as time went on.

In contrast to the cases of Charles I, who lost in the English Civil War, and Nixon, who was forced to resign, the Canadian case has defied resolution. Rather, it has returned to a state of "settled unsettlement," a situation that political elites, with the complicity of the public, appear to find the most acceptable. This equilibrium has been based to some extent on the creation of new abeyances, which emerged after the referendum, specifically surrounding the Clarity Act and Quebec's response.[3] The Supreme Court has been complicit in this story, leaving areas of abeyance unresolved while giving just enough specificity to keep different communities sufficiently happy with the status quo. Such agreements fulfil the basic needs of an abeyance in that they remain sufficiently vague and, therefore, untroublesome.

The shift that moves these abeyances from poorly understood gaps in the Constitution to being taboos covers a lot of ground, however. The abeyance must first be exposed, the danger recognized, before the abeyance can be subsequently restored. Thus, the traditional under-standing of abeyances is couched in the language of "disjuncture," of being "barely sensed" and in general hidden or at least generally un-acknowledged. In Canada's case, this definition does not hold. If any-thing, the issues underlying abeyances are overexposed, well defined, and widely acknowledged. As they have been subjected to bureau-cratic, legal, and philosophical scrutiny, there is no longer ambiguity on the question of abeyances and their root causes in Canada. Instead, in light of this new clarity, they have been reburied.

Quebec as the New Taboo: Restoring the Abeyance

Even if an abeyance comes to the surface and results in political conflict, is it possible that it may be restored later, perhaps even after a crisis? Can conditions emerge that encourage actors to forget that they ever brought it up? This describes the current situation in Canadian feder-alism vis-à-vis the Quebec question. There has never been an agree-ment or even a tacit understanding among different stakeholders that the Constitution is closed, or that Quebec is fine with the status quo, or that there will never be any reforms in the future. Rather, federalists do not see any incentive to bring up the topic and risk creating another crisis. This has been the case since around 2000, after which federalists refused to engage with the question, offering small concessions when necessary, but otherwise refusing to admit that the Constitution is a priority or that there is a "right" view of it outside of their own. In other words, the abeyance has been restored in the form of a taboo.

Tracking this process is the central contribution of *Sleeping Dogs* when it comes to the theory of abeyances. Scholarship on abeyances suggests that once a conflict has been exposed, it sets up a zero-sum type of thinking, especially when it is made a political issue. Given the high stakes involved, a climb-down is difficult for the parties once the prob-lem is out in the open. However, this book seeks to demonstrate that such constitutional gaps can be maintained even after they are exposed. The situation emerges if different actors realize that the problem can-not be resolved at an acceptable cost – or, put another way, if winning the battle means losing the war. The conditions that lend themselves to a conversion into a taboo rest on a political calculation. Similar to the way in which the emergence of abeyances as political issues hinges mostly on electoral calculations, these calculations weigh heavily on those in a position to keep an issue alive when the incentives to do so dry up. Once a stalemate becomes the best option for those otherwise committed to the constitutional system, turning the matter into a taboo becomes the best solution. Thomas wrote that the notion of abeyances as taboos was once suggested by David Cameron in the context of the refusal to talk about what might happen after a yes vote in Quebec, but the idea has never been fully developed (Thomas 1997, 27; Cameron 1974, 126–9). Such taboos occur at a higher order of consciousness than abeyances do, which occur at a proto-level of awareness: an abeyance might be a disjuncture, barely noticeable in a constitution, or it can be recognized and consciously maintained to avoid confrontation. How does this occur?

Restoring abeyances requires returning to a state similar to that which prevailed before the abeyance collapsed. At the very least, it requires strategies to de-escalate the situation but in a way that accounts for the fact that the matter has emerged and remains unresolved. As in a situation prior to an abeyance collapsing, the strategy for the restoration of an abeyance will manifest itself in the following ways: issue avoidance by political leaders, some level of moderate compromise in recognizing different visions without sacrificing one's own, and conflict isolation and depoliticization when the abeyance must be addressed. Politicians will adopt strategies to navigate the situation as best as they can. Today, that describes *all* of the major federal parties in Canada as well as all of the parties in Quebec with the exception of the PQ. *None* is interested in pursuing major, multilateral constitutional change. There is a belief that it is a waste of time, leads to irresolvable questions, and risks putting the country in jeopardy. There is a sense that the public is not interested in constitutional politics either.

That is a big change from previous decades, when constitutional discussions had considerable appeal – and not just among academics. The process itself had huge appeal for the people involved. Intergovernmental relations provided an important outlet for premiers and policymakers to build their careers and show off on the national stage. As Roger Gibbins saw it, executive federalism was attractive to ambitious politicians who would not have had much national exposure otherwise:

I think during the '60s and '70s the national movement in Quebec provided a stage, an opportunity, an opening if you want for provincial governments to play a much larger role and created a constitutional stage, and created roles and opportunities for people like Peter Lougheed to step on to that stage … Lougheed in the late '70s was often cited for the [leadership of] the federal Conservatives, Progressive Conservative Party, at that point. But it became clear that his lack of ability in French shut him out of that national role; it was no longer possible. And so interprovincial relations was a pretty good substitute for that. So for people like Lougheed and Blakeney and others, this had really allowed them to achieve the status of national politicians, national leaders that would not have been possible without that constitutional stage and the intergovernmental stage. (Gibbins, interview, 2014)

Intergovernmental institutions became quite prestigious and powerful places for bureaucrats, and very useful to the political leadership of the different provinces (Mel Cappe, interview, 2014). Nearly all of the dedicated offices were close to the premier or prime minister and were used for politics at the highest level. They became associated with constitutional issues, which increased their cachet (Pollard 1986, 20). One interviewee spoke of these types of organizations as places that were much sought after by people who were seeking to make a career in the public service, second perhaps only to the Department of Finance in the 1970s (Mel Cappe, interview, 2014). The fact that they were also deeply connected to matters of the public purse also meant that they had the capacity to make an impact on the day-to-day lives of ordinary Canadians. They also arrived at a time that was often thought to be associated with the growing power of first ministers in relation to their cabinets (e.g., see Savoie 1999 for the leading thinker in this vein; White 2010 for a competing view that nevertheless recognizes the dominant position of first ministers, especially at the provincial level).

The mega-constitutional era ended this style of IGR. After widespread criticism of the process as elitist and counterproductive there was a long-term shift away from the apex style of meeting (Cameron and Simeon 2002; Schertzer, McDougall, and Skogstad 2018; É. Montpetit 2007a, 2008, 2012; Inwood, Johns, and O'Reilly 2011). It was also criticized for linking complex issues together into irresolvable bundles (see for example Cameron and Krikorian 2008). In essence, the modern IGR style in Canada is far less confrontational, more collaborative, and built on consensus. It has been styled "non-constitutional renewal" and reflects the stripped-down, lower profile of solving problems (see for example Lazar 1998). It also reflects a willingness on the part of the federal government (in particular that of Stephen Harper with the concept of "open federalism") to stay out of provincial jurisdiction as much as possible (health and infrastructure excluded) (Fox 2007; Norquay 2012). Generally, the last twenty years have seen a mixture of what has been styled federal provincial multilateralism mixed with bilateralism – or a framework in which national program objectives are identified and bilateral agreements are then reached with each of the provinces individually. This is how active labour-market policies have been devolved and periodically renegotiated since 1996 (e.g., Wood 2018), immigration policy since 1991 (Paquet 2014, 2019), and agricultural policy in the latter part of the twentieth century (Skogstad 1998), as well as health-care funding arrangements. In each, Ottawa announces a set of objectives, usually through or with an apex policy-area forum (the Forum of Labour Market Ministers in labour policy, for example), but then breaks out into discussions with each province. This ensures a level of asymmetry without losing sight of national standards. The refusal to announce *de novo* programs, such as one on pharmacare, has kept any real violation of the norm off the table, with the possible exception of the Canada Research Chairs in 1998, although the impact of this was limited. Although the government of Justin Trudeau has embraced the summitry of earlier years, the surrounding politics is nothing like it was in the 1980s.

The apex of this style of IGR was reached under the government of Stephen Harper. Ottawa's disengagement was widely panned in many of the interviews that were done for this study. At the same time, nearly everyone interviewed understood the reasons behind Ottawa's decision not to engage in high-stakes federal negotiations: the opportunity they allow for the provinces to "gang up" on Ottawa, the perennial demands for more money, and the tendency of the meetings to highlight intergovernmental conflict. Still, Jim Eldridge, a long-time advisor to the Manitoba government, captured the frustration among the provinces that was brought on by Ottawa's refusal to meet with them:

> The biggest difference I see, now, is that there is virtually no dialogue, multilateral dialogue, between the federal government and the provinces at the highest levels. There's bilateral dialogue, and occasionally as happened in the recent Canada Job Grant negotiations or discussions, the provinces allied themselves and forced the federal government to sort of deal with them collectively through emissaries. But there hasn't been a first ministers' meeting since 2009, and the general view is that that is no way to run a federation … [P]ost '95 the federal government pretty much started winding down the formalized first ministers' meetings and so on, and, believe it or not, there hasn't been a formal meeting of IG deputies with the federal deputy since 1997. (Jim Eldridge, interview, 2014)

This analysis exaggerates the situation somewhat as Eldridge notes that the deputies have been in the same room and attended the same events, and that there is coordination taking place at lower levels. The formal structures that existed previously, however, are in decline as was noted by several people interviewed for this study (Mel Cappe, interview, 2014; Alfred LeBlanc, interview, 2014). Former Harper chief of staff Ian

Brodie recounted that IGR machinery was never seen as a priority for the Harper government. "Remember, we never even appointed a very senior Cabinet-level minister or anyone to run the government's position [on IGR]," recalled Brodie. "There was that minister, Chong, first, and then Peter Van Loan, but really there was no high-level federal direction" (Ian Brodie, interview, 2014). Instead, to the extent that the federal government wants to meet with the provinces, it only happens bilaterally and largely out of sight. Additionally, even at the provincial level, many of the IGR deputies have been given other responsibilities that overshadow their responsibilities in this area (Jim Eldridge, interview, 2014).

Perhaps tellingly, the decline of these meetings may have coincided with their greater democratization since Charlottetown when the process was widely derided as elitist and anti-democratic. Since then, responsibility for the processes of executive federalism has increasingly moved to the political staff or the various Cabinet secretaries, in particular. Some have argued that open federalism does not extend to better engagement with the public (Inwood, Johns, and O'Reilly 2011, 74). While there have been some efforts to raise the level of accountability in the process (increasing the transparency of which government is doing what), open federalism has generally been more about maintaining the level of government-to-government interface at the highest level rather than seeking more public input. The relevant links are more closed off, more political, and more fluid than they were in the past. For example, in 2014 Jim Eldridge described how the federal Cabinet secretary had begun to play an important role in maintaining the relationships among governments at the expense of the traditional IGR machinery:

> The federal Cabinet secretary and clerk of the Privy Council ... has maintained something that has existed now for more than ten years, which are regular meetings of clerks. So there is a regular set of meetings of the federal, provincial, and territorial Cabinet secretaries. They meet at least twice a year and do occasional videoconferencing and teleconferencing and they have become a very important instrument for multilateral, intergovernmental discussion. It's kind of formal and informal, and in some ways has replaced the intergovernmental deputy, F-P-T network. The federal clerk for these discussions is the "fed-prov" deputy and they deal with very high-level stuff like governance best practices, and security issues, and stuff like that. But it is working, it is very positive, it is well regarded by the Cabinet secretaries at all levels of government, and so it is

a new approach, and the beauty of that is that these are the people in the provincial and federal governments who have the closest access to the first ministers. (Jim Eldridge, interview, 2014)

Most interviews suggest that the *need* for intergovernmental coordination has not declined, but there has been a rejection of the traditional *process*, the very public and open summit IGR that characterized earlier eras. Instead, there has been an increasing use of the back channels and less involvement by the prime minister in visible conferences with other premiers: "You can imagine that there are huge national security issues that require good regular communications and the ability for government A to talk to government B on an urgent basis if necessary, and this network encourages that, but it also encourages good discussion on governance improvements and everybody trying to provide better public services at reduced cost, and it's doing some quite good stuff" (Jim Eldridge, interview, 2014). Alfred LeBlanc, formerly the assistant secretary to Cabinet for federal-provincial-territorial relations in Ottawa, acknowledged that the decline in summit IGR clearly had some benefits for Ottawa, but he felt that work could still proceed effectively without the political visibility.

> There is a lot of engagement over all kinds of files at many different levels. Some of it [is] at the officials' level, and also it tends to take place at what makes sense in terms of sectoral focus. So they [officials] may meet on infrastructure, they may meet on labour-market agreements and labour-market training, they would meet federally [and] provincially, at first at the officials' levels, making sure you know what could possibly work and [to understand] the concerns of provinces. And then eventually you would meet at the lead-ministerial level. And that tends not to produce the same kind of thirteen-against-one broad demands. So it might produce a gang up – "We don't like the Canada Job Grant the way you have designed it, we want it done differently" – but it is not the same dynamic as a first minister's meeting where the Prime Minster is really much more exposed. (Alfred LeBlanc, interview, 2014)

LeBlanc took a slightly different view of the question of capacity reduction, suggesting that it was also a reflection of the fact that there was less to do in intergovernmental relations than in the past. As well, while the centralization of power in the prime minister's office was connected to the government's overall deficit-reduction strategy, it also reflected a shift in issue management:

There's a logic to what's been done. It is partly a reduction of capacity but also a reorganization of how these issues are managed within
the Prime Minister's department. And in a longer-term perspective this
place and this function has gone through big cycles. So you know this
was a big place in 1993, 1994, and in all the constitutional era. It has not
always been this big; in fact at some points it didn't exist. So, yeah, there
has been a reduction in capacity, but to some extent you could say, well,
I think most people's assessment of federal-provincial relations is that
relative to the '60s, relative to the '70s, relative to the '80s, relative to half
of the '90s, [they] have been in a reasonably harmonious state with low
risk, low engagement – maybe too low for some people's interests – but
it's not a boom time for federal-provincial relations. (Alfred LeBlanc, interview, 2014)

The government of Justin Trudeau has been more open to meeting with
the provinces but has been more consistent than not with the Harper
style. To a degree, it has been easier because, unlike that of Harper,
it has had to deal with only federalists elected at the provincial level
in Quebec or, in the case of the Coalition avenir Québec (CAQ), at
least those with no interest in another referendum. But there still has
been a studious avoidance of constitutional questions, a resistance to
becoming involved in provincial affairs, and a desire to emphasize
partnership on key issues. Constitutional questions are never on the
agenda with the annual premiers' meetings. The renegotiation of the
North American Free Trade Agreement (NAFTA) was notably muted
when it came to the talks and lacked a highly visible confrontation with
the provinces. Other major issues, such as cannabis legalization, were
sorted out behind the scenes and with no federal interference. Taken together, we see a smaller "shop" in IGR with more political management
of controversial issues to ensure less visibility, and fewer meetings with
the premiers that could get out of hand.

The role of the Supreme Court is absolutely vital to this story. Politicians rely on the Supreme Court for its neutrality in negotiating tricky
issues, but the Court is also interested in avoiding major constitutional
crises for its own reasons. More than any other institution, it is implicated in the resolution of conflicts between different actors and orders
of government, including on the most divergent views of the state. At
several points, the courts have been forced to rule on the roots of the
abeyances. Courts serve as neutral arbiters where disagreements can be
punted, where a political issue can be converted into a legal one. The
benefits of doing so can be that no party ends up being blamed directly
for a result – they have the legitimacy of being vindicated in front of

a trusted court. It also means that the issue can be framed as having been a legal one all along, and less vulnerable to the charge that what is occurring is a clash of visions rather than of laws. It also keeps the question isolated in that it can be hived off into a court case rather than linked to a broader constitutional discussion.

There is evidence that, in the Canadian case, the Supreme Court will not be painted into a corner. If the matter of whether Canada is a contract or a compact remains the mega-abeyance, the Court has done little to make a definitive finding on who is right. Jeremy Webber has called this "agnostic constitutionalism" and demonstrated how the court maintains ambiguity around constitutional visions so that several can coexist at once effectively (2021, 8). Looking at the Supreme Court of Canada and its view of the federation, Robert Schertzer notes that it has been neither unanimous nor consistent over time. Canada has been conceived as a multinational compact, a contract among the provinces, and as a broader pan-Canadian union that rejects the first two views. None of these positions has been definitively accepted by the courts (Schertzer 2012). Of the *Secession Reference*, Schertzer states: "Recognizing the contested nature of the norm [of what the federation is], the Court went to considerable effort to highlight that there is no single way to approach federalism in Canada" (2008, 114–15; see also Schertzer and Woods 2011; Woods, Schertzer, and Kaufmann 2011; LeRoy 2004). Rather, federalism is a norm or a process through which to navigate that ambiguity. The multinational, pan-Canadian, and provincial equality visions are *all* relevant to some extent, and the country would never have united if there had not been space for each.

There are other examples. The rejection of Justice Marc Nadon's appointment to the Supreme Court of Canada on the grounds that he was not a member of the Quebec bench or bar was important not just for that specific point. The Court suggested that appointing Nadon would upset a basic understanding of the Canadian constitutional structure which requires that French Canadians feel secure that the Court protects not just their legal tradition but also their social values (Reference re Supreme Court Act, ss. 5 and 6, 2014, at para. 59). This interpretation protects both the functioning and the legitimacy of the Court (Reference re Supreme Court Act, ss. 5 and 6, 2014, at para. 49). While not proclaiming Canada a dualist society, such a ruling leaves that interpretation in play. Conversely, the finding that Quebec does not have a veto might be taken to negate a dualist interpretation, but the proviso of substantial provincial consent as a recognized convention did not mean that Canada was a true contract either (see Reference re Resolution to Amend the Canadian Constitution 1981).

The nature of common-law judging makes it very useful for contributing to the maintenance of abeyances. To that extent, the courts are being used to further the ends of a party who wants to make use of their assumed neutrality. The courts may not be entirely neutral, but their legitimacy depends on that fiction being maintained, and there is an interest on all sides in their remaining balanced or appearing to be so. Superficially, it is easy to see the Court as complicit in maintaining these abeyances – and perhaps it has been. Occasionally the courts have been forced to confront an abeyance head on. Usually, though, courts have been more circumspect. It is no secret to legal scholars that the courts remain fundamentally conservative institutions, living up to the claim of Alexander Hamilton that they are "the least dangerous branch." Nor is it a surprise that they work to protect their legitimacy, which rests on a more tenuous ground than other political institutions do (Radmilovic 2010, 845–6). The lack of budgetary or coercive control leaves courts vulnerable and dependent on the other branches, and judges must be wary of not sacrificing their authority (845–6; see also Spiller and Gely 2008; Gibson, Caldeira, and Baird 1998). Reflecting in part that the lack of independent budgetary or coercive powers leaves courts dependent on other political actors to function (as first identified by Alexander Hamilton in the *Federalist*, no. 78), as well as the absence of periodic elections for legitimacy renewal, courts must be careful to maintain their position in the political system (Radmilovic 2010, 845). Cass Sunstein has written that this circumspection is essential in well-functioning legal systems, in which participants will try to cultivate "incompletely theorized arguments on particular outcomes" when there are many values in tension (1995, 1735). To give an example, one might support unions for a variety of reasons: they have a democratic character, they protect peace in the workplace, or they protect the rights of workers (1736). A judge may rule for a union because he or she supports all of these, but it is usually not necessary and often counterproductive to offer a complete theory justifying unions in a particular case. The failure to do so might reflect a fear by a judge of finding himself in the minority if the point is pressed, or perhaps out of a fear of the precedent it might set. It may reflect an unwillingness to close the argument for good. Sunstein points out that none of this is strange to courts. "Disagreement on foundations may produce disagreement on particulars," he notes. Further, "What I am emphasizing is that, when closure cannot be based on relative abstractions, the legal system is often able to reach a degree of closure by focusing on relative particulars. Examples of this kind are exceptionally common. They are the day-to-day stuff of law" (1737).

The tendency of courts to remain *in general* at the highest level of abstraction allows for the preservation of abeyances *specifically* and is likely a key part of why democratic federations (which depend on abeyances) are able to stay together in spite of considerable disunity. Faced with competing visions, the Court need not come down on one side; it must only resolve the matter in a way that is sufficiently clear for the matter at hand. This results in judicial decisions that are often partial and ambiguous and leave a range of possible pathways for an issue to follow. In 2005, surveying the role played by the Supreme Court, James Kelly and Michael Murphy argued that the Court's role is essentially "meta-political" – it does not and has not usurped the role of the political actors on questions of division of power (2005, 218). Rather, the Court supplements these debates, assisting the actors where it can in the system and offering guidance only when these political processes fail. Kelly and Murphy argue that the Court has fostered an inter-institutional dialogue that never closes off a particular interpretation but is something that "challenges the argument that judicial review represents the final word on the scope and content of constitutional provisions" (219). Jan Erk and Alain-G. Gagnon made a similar argument as far back as the year 2000, focusing on the extent to which the justices appear to have noticed that ambiguity is essential in maintaining the understandings that underpin Canadian federalism (2000). The Supreme Court was asked to rule on several clear questions in the 1998 *Reference re Secession of Quebec*. The ruling, however, left a considerable amount unclear. While the Court found Quebec did not have a *unilateral* right to leave Canada, there was still a duty on the part of the rest of the country to negotiate in the event that the population gave its clear desire to go. The Court kept that threshold ambiguous.

Courts cannot do the job alone, though, as the restoration of abeyances is a political choice. If there is enough agreement on the overall constitutional system, then actors who have a stake in it will operate to play down their differences. One will see abeyances score lower on the political agenda than they did previously, differences of opinion will be tolerated and perhaps gestured to without genuine acceptance, and possibly tricky questions will be hived off, depoliticized, and endlessly postponed.

Conclusion

None of this would be possible were it not for evolving conditions in Quebec that have given the space needed by politicians to dodge the issue of settling Quebec's place in Canada. The experience of exposing the abeyance and trying to solve it did not lead to resolution in the form of one "side" simply losing the fight once it began. Instead, it nearly led to the collapse of the Constitution, and those who had an interest in national unity realized that perhaps it was better to leave the national question alone. Rather, the abeyance, now revealed, has become a taboo, maintained by those with an overriding interest in the stability and unity of the country. It is a taboo because the troublesome and unbridgeable ambiguity has been exposed but the danger is so great that no one wants to talk about it any more. So the abeyance is replaced. Today the gaps are forbidden subjects in the political discourse. There is a broad consensus among federalist governments, political parties and their leaders, the courts, and, to no small extent, the general public not to reopen the debate – not because these problems do not exist or are unimportant, but because *no one can resolve them at an acceptable cost*. The sole exceptions are the PQ, which has an interest in breaking up the country, and the BQ for the same reason. The result has been a return to what Thomas has called a "settled unsettlement" (1997, chap. 3).

The following chapters examine the political conditions that have allowed this situation. While it is clear that political management has been critical in keeping a lid on the issue, there are other forces at play that have taken the heat off the political class to address this constitutional gap. None of these was inevitable, but they have come together to create an environment that has benefited federalist leaders at the expense of their antagonists. Importantly, it is not guaranteed to continue; the situation could easily change, pushing the national question back into the spotlight.

3 Constitutional Fatigue

In the aftermath of the closely fought referendum in 1995, Quebec premier Jacques Parizeau told his supporters to prepare themselves for the next opportunity to fight for an independent Quebec, an opportunity that would come sooner rather than later. "I really would have liked for it to happen," he said of winning independence. "I so wanted it to happen. We were so close to having a country. Well, it's pushed back a little bit. Not long. We won't have to wait another 15 years this time. No, no no" (Patriquin 2015).

Unsurprisingly, Parizeau's belief was also the consensus opinion of most outside observers (e.g., Broadbent 1996; Cameron 1996). The federal government tried desperately to get ahead of what it assumed would be a third referendum, likely to be held soon after the next provincial election, due in 1998. Indeed, former prime minister Jean Chrétien admitted that the terror of an imminent referendum drove the planning that went into the publicity programs involved in the so-called sponsorship scandal and aimed at raising the country's profile in Quebec in the late 1990s (Gomery 2005, 65–7). The political stars, as well, appeared to align. Parizeau resigned within hours of his speech, and Lucien Bouchard moved quickly to fill his shoes and finish the job.

Still, it was clear that a time gap was going to be necessary. By law, the PQ could not hold another referendum on the same question within the same mandate. There would have to be another provincial election – presumably one the PQ would win – before another poll could be held. Since Parizeau had moved so quickly after being elected, the earliest a third referendum could realistically take place was 1999 or 2000. Parizeau, now out, left it to Bouchard to steer the path forward. When it came to the timing of the next vote, however, Bouchard was far less aggressive than his predecessor. He sensed that there was no support for a snap election or referendum and was happy to push it off for a time in order to consolidate his position. That meant that both sides needed a bit of a delay. Bouchard turned his attention to other questions, in particular those on the economy, which reflected the fact that his roots were more conservative than Parizeau's. He launched into building the "social economy," a twist on capitalism that arguably made Quebec more progressive than other provinces and was rooted around stronger social programs in health, childcare, and education (see generally Arsenault 2019). Even after winning the 1998 election, however, Bouchard sensed that the appetite for another vote had not returned. Instead, he continued the search for the elusive winning conditions that he needed before committing to another referendum. Not finding them, and disillusioned with the quest, he stepped down in 2001.

The push towards sovereignty was reignited when Bouchard was replaced by Bernard Landry, a much more hard-nosed separatist and one more closely in line with Parizeau. Though Landry's election signalled a return to a more aggressive posture, he too failed in finding the conditions needed for a third referendum. As the years passed, and it was clear the public did not want another referendum, people began to search for reasons for the lack of appetite. The first explanation to emerge was that the public was simply suffering from "constitutional fatigue"; basically, people were tired of talking about it. By this point the people of Quebec had been fighting the separatist battle for close to forty years, and there was a sense that the electorate wanted to move on to something else.

The sudden drop in the public's interest in a topic is usually characterized as a question of *salience* for the voters, and it is from this perspective that the chapter examines the question. As mentioned in chapter 1, I define *constitutional fatigue* as the sudden drop in the issue salience surrounding the politics and process of finding a permanent solution to Quebec's status within Canada. This drop affected both the public and the political elites, a distinction that will become important later in this chapter. Beginning in the mid-1990s, there was a belief that Canadians everywhere had been oversaturated by the time spent on the issue, leading to a sense of intractability and a desire to move to other topics. The public-policy literature on salience (Krosnick 1990; Dennison 2019) suggests that once an issue drops in importance, it becomes a problem of agenda setting for elites who wish to pursue it as a political objective (Jones and Baumgartner 2005; Baumgartner and Jones 2009). At that point, there is a clear advantage for politicians willing to discuss other, more important topics in the electoral arena. This exhaustion seemed to exist after 1995 – both among the population of Quebec and that of English Canada – and this, in turn, created an incentive for politicians to leave the issue in abeyance.

This chapter first traces the origins of the term *constitutional fatigue* as it pertains to the national question in Quebec. From there, the chapter situates constitutional fatigue within the broader public-policy literature on salience and agenda setting in order to give it a firmer theoretical foundation in political science. To demonstrate why this lack of salience mattered, I suggest that pursuing sovereignty, no matter how it was defined after 1995, was no longer seen as a solution to modern political or policy problems that was strong enough to get its pursuit to the top of the political agenda. Still, I argue that, while it is reasonable to conclude that there was a drop in issue salience right *after* the referendum, constitutional fatigue alone cannot be held as a complete explanation for why the national question fell as a priority to the point that the issue could be dropped by elites for almost three decades. Rather, it makes more sense to see constitutional fatigue as a key explanation for the late 1990s, but that deeper factors explain fully why the national question fell off the agenda in the decades that followed.

History of the Term

The origin of the term *constitutional fatigue* is unclear in Canadian politics, but it seems to have come into common parlance by about 1990. Not surprisingly, it appears first in Quebec, where there are sporadic references to it in the press throughout the 1980s. Its application to English Canada came a little later, although during the first referendum former Quebec Liberal leader Claude Ryan had warned that a "constitutional fatigue" could hold Canada back from negotiating an economic partnership with an independent Quebec (Assemblée Nationale du Québec 1990, 4341).

By 1990, it became more common to refer to constitutional fatigue as affecting the whole country and to a common desire to drop the constitutional debate entirely. In that year, *Maclean's* magazine ran an editorial by the editor-in-chief, Kevin Doyle, who noted that the term "was gaining some currency" after the collapse of Meech Lake and the move towards the Charlottetown Accord (1990). His use of the term is unattributed, making it unclear about whom he was speaking, but references to constitutional fatigue appeared in the news, the National Assembly in Quebec, and at political press conferences around this time (e.g., Contenta 1990; *Journal des débats de la Commission des institutions* 1990; Robert Bourassa 1992; *L'actualité* 1993, 28). *Constitutional fatigue* as a term continued to gain traction in the popular media, and it peaked in both English and French in 1992 with the failure of Charlottetown.[1] Although popular use of the term declined afterwards, it appeared in the political-science literature as early as 1993 and then was continually reproduced, probably first in English by Peter Russell and then by others (Russell 1993, 36; Vipond 1993, 52). By the late 1990s, constitutional fatigue was a common explanation for the public's lack of interest in constitutional change. It appeared in the introduction to the Institute of Intergovernmental Relations' 1998 Canada: State of the Federation series on non-constitutional renewal as a problem afflicting Canadian politics (Lazar 1998, 4). Today it is not hard to find the term in both the English and the French Canadian literature on federalism and intergovernmental relations where it is typically used to explain the public's disinterest in mega-constitutional politics, Quebec sovereignty, and constitutional change (Gibbins 1999, 273; Knopf and Sayers 2005, 16; É. Montpetit 2007b, 111; Simeon, Robinson, and Wallner, 2014, 81; B. Gagnon 2015, 117; McGill Law Publications 2016; Vachet 2019).

For the most part, constitutional fatigue has been used as a shorthand for the public's exhaustion with the national question in Quebec, but there has been no systematic or theoretical treatment of the concept outside of this use.[2] The idea is similar to other terms that refer to the tendency of people to become overwhelmed by, and in turn indifferent to, intractable and difficult situations. *Compassion fatigue*, for example, is used in the medical community to refer to those who suffer from burnout in caring for others (see Figley 1995 for the original conception of the idea in the medical community). Journalists also talk about compassion fatigue as the tendency of the public to lose interest in a war or disaster story or to become immune to the chaos of the world around them (e.g., Moeller 2002). Academics have developed the idea of *war fatigue* to refer to populations who become indifferent to the conflicts through which they are living or to who might win them (see Ramazani 2013 for a description of the term's origins). Perhaps the most rigorous work has been on *voter fatigue* or *choice fatigue*, which is concerned with how voter turn-out is connected to the spacing of elections (see Garmann 2017). There has also been experimental work of examining how, in a controlled setting, voters respond to a ballot with a large number of options and whether they are more likely to take short cuts and select according to the position of a choice on the ballot (Augenblick and Nicholson 2016). However, this work has evolved without much connection to constitutional politics in Canada. And there is very little theoretical treatment of the way in which voters respond to a large bundle of connected issues over a series of decades, as was the case with the mega-constitutional era in

Quebec, which came to be associated in the minds of Canadians as a single thread of insoluble problems.

Still, what are we to make of constitutional fatigue? Ignoring the loose meaning of the term, we can see how it has shaped the way in which both citizens and politicians think about Quebec, the Constitution, and the scope of possible reforms. In a 2000 interview Jean Chrétien cited constitutional fatigue as a reason he would not re-enter the constitutional debates of the previous decades: "[Constitutional fatigue] is not a temporary fatigue; it's a very deep fatigue. It's not the type of fatigue where we say go take two weeks' vacation, or a year of vacation, or a year-long sabbatical and we will come back to it ... What people want is to move onto other things" (author's translation, adapted from H. Young 2000).

What is constitutional fatigue, beyond a series of buzzwords? How does the public become tired of an issue? And how important was the Constitution to the people of Canada, even at the peak of constitutional politics in the 1970s, 1980s, and 1990s? To answer these questions, the chapter conceptualizes the term theoretically within the public-policy literature on issue salience and agenda setting. It examines why the public and elites prioritize some issues over others.

Issue Salience and Agenda Setting

If an issue falls off the political agenda, a few possibilities come to mind to explain why. It could be that politicians have decided they no longer want to pursue the issue regardless of public opinion. It could be that there is a drop in the number of people who are interested in the issue in the first place. Regardless, the disappearance of an issue usually reflects a drop in issue salience, something that will be familiar to people who study electoral behaviour or the public-policy process.

An issue can become less salient if people care less about it. The issue may not disappear, but it might not be top of mind either. Salience is a concept that has received wide attention in political science, going back to the last two decades of the twentieth century (Dennison 2019; Krosnick 1990). The idea is central to public-policy literature, but while there is no shortage of definitions, it remains a somewhat under-specified term (e.g., Miller, Krosnick, and Fabrigar 2017). The study of salience can be split between *elite salience* – when an issue is particularly important to a political party, say – and *issue salience* for the public in general, which is usually studied as an outgrowth of electoral politics. The former, sometimes called supply-side issue salience, has received less attention than the demand-side issue salience. This latter category of issue salience can be further subdivided into two strands of literature that examines why issues are important to individuals (Dennison 2019, 437). The first is characterized as studies that are psychological in nature; they define salience according to how importantly a person might describe an issue, or how much they say they think about it when asked. The second, and arguably broader and more influential strain, has been described as the behavioural strain of literature. This branch studies issue salience from a rational-choice perspective, exploring how people demonstrate issue salience through voting behaviour and why they make the choices they do at the ballot box (437). This literature has made major contributions to issue-voting theory, as a weight in spatial models, and to study interaction and direct effects on questions like a voter's party choice (441).

Why issue salience varies over time, if at all, is a far less understood concept (Dennison 2019, 442). For example, is an issue rising or dropping in salience, or is it just standing still, overtaken by the relative movement of other issues? Some models have assumed that issue salience is relatively static for individuals, especially for scholars who rely heavily on assumptions about preference formation happening early in childhood (this will be particularly important in the next chapter when we examine the explanations connected to generational change). Krosnick's 1990 study identified the three factors of self-interest, values, and social identification as the basis of a well-known framework for understanding the basics of stability of issue salience. Variation in issue salience only occurs in the light of major events of significant public or political importance (Dennison 2019, 442; Krosnick 1990, 74; see also Jones and Baumgartner 2005).

The rest of the chapter assesses the reason the national question has failed to reach the top of the political agenda. The mega-constitutional era gave rise to a sense of the intractability of constitutional issues on the part of the public, and of many politicians. That is, there was a drop in both issue and elite salience. It is not clear what problems exist that independence could solve. Too many experts have offered too many views on the benefits or costs of separation to be credible, and the inability of elites to solve the problem through executive federalism has eaten away at their desire or support to bring the national question to the top of the agenda. The reluctance of federalists to be dragged into constitutional debates has robbed sovereigntists of opportunities to create focusing events that would raise the salience of the issue and bring it to the surface. This has enhanced the conditions for leaving Quebec's status in the federation as a constitutional abeyance among the federalists themselves.

Struggling to Reach the Top of the Political Agenda

What were the problems that independence was supposed to solve?[3] In a study of why people supported the sovereigntist option, Matthew Mendelsohn found many factors at play. Disaffection from the country and the perceived lack of respect that Quebec received from the rest of Canada was the major but hardly the only reason that people were willing to vote for independence (Mendelsohn 2003, 511–18). Cost-benefit considerations for the economy were also important, a calculation which suggested that for some people gaining independence was partially a means to an end. Constitutional questions are necessarily elite issues and often lack support when not otherwise connected to more bread-and-butter issues like jobs, health care, and the economy. Independence made no sense if it did not contribute to solving the everyday problems that people faced. The evidence for this is not hard to find; the academic community has generated a vast literature on the economic reasons for voting either for or against independence, which will be looked at in the chapter on globalization (e.g., Pinard and Hamilton 1977, 1984a, 1986; Howe 1998; Blais, Martin, and Nadeau 1995). Thus, while the lack of respect Quebec faced in Canada rooted the project, it was always clear that support for separation was contingent on believing that life would be better outside of Canada.

The PQ has known this and, from early on, has always been forced to fight for independence on the ground of "sovereignty association." The sovereignty-association concept developed in the 1970s as a method of reassuring the public that the economic risks of independence were minimal, while offering a path to secure the national respect that Quebec deserved (Pinard 1992, 481). It formed the basis of the successful pitch that the PQ made for power in the provincial election of 1976 and was central to the strategy in the 1980 referendum (Cloutier, Guay, and Latouche 1992). Although the Quebec public was always supportive of the nationalism of the PQ, the idea of outright independence struck many voters as being a step too far (D. Smiley 1978, 203). Even after the PQ took power in 1976, experts who studied public opinion found little appetite for an outright break. Around 90 per cent of people who supported independence voted for the PQ in 1976, the year the party were first elected, but a review of the polls from 1962 until that date found an absolute ceiling of 23 per cent in support of independence (Pinard and Hamilton 1977, 230; D. Smiley 1978, 203). In response, the PQ embraced a "go-slow" approach so as not to scare off more moderate voters. This strategy of *étapisme* was then combined with a promise that the party would never make a move towards independence before first getting approval in a popular referendum (D. Smiley 1978, 203). To make it more palatable, the PQ promised voters that it would only pursue independence in the context of a partnership with Canada and then only after a consultative referendum had been held (203). The run-up to the election in 1976 saw the party focus more on bread-and-butter economic issues and play down the separatism option (203). This strategy was very effective and led to the dominating performance in the election that followed. This cautious and careful approach remained the thrust of the PQ's commitment so long as René Lévesque was in charge. It could not, however, paper over the fact that it was only one strain of thought on the topic and that there were many other hardliners who saw the commitment to a partnership as little more than a tactic to achieve full independence.

Lévesque famously accepted the 1980 defeat for what it was and encouraged the party to take the *beau risque* of a continued federalism with Canada. But his view was increasingly not that of the rest of the PQ. As the 1980s wore on, the elite of the PQ began to lose interest in a close relationship with the rest of Canada and saw true independence as the goal. An offer of association might be necessary, but it should be a loose one. As hardliners such as Parizeau and Landry moved to the centre of the party, the party's stance hardened. Still, even as the elites moved in this direction, the public remained interested in the issue but not committed to outright independence. Questions remained about what the debate on the Constitution was achieving. Consistent with theories of both issue salience and agenda setting, research on public opinion showed that the salience of independence rose and fell with the debates undertaken by elites. That meant that the absolute peak came in 1990 with the collapse of the Meech Lake Accord and rallied again after the collapse of the Charlottetown Accord.

At this time, independence was enjoying the apogee of its appeal to solve a wide variety of problems for Quebec. By the late 1980s not only the PQ but even the federalist Liberals were promising a referendum if the province's demands were not met, suggesting a consensus that Quebec was better off out of Canada. Maurice Pinard argued in an article entitled "The Dramatic Re-emergence of the Quebec Independence Movement" that it was clear that independence had hit a strong new wave by 1992. For Pinard, the failure of the Meech Lake Accord was the obvious catalyst. But there was more to it. More people saw independence as a path to prosperity, and, although the number never reached a majority, the change was dramatic. Between 1970 and 1991, the number of those who saw independence as a risk to Quebec fell, from 63 to just 47 per cent (Pinard 1992, 495). Those who thought independence would improve conditions or at least stay the same went from 14 and 7 per cent – low by any measure – to 25 and 19 per cent respectively (Pinard 1992, 495). Beyond the forces generated by the perceived rejection by Canada and by economic issues, Quebec independence was probably motivated by a belief that it could solve problems that are commonly identified with other nationalist movements, including concerns over resource control, worries brought about by post-materialism, and cultural insecurities. By the early 1990s, independence was now a mainstream idea supported by a fully mature political movement with competent political leaders. Thus, it was not just one problem that independence seemed to be able to solve; for many voters in 1992, it could solve almost all of them.

The 1995 referendum was a key moment in which Quebecers were encouraged to make that jump. A critical PQ tactical move was to reassure the public that there would be a deal with the rest of the country, no matter what – something many in the PQ did not want but knew was necessary. The most visible example of this was the depiction of the one-dollar coin as part of the "Oui" sign, and the suggestion that people would be able to use their Canadian passports and even send Members of Parliament to Ottawa. Polls at the time suggested that a large segment of the population bought into these ideas. The rest of the country never accepted the idea of a deal, of course, and made no secret of the fact that it was willing to use the economy as a bargaining chip in stabilizing the country (Martin 1995, 56). Nevertheless, perhaps the key move was the change of salesman, when Parizeau, in the face of a floundering campaign, stepped aside and allowed Bouchard to take the helm. Viewed as a much more pragmatic politician who could get things done, and supported by a winning story of overcoming adversity after he had lost his leg to a terrible disease shortly before the referendum, the public rallied to the cry.

Even before the referendum was narrowly lost, a shift had started in the narrative that the Constitution was in reality a distraction in the search for solutions to ordinary problems. This approach also appeared to have an electoral following. The federal Liberals won a huge majority in 1993 by promising to provide "jobs, jobs, jobs" and to move away from the constitutional issues that were dominating the headlines at the time. While the period after 1995 was gripped with a sense that another referendum might be coming, it never materialized. By the end of the early 2000s, there was a clear political strategy on the part of federalist parties to paint the Constitution as a distraction. To take one example, the Quebec Liberal Party slogan in 2013 was *L'économie d'abord OUI* (YES, the economy first), and later in 2014, *Ensemble on s'occupe des vrais affairs* (Together let's take care of the real issues). This was a far cry from 1960, when the slogan was *C'est l'temps qu'ça change* (It's time for a change) or, famously, in 1962, *Maîtres chez nous* (Masters in our own house).

Public-opinion polling suggests that independence is no longer seen as a solution to ordinary problems. In fact, the priorities of Quebecers are not radically different from those of other Canadians. Vote Compass, an organization that tracks public opinion in Canada, has asked Quebecers whether their top priority for the past decade has reliably been the economy, health, or education (J. Montpetit 2018). In the three polls conducted, there was little change among these priorities, with the economy taking the lead position in the 2012 survey at 37 per cent, and an ever-larger lead in the 2014 survey, where it topped out at about 47 per cent (J. Montpetit 2018). As the economy recovered after the financial crisis, it eventually fell behind education as a public priority. Education took the lead spot at 32 per cent, with the economy coming in at 24 per cent. In all three iterations of the survey, independence never received more than 12 per cent support, where it was tied with education in 2014 (J. Montpetit 2018). In all three surveys the top three results all topped 50 per cent. The question surrounding sovereignty directly was no longer being asked.

How Much Did Pursuing Independence Really Matter in the End?

The question of how salient constitutional issues have ever been for the Canadian public has always dogged those politicians who want to pursue them. It was a question that Pierre Trudeau faced in the late 1960s when he began the first round of the patriation process and wondered whether it was worth the time and effort when there were so many other pressing issues facing Canadians. He notably dropped the project after the failure of the Victoria Charter in 1971 on the belief that there simply was not enough interest to continue pushing it. Brian Mulroney also faced the question when considering whether or not to relaunch constitutional discussions in 1984 after taking office following John Turner's defeat. Such abstract constitutional issues may be alluring for the perceived stakes and cachet they bring to those involved, but they risk coming across as very remote to the concerns of ordinary Canadians. Even among the PQ in its heyday there was always the question hanging over the project of just how engaged the public ever actually was. In this telling, *elite* salience is the driver of the question in the politics stream, but it was never that important for the public and is increasingly less important to those in charge.

Beyond the substantive content of constitutional politics, the process involved has often been accused of being too remote from the concerns of ordinary people. Intergovernmental relations in general is the study of the internecine battles among the political class – theorized as "elite accommodation," "executive federalism," and so on, often done without reference to the people who are actually being governed. It is this characteristic that makes the study of constitutional politics not only fascinating but also often subject to the criticism that this style of politics is both undemocratic and unaccountable. Following the collapse of the Meech Lake Accord, there was a notable public backlash against this style, forcing a referendum on the subsequent Charlottetown Accord and arguably ushering in the conditions for a rise in the populism and anti-elitism later seen in other countries. This sentiment was reflected in the rise of the populist Reform Party in 1993, a rise in interest in citizen's assemblies, and a period when many provinces flirted with changing their electoral systems. By the time the rest of the world was having its populist moment in places like Britain with Brexit, or America under Donald Trump, Canada had already experienced a similar wave and did not experience these forces.

Regardless, the role of policy entrepreneurs needs to be considered in the way that issues come to the top of the political agenda. There is no doubt that much of the instability of the 1970–90 period reflected the power of charismatic individuals who were able to push their projects forward. The concept of policy entrepreneurship is associated with Kingdon (1984) but has flowed through to the current day in many different policy areas (e.g., Mintrom 1997; Corbett 2003; Font and Subirats 2010). These leaders have the ability to transcend adverse or otherwise unpromising political conditions to open the policy windows they need in order to achieve their particular projects.

Most academics agree that the mega-constitutional era's peaks and valleys tracked the political agenda of the elites, at least to a degree (e.g., Institute of Public Administration of Canada 1979; Banting and Simeon 1983; Pinard 1992; Simeon 2002, 2006). As politicians lost interest in the national question in Quebec, one interpretation of the idea of constitutional fatigue is that public support for independence simply fell to normal levels once there was no opening for it to rise again. Without question, in more recent years politicians have learned their lesson and avoided anything that would visibly raise the profile of the Constitution. As discussed in the introductory chapter, the unwillingness of Jean Chrétien to discuss constitutional questions after 1993 contributed to taking the heat out of the question. This approach was adopted by all federal governments that followed, first by the short-lived government of Paul Martin and then by the government of Stephen Harper, who refused to be drawn into any debates with Quebec. Harper pointedly refused to meet with the premiers together on almost any subject, taking the view that first ministers' meetings only served to make the federal government look bad. Furthermore, Harper stuck to a view that federalism (couched in the term of *open federalism*) was fundamentally about the different levels of government restricting themselves to matters that were in their jurisdiction, and avoiding overlap. While making exceptions for health care and infrastructure, he never deviated from his philosophy that Ottawa and the provinces should interact as little as possible (Fox 2007; Harmes 2007; Dunn 2008; Gotz 2010). And it seemed to work.

Never was the efficacy of Harper's approach more evident than during the era of Pauline Marois, the PQ premier of Quebec between 2012 and 2014. She came to power on the specific promise to resurrect the moribund movement. Understanding that interest in the topic had waned, she committed herself to opening a discussion with Ottawa to transfer as many powers as she could and to be much more confrontational with the federal government. Notably Bernard Drainville, who would eventually serve as Minister of Democratic Institutions, got the party to commit to holding a series of citizen's referendums on devolution, which he felt were a guaranteed winner politically (Canadian Press 2012). Harper simply refused to take the bait, dismissed this and other provocations as the "old tricks," and suggested that Quebecers wanted to move on to other topics. For his part, Justin Trudeau has taken a similar position towards federal-provincial relations, although he has been more willing to meet with the premiers than his predecessor was. Regardless, he has shied away from any suggestion that he reopen the Constitution, whenever an opportunity to do so arises. Like Harper, Justin Trudeau ignored Phillipe Couillard's musings about a constitutional discussion to find a way for Quebec to sign the Constitution in time for Canada's one-hundred-and-fiftieth anniversary, and he was similarly unsympathetic to former Alberta premier Jason Kenney's request for constitutional talks about equalization after the provincial referendum in 2021 (Canadian Press 2014; McGregor 2017; Amato 2021). As a result, the options for stirring up trouble on the constitutional front are minimal.

Right now, the best evidence that constitutional questions are not on the political agenda in Quebec comes from the stance taken by the Coalition avenir Québec government under François Legault. The CAQ, elected in 2018 and then re-elected with a huge majority in 2022, represents a watershed moment for the province as it is the first time in decades that a party other than the Liberals or the PQ have held power. The present CAQ is the product of a merger with the Action démocratique du Québec (ADQ), which was formerly led by Mario Dumont and was well known to Canadians for supporting the PQ in the drive to independence in 1995. After that election the ADQ remained an important force in Quebec politics, eventually becoming the official opposition after the election in 2007 and relegating the PQ to third-party status. After that high-water point, the party declined badly and eventually merged with the CAQ in 2012. The CAQ was notable from the beginning for its commitment to move away from the national question and put economic questions at the heart of its policies. While it was clearly a nationalist party, it was not a separatist party and had no interest in that agenda. Instead, the CAQ staked its political future on the idea that the Quebec welfare state was too big and that the economy could do better with the right reforms, but also that there were clear cultural values at the heart of Quebec society that needed protecting (Boily 2018, 48–51). To that extent, it embraced the Bouchard-Taylor Commission's recommendations on state secularism and broadly supported the move to introduce some form of a law limiting religious displays in the public sphere.

At the same time, the CAQ made it very clear that it saw the constitutional debate as being over, and François Legault has held firmly to that position. He has concentrated instead on the politics of nationalism – moving aggressively on the politics of language and state secularism, and arguing that Quebec can recognize itself as a nation without the recognition of the rest of the country (a position that most experts reject as illegal) – which has demonstrated his lack of interest in multilateral constitutional discussions or accords or in returning to the debate about independence. The CAQ message had appeal partially because of the person who was selling it. Legault was the founder of Air Transat and had the private-sector business credentials that lent force to his modernizing and fairly neoliberal message. Legault notably decried equalization as a program that was infantilizing for the province, and he would like nothing better than for the province to do well enough that it could do without it. Perhaps more importantly, his abandonment of the sovereignty cause had something of a "Nixon goes to China" element, given that Legault was himself a former PQ minister. The fact that he had split with the party and decided that the province needed to go in a different direction lent credibility to what he was saying (although some questioned his sincerity and willingness to abandon his earlier views) (Boily 2018, 33–4). Indeed, he went so far as to reach out to the anglophone community and announced that should the CAQ come to power, he would never hold a referendum on sovereignty. The hope was to pry at least some of the English vote away from the Liberals, who have historically benefited disproportionately from their popularity among anglophones given the latter's heavy concentration on the west island of Montreal and ability to deliver a solid number of seats. While efforts among anglophones did not pay off, the strategy did work with the broader francophone community, and the CAQ shot to the top of Quebec politics. On 1 October 2018 the CAQ was elected with a large majority and decimated both the Liberal Party and the PQ. Since then the CAQ has implemented much of its program, first by bringing in a secularism bill and making a number of other changes around school boards and the economy. But the CAQ did not deviate from the commitment to leave the national question alone, and Legault has done little to pick fights with Ottawa. One opportunity that presented itself for such a conflict was Bill 21 (an Act Respecting the Laicity of the State), which many see as unconstitutional. But the federal government has refused to become dragged into the debate. A similar situation arose after Legault claimed that he could unilaterally amend the Canadian constitution to have Quebec recognized as a "nation" in the context of Bill 96 (an Act Respecting French, the Official and Common Language of Québec), which strengthened the provinces' language legislation. Even though most experts agreed he had no such power, the federal government again refused to be involved, and Legault refused to demand anything more from other Canadian partners, satisfied to leave the question to the courts. This approach has proved very popular, and Legault returned to power with a huge majority in the provincial elections of October 2022 (CBC News 2022).

The one bright spot for the separatist movement has been the return of the Bloc Québécois. After experiencing a series of disasters, the BQ had a breakout success in the federal election of 2019. After unifying behind an articulate and capable new leader, Yves-François Blanchet, the party ran a very competent and steady campaign, which paid large dividends. The BQ won thirty-two out of seventy-eight seats in Quebec, the best performance it had seen in years (Elections Canada 2019). This win also allowed the party to regain official party status, which it had not held since 2011. Commentators watched and wondered whether or not this meant that the movement was once more on the rise.

A close inspection shows that it is not. Blanchet ran as a separatist, but he was very much the product of the same forces that had brought the CAQ to power the year before. The message that Blanchet brought was the same as that of the CAQ, focused on cultural insecurities but avoiding direct talk of future referendums. Rather, he played to the debate on reasonable accommodations and concerns about the security of the French language. But the party has essentially risen alongside a promise not to reopen the debate, at least not yet. The BQ has advanced the position that it is the party best placed to defend the interests of Quebec, and that for now those interests do not include another referendum on independence. The BQ continued to take this line in the federal election of 2021 and matched its seat count with a nearly identical vote share (Elections Canada 2021). Taken together, all parties, including those that are openly advocating for the break-up of the federal system, have admitted that they do not see the question of independence as being one that they can or should bring to the top of the political agenda right now.

Still, there is always a chance that a policy entrepreneur who, given new conditions or a new message, may be successful in bringing the national question back to the top of the political agenda. There have been some, as noted earlier, who have tried, albeit not successfully. Although this book has focused on the reasons why this has become more difficult, it is by no means impossible. The election of the PQ in 1976 was an absolute shock to many people, and Quebec politics can be quite volatile. Furthermore, polling suggests that there remains a solid group of people who would be willing to vote yes in the event of a referendum and who would likely be open to a discussion about the national question in Quebec; they just do not see it as a priority at the moment (e.g., Bourgault-Côté 2013). It cannot be discounted, therefore, that one day there may be a person who will be successful in bringing the national question to the top of the agenda. That day, however, has not yet come.

Constitutional fatigue has been a popular explanation, but it is unlikely to be the only force at play in the decline of the salience of the national question. Fatigue does not explain why the younger generation has so little interest in this issue, given that they were not around for (and have no memory of) the mega-constitutional era (e.g., G. Hamilton 2004; K. Gagnon 2014a; Mahéo and Bélanger 2018). Other countries have struggled with constitutional questions for even longer periods and have not always seen the same effect; indeed, long struggles can often *increase* the passions of those involved, not the other way around. Constitutional fatigue also cannot account for why other issues may have grown in importance all on their own, without reference to the constitutional context. Thus, a drop in salience, relative or absolute when compared to other issues, is unlikely to solve the puzzle alone. Rather, it is best contextualized as a force that had pull in the months and years after the end of the mega-constitutional era in 1995. Beyond that time period, it becomes necessary to look for other explanations as well.

Conclusion

This chapter has reviewed the history and conceptualized constitutional fatigue theoretically as an explanation for the decline of the Quebec sovereignty movement. It has done so by defining the concept as a drop in issue salience that was brought about in the public by the elites' oversaturation of a question to the point that the public believed the problem had become intractable. To that extent, the constant discussion of the issue and the failure of the political leaders to reach a consensus meant that Quebec sovereignty declined in importance for the average voter. There were policy entrepreneurs who tried to bring it to the top of the agenda, but this became much more difficult after 1995. The term *constitutional fatigue*, most likely Canadian in origin, peaked after the collapse of the Charlottetown Accord and was driven by the sense of intractability that the public felt with mega-constitutional politics. After 1995 it became a shorthand used to explain why the appetite for major constitutional change never returned. It does, though, raise questions about how relevant mega-constitutional politics ever was. Even within Quebec there is a plausible argument that separatism was never high on the agenda and that it relied on political elites to open policy windows and create the right winning conditions to trigger a referendum – considerations that ultimately proved impossible to create.

In total, constitutional fatigue looks like the most convincing explanation for the lack of interest in the Constitution in the period directly after 1995. But it cannot be disaggregated from the other forces that were at play, and it becomes a poorer explanation as time goes on and memories fade. Other explanations need to be taken into account, including social and economic developments, generational effects, economic change, and the accommodations that have been made for Quebec by the rest of Canada over the last fifty years. It is to those forces that the book now turns.

4 Non-constitutional Accommodation

The question "What does Quebec want?" defined Canadian federalism throughout the second half of the twentieth century. There were no easy answers, and opinions varied depending on who was asked. It became a matter of serious concern in the 1960s, triggering the national unity crisis. Depending on who was governing in Quebec City, the question seemed to have no clear or fixed answer, giving rise to a degree of frustration by Canadians outside Quebec. The closest Canada and Quebec ever came to answering the question was the Meech Lake Accord, signed in 1987 by the prime minister and all ten premiers and focused on amending the Constitution in such a way as to obtain Quebec's signature. The failure of the Accord was damaging to the federation because it seemed to signify that the problems faced by Canada truly were irresolvable. During the "Quebec round" of constitutional negotiations at Meech Lake the province put all its demands on the table, even while agreeing to some compromises with Canada. Still, the effort did not succeed. The fallout was severe; polls showed the number of Quebecers who would vote yes in a referendum held after the debacle of Meech Lake at 60 per cent or so, reaching a high of 64 per cent of the francophone community in November of 1990 (Behiels 2007, 276). The political situation was so bad that even the leader of the Quebec Liberal Party, Robert Bourassa, suggested that if there was not another effort at constitutional change, he would call a referendum himself.

Meech Lake gained iconic status after it failed, almost akin to Quebec's "Night of the Long Knives" that led to the province's self-imposed ostracism after the patriation of the Constitution in 1982. Meech Lake was seen as another betrayal by English Canada, yet another example of the inflexibility of federalism and the need for Quebec independence. In many ways, it was as much a disaster for Canadian federalism as was the fallout from the patriation of the Constitution, given that, following its failure, the chances of securing Quebec's support and solidifying its place in Canada seemed more remote than ever. It was certainly a bigger failure than the subsequent Charlottetown Accord, which was seen as the "Canada Round" and rejected by a majority of the entire country, including Quebec, in a referendum.

What is striking at this point in time, however, is the extent to which Quebec has achieved much of what it wanted in the Meech Lake Accord, some of it even through quasi-constitutional means by way of rulings of the Supreme Court. This achievement has happened on a piecemeal basis, through "non-constitutional renewal," through a lower-keyed process, and to little fanfare (for the term's origins see generally Lazar 1998). But it happened nonetheless. Whereas the literature on non-constitutional renewal has argued that this new, depoliticized process has worked to reduce federal-provincial tensions in Canada, this chapter argues that much of the content of the Meech Lake Accord has in fact now been delivered, eliminating many of the obstacles that once stood in the way of both Ottawa and Quebec (for an excellent recent study on the importance of flexible political arrangements in determining whether a nationalist movement embraces secessionism or remains more autonomist in outlook, see generally Lecours 2021).

Many of the developments discussed in this chapter overlap with the conduct one expects to see around abeyances, suggesting that there is endogeneity here with the framework that is outlined in chapter 2. Still, while abeyances are about preserving ambiguities and failing to push constitutional visions too far, this chapter argues that substantive developments around the major demands of Quebec can independently reduce support for independence by reducing what is left to fight over. It becomes a virtuous cycle: the abeyances become easier to preserve as constitutional edges are rounded off. Quebec did not achieve everything it wanted (notably with regards to constitutional recognition of its demands), but chipping away has resulted in important gains and left less to fight about. What is left becomes harder to justify separating over. In terms of structure, the chapter begins with an overview of the Meech Lake Accord and some of the controversies that surrounded it. From there, it argues that the content of the Accord has been addressed in different ways over the last thirty years, with a result that much of the substance that was promised to Quebec in the late 1980s has since been delivered. The issues were dealt with separately and incrementally, but they were all addressed. Thus, this chapter argues that Canada did not accommodate Quebec's demands in general but that over time Quebec has won most (but not all) of what it asked for at Meech Lake.

The Meech Lake Accord

Could the question of Quebec's place in Canada have been dropped after the patriation of the Constitution in 1982? The "incalculable consequences" that René Lévesque warned about did not materialize, and, with the PQ clearly headed for a defeat, it is tempting to think that the question could have been effectively put to the side. But the dominant belief is that the Progressive Conservatives had very little choice but to return to the constitutional table after 1984. Senator Lowell Murray, a former government leader in the Senate under Brian Mulroney, certainly thought so:

> Oh come on. I mean, I've heard that, of course, "Aren't you sorry you reopened the Constitution?" We felt – I think we would never have been forgiven [if we had not]. We would have been attacked, vigorously and legitimately, if after the election of a majority Conservative government in Ottawa under a Quebecer, with strong representation from every region, at the same time a majority government, federalist government under Bourassa in Quebec who had put forward five conditions, all of which had been offered by previous governments, and as my sometimes friend [former Liberal politician Jack] Pickersgill said, the most reasonable conditions that had been forwarded in living memory – no, we could not ignore that and we did our best to bring it along, push it forward. So that's not really sensible; we would never have been forgiven if we hadn't. (L. Murray, interview, 2015)

Former senator Hugh Segal argued that a lot of the pressure actually came from the rest of the country rather than Quebec, namely from some of the other premiers and some Liberal senators who saw an opportunity in Bourassa, one that Prime Minister Mulroney could take advantage of. Mulroney had also promised to bring Quebec into the constitutional fold, which added to the pressure on him to act: "For Mulroney, coming in with a strong Quebec base, and a national mandate, and the largest majority known to the time, and a commitment that had been made to Quebecers, the notion of not trying after the anglophone premiers had said, 'You really should,' would have been unconscionable. It would have been a complete violation of his sense of mission and the government's commitment to bring Quebec into the family" (Segal, interview, 2015).

Whether or not reopening the discussion was a good idea, it was the strategy that the opposition Conservatives adopted in the run-up to the federal election of 1984. Mulroney exploited the still volatile situation, having brought Lucien Bouchard on board as a speechwriter to reach out to nationalists, and made bold but vague commitments to the people of Quebec that he would do what he could to "convince the National Assembly of Quebec to give its consent to the new constitution with honour and dignity" (Behiels 2007, 257–8). The Progressive Conservatives' subsequent win in Quebec made it even more difficult for Mulroney to back down. In Quebec, Bourassa also campaigned on the issue, promising that his government would restore the province's veto, develop Quebec's hydroelectricity, and bring peace to the language front (261). Mulroney's efforts held significant appeal among Bourassa's supporters; in the 1984 election half of the membership of the provincial Liberals and some 20 per cent of the provincial Liberal riding associations were supporting and, in some cases, even working for the PCs (257). The result was a very strong Mulroney-Bourassa axis that was fundamentally committed to bringing Quebec back into the Constitution, notwithstanding the absence of consensus on what that would look like.

The Meech Lake Accord represented the first of two efforts that the Progressive Conservatives undertook (the other being the Charlottetown Accord) in which Canadian political leaders attempted to resolve the points of disagreement that underlay the abeyances in the Constitution. These actors shared a common commitment to finding a magic-bullet solution that would reconcile different visions of the country sufficiently to overcome the failure of 1982. Their strategy was to link all of the problems together into a single accord consented to by all actors. The Meech Lake Accord negotiations thus represented the peak of the style of highly visible elite accommodation that defined the era, or what this chapter calls summit intergovernmental relations (or summit IGR) in the search for constitutional clarity on Quebec's demands (Jeffrey 2006, 120). It reflected the desire of both Bourassa and Mulroney to find an agreement in a non-conflictual way and to demonstrate symbolically the effectiveness of Canada in meeting the aspirations of all its people. The Accord itself is an admirable attempt to square the circle of the various visions.[1] Whether it was a good idea was not as relevant as the fact that it was being tried at all. It is not necessary to offer a blow-by-blow account of how it collapsed, except that it did so through an escalating series of attempts to bring constitutional clarity to questions on which there was no fundamental agreement. That inability to agree on the fundamental questions at stake ended with the Meech Lake Accord becoming the most spectacular failure of the mega-constitutional era and the one with the most wide-ranging repercussions after 1982.

What did Quebec actually want? The answer only became clear in the lead-up to the negotiations. On the Quebec side the PQ opened the discussion in 1985 with its *Draft Agreement on the Constitution: Proposals by the Government of Quebec* (Quebec 1985). There was little doubt that the *Draft* was something of a wish list, given that Lévesque was having difficulty holding his party together and it was correctly assumed that he would soon be out of office (Behiels 2007, 259). Nevertheless, in many ways the *Draft* resembled the ideas that would be advanced by Robert Bourassa in 1986. It proposed: (1) the constitutional recognition of Quebec as a distinct society; (2) the right to opt out of national programs with compensation for future programs in provincial jurisdiction; (3) an expanded provincial veto over constitutional amendments; (4) a provincial role for future Supreme Court appointments; and (5) constitutional entrenchment of Quebec's role in immigration (Gibbins 1990, 257). The final Accord tried to recognize Quebec's view on the cultural duality of the country, while withholding powers that were not enjoyed by the other provinces. It recognized Quebec's three seats on the Supreme Court, while giving an expanded say to other provinces on the appointment of judges (1987 Constitutional Accord, s. 6, cited in Monahan 1991, 301–2). It recognized Quebec as a distinct society, while insisting that recognition had no impact on the "powers, rights, or privileges" of either the federal or provincial governments (1987 Constitutional Accord, s. 1, cited in Monahan 1991, 299). Without mentioning Quebec, the Accord expanded Quebec's veto powers by making more areas subject to the rule of unanimity (1987 Constitutional Accord, ss. 9–12, cited in Monahan 1991, 303–4).

In opposition, the federal Liberals and New Democrats were initially supportive of the Meech Lake Accord, suggesting that their parties would play ball. But as time went on, constitutional reform would ultimately split the Liberals and, to a lesser extent, the New Democratic Party (NDP) (Behiels 2007, 266). Former Liberal prime minister John Turner initially argued that the Accord was a good deal (Cohen 1990, 143–5). He stuck to this position even as many of his colleagues began to pull away from Meech Lake, in particular following the negative intervention of Pierre Trudeau (see e.g., Trudeau 1987). Eventually, although major divisions emerged in both parties, it served neither the federal Liberals' nor the Conservatives' interests to seriously damage the Meech Lake Accord once it had been agreed. The Liberals had always relied on Quebec for significant electoral support and had little interest in antagonizing that base, and the NDP had always maintained a positive position on questions such as a distinct status for Quebec (Monahan 1991, 81, 101). The Accord was ultimately neither party's responsibility, and their attitude towards it was overshadowed by other issues that they felt were more important, such as the free-trade deal with the United States. However, the fact that such deep divisions could exist in both parties demonstrates the divisions that tackling abeyances could involve.[2]

Nevertheless, despite the insistence of Conservative senator Lowell Murray that the agreement was a "seamless web," the Accord began to disintegrate soon after it had been signed. This led to further bargaining in a desperate effort to save it (Behiels 2007, 269). Subsequent proposals, meant to address in particular the concerns of women and Indigenous Peoples, as well as the specific objections of Newfoundland and New Brunswick, contributed to an air of crisis. The premier of New Brunswick, Frank McKenna, was the first to suggest the idea of a parallel accord that would clarify the Meech Lake Accord on the more controversial points and hopefully save the deal (271–2). The subsequent Charest Report led by Progressive Conservative Member of Parliament Jean Charest to salvage the Accord and its insistence on a future "Companion Accord" testified to the inability of the Meech Lake Accord to do the job it was supposed to do (271–2).

The highly visible process through which the Accord was negotiated – linking all the issues together and attempting to solve them through executive federalism – is now seen as the central cause of its failure. In his influential book on the Accord, Patrick Monahan argues that it was the effort at clarity itself that doomed the Accord. "Constitutions do not generally resemble the Income Tax Act. The point of a constitution is to set down basic, fundamental principles that are to govern the making of laws in a society" (1991, 255). But even when one focuses on the symbolic parts of the agreement, Monahan argues that the competing symbols that lay at the heart of the agreement, and in particular the distinct-society clause, turned off English Canadians, Indigenous Peoples, and others. Alan Cairns's work on the dialogue of the Constitution observes that the effort to accommodate Quebec's need for special status could not be reconciled with the perception that a distinct status for Quebec would rob others of status at the same time:

> The bitterness and passion that inform the presentations of the numerous groups objecting to the Accord are not based on a narrow instrumental calculation of its effects on the future flow of material benefits. Their anger is not driven by the fear of tangible gains foregone, but by a more complex battery of emotions. The representatives of women's groups, of aboriginals, of visible minorities, of supporters of multiculturalism, along with the northerners and basic defenders of the Charter, employ the vocabulary

of personal and group identity, of being included or excluded, of being accepted or being treated as an outsider, of being treated with respect as another participant or being cast into the audience as a spectator as one's fate is being decided by others. They employ the language of status – they are insulted, wounded, hurt, offended, bypassed, not invited, ignored, left out, and shunted aside. They evaluate their treatment through the lens of pride, dignity, honour, propriety, legitimacy, and recognition – or their reverse. Their discourse is a minority, outsider discourse. They clearly distrust established governing elites. They are in, but not of, the constitution. (Cairns 1988, 139–40; quoted in Gibbins 1990, 262)

David Taras has argued that the level of media attention essentially meant that the actors were bargaining in two different venues, with each other on the one hand and in front of the country on the other, making the process of negotiating much more difficult than it had to be (1991, 169, 178). The atmosphere certainly constrained the parties in front of their publics, and they were fearful of appearing weak at the table (Meisel 1991, 150). Complicating matters, the high-stakes nature of the negotiations fed into what John Meisel has called an environment of "high exposure / low comprehension" on the part of the Canadian public, in which people were unsure of what the deal meant or what to think of it (148). A 1990 poll for the CBC / *Globe and Mail* showed that some 71 per cent said they knew little or nothing about the Accord, against 28 per cent who knew "a fair amount or more" (148). Nevertheless the public was highly engaged, especially during the meetings of first ministers. It has been estimated that some four million Canadians watched at least some part of the conference (148). It was in this highly charged context that Trudeau intervened with his devastating and highly effective written critique of the Accord in the *Toronto Star* and *La Presse* of Montreal, which helped to rally opposition to the agreement (Russell 2004, 139).

In so far as the process used to negotiate the Accord did not ease intergovernmental tensions either, the concept of summit IGR received increasing scrutiny. In keeping with its decentralizing tenor, the Accord took steps to increase institutions of executive federalism. It committed the first ministers to holding annual meetings on the economy and the Constitution (1987 Constitutional Accord, ss. 8, 9, cited in Monahan 1991, 303–5). Although executive federalism would remain the format for the second round of constitutional negotiations, and demonstrated a commitment by elites to this type of negotiating process, critics increasingly saw the IGR process itself as an obstacle.[3] Alan Cairns felt that the Charter of Rights and Freedoms, which had politicized groups in the constitutional context in ways that had not previously been the case, was at least partly to blame for the political backlash to the Meech Lake Accord (1988). Russell argued that Canadians were rejecting having the country's sovereignty exercised solely by elites (2004). Before the Accord had even collapsed, Roger Gibbins noted that while conflict and coordination around technical details was fine in a federal system, the system of summit IGR could run into problems when it went beyond the details to channel more fundamental disagreements: "Intergovernmental conflict becomes a more serious matter when it serves as an outlet for major cleavages within the Canadian society. Conflict between Ottawa and the government of Quebec, for example, may go well beyond the intrinsic problems of governmental coordination to a fundamental debate over the place of Quebec within the Canadian political community. At issue is which government best speaks for Quebec when the two governments pursue quite different political visions" (Gibbins 1990, 264). Nevertheless, the commitment of the different actors to these provisions in the Accord suggested that summit IGR was now a primary vehicle for resolving ambiguities in the Constitution.

All told, however, the collapse of the Meech Lake Accord led to a significant increase in media attention on the debate and on grievances that different parts of the country had with each other (Monahan 1991, 174–5, 213). The defeat of the Accord played into a national victimhood narrative within Quebec, something that had been part of the political culture for decades. That narrative was now further accentuated with the language of betrayal, rooted in the inability of the rest of the country to overturn the injustice that had been committed during 1982 (Fournier 1991; Behiels 1992, 136). Michel Behiels has argued that this narrative of betrayal was never actually challenged by the federalists and was in fact embraced by them, since it formed the basis of the problem that they were all trying to solve. Once that failed, the legacy of that narrative considerably complicated the situation heading into Charlottetown, when it was too late to revise the historical record even if they had wished to do so (Behiels 2007, 274).

Subsequent Evolution of the Meech Lake Accord

The decoupling of the issues at the heart of the Meech Lake Accord appears to have allowed them to develop on their own, at different speeds, and to deliver much of what Quebec wanted. The remainder of this chapter reviews this progress.

To reiterate, the major pillars of the Accord were as follows:

1 the constitutional recognition of Quebec as a distinct society;
2 the right to opt out of national programs with compensation of future programs in provincial jurisdiction;
3 an expanded provincial veto over constitutional amendments, in particular with regard to national institutions;
4 a provincial role for future Supreme Court and Senate appointments; and
5 constitutional entrenchment of Quebec's role in immigration.

This chapter will take them each in turn, although the question of the veto will be combined with the discussion of national institutions, since the two were largely combined in the final agreement.

Distinct Society

There is perhaps no more emblematic idea or phrase that comes out of the mega-constitutional era than that of *distinct society* for Quebec. For many it encapsulated the idea that Quebec was unique, and offered the symbolic recognition that is so important to national minorities in multinational states. Failing to receive the symbolic aspect of recognition can delegitimize the national project, even if those symbols mean little in instrumental terms for the minority to achieve its goals (Basta 2021, 45–6) The origin of the phrase can be traced back to Quebec premier Jean Lesage, and it was more fully developed in the Royal Commission on Bilingualism and Biculturalism (see some discussion of this in the first volume of the report on Official Languages in Canada 1967, xxxiii–xliv). For Lesage, the concept was a way of protecting the cultural distinctiveness of the province, and he wanted it included in any reform effort. Whether or not it was ever supposed to have substantive legal content, however, is debatable. Peter Hogg has argued that Quebec has always been recognized as a "distinct society," citing a number of important features of the Constitution (for example, see Hogg 1988). Quebec always had certain guarantees pertaining to the language, the Roman Catholic religion, and the civil law tradition.

During the Meech Lake negotiations, gaining distinct-society recognition was one of five preconditions that Quebec set before it would sign the Constitution. That process began at a conference held at Mont Gabriel in May of 1987, which started with a speech by Quebec's intergovernmental affairs minister Gil Rémillard (Russell 2004, 144). The meeting was based around a document called *Mastering Our Future*. Written by the Quebec Liberal Party, the document outlined Quebec's constitutional positions and set a minimum bar on what the province would accept (Monahan 1991, 56). Few of the conditions were truly new, but even then it was not entirely clear what *distinct society* meant. In theory, it would ground the cultural distinctiveness of the province in the Constitution and preserve its francophone character. But there was very little on the specifics, including where in the Constitution such a provision should go. Rémillard was silent on this question, but observers generally assumed that it would go in the preamble, which had been suggested in the past (see Monahan 1991, 56, for an excellent account). Having such a guarantee appear in the preamble made sense from Ottawa's perspective, too, because the federal government had committed itself to the principle of equality of the provinces, and that would leave it as an interpretive provision (51–2).

In the end, however, the inclusion of Quebec as a distinct society was to be in the body of the Constitution Act 1867, as a new section 2. It would have four subsections. The first subsection had two subparts that were, in turn, supported by the three following subsections. First, the Constitution of Canada should be "interpreted in a manner consistent with" (a) that the French-speaking community is centred in, but not limited to, Quebec, while also noting that English was present in Quebec and represented a "fundamental characteristic" of Quebec and Canada. Subsection (b) provided "the recognition that Quebec constitutes within Canada a distinct society" (Monahan 1991, 299).

In subsection 2, Parliament and the provincial legislatures were committed to safeguarding that fundamental characteristic within the limits of their authority. Subsection 3 went on to specify that it was the "role of the legislature and government of Quebec to preserve and promote the distinct identity of Quebec referred to" in subsection 1(b) of the document. But the agreement also specified in subsection 4 that nothing in that section "derogated from the powers, rights or privileges of either the parliament or government of Canada or of any of the provincial legislatures." This was included out of a fear – voiced most clearly by Newfoundland premier Clyde Wells – that the identification of Quebec as a distinct society might have the effect of leading to an interpretation of the division of powers that would allow Quebec to gain some additional powers connected to things like broadcasting or other cultural programs (Monahan 1991, 217). Wells accepted that this could be limited with the final addition (Monahan 1991, 230).

However irrelevant many thought that this would be from a legal perspective, the political implications were toxic. It was also the part of the agreement that Brian Mulroney and the federal Progressive Conservatives had the hardest time justifying to the rest of the country. There was a sense that, when he was in English Canada, Mulroney waved away the clause as being essentially meaningless, but when he was in Quebec, he attached great weight to it. The doublespeak was not a great look for the prime minister and gave the impression that he was not being truthful about the Accord. Although the promise of a distinct society saw a revival in the Charlottetown Accord, the collapse of that agreement appeared to put an end to it. Nevertheless, the idea that Quebec is a distinct society has not died. It lives on in certain political pronouncements and some subsequent constitutional jurisprudence.

To start, it is important to remember that the distinct-society clause was always supposed to be an *interpretive* mechanism. In that sense, it was not particularly different from section 28 of the Charter, which guarantees equally the rights provided within it to both male and female persons. After the collapse of the Meech Lake Accord, subsequent political and juridical developments have meant that the Constitution *is* interpreted as though Quebec is a distinct society. First, there were three *political* recognitions of Quebec as a distinct society that came after the Accord, which meant they were more symbolic than legal guarantees. But they shape the expectations of what political leaders can do, and these commitments have been made by both Liberal and Conservative leaders, as well as by the premiers. The first of these changes came directly after the 1995 referendum during the so-called Plan A phase of Ottawa's response to that event. As part of the package of those reforms, the Government of Canada under Jean Chrétien passed a parliamentary motion that held:

Whereas the People of Quebec have expressed their desire for recognition of Quebec's distinct society;
1) The House recognize that Quebec is a distinct society within Canada;
2) The House recognize that Quebec's distinct society includes its French-speaking majority, unique culture and civil law tradition;
3) The House undertake to be guided by this reality;
4) The House encourage all components of the legislative and executive branches of government to take note of this recognition and be guided in their conduct accordingly. (O'Neal 1995, 21)

This statement was more direct about Quebec's distinctiveness than the committee's written statement in the Meech Lake Accord, although, as a mere resolution, it had more symbolic value than anything. Still, it was the first time that Quebec had been so expressly recognized as distinct, given the failure of two previous efforts in Meech Lake and, later, at Charlottetown.

Secondly, Quebec was also recognized as a distinct society a year later, in the "Calgary Declaration" that came out of the Annual Premiers' Conference of 1997. Whereas the House motion applied only to the federal government, and specifically to the House of Commons, the Declaration embraced not just Ottawa but all the provinces and territories as well. That document, a joint statement of all the premiers except Lucien Bouchard of Quebec, who stayed home, recognized the "unique character of Quebec society," which differed from a formal declaration of Quebec as a unique society ("Calgary Declaration" 1997). Like the Meech Lake Accord, it stressed the equality of the provinces, suggesting an "all things to all people" approach. Thirdly, in 2006, Stephen Harper passed the Quebec "nation motion," in which he essentially caught the Bloc Québécois flat-footed when he agreed that Quebec would be recognized as a "nation" inside of a "united Canada." This motion cost Harper his intergovernmental relations minister, Michael Chong, but it passed the House with the support of all parties, including the Bloc Québécois, effectively ending the debate from a political perspective.

As political pronouncements, these actions did not directly change the constitutional status quo, but there has been movement here too, by way of the Supreme Court, which nodded to Quebec's distinct status and valid cultural concerns in some of its decisions. These cases have established that the Constitution must encompass the view that Canada is a bijural country and that attention must be paid to Quebec's distinctiveness when interpreting relevant parts of the Constitution. The Court began moving strongly in this direction in the 1998 *Secession Reference*. The key finding of that ruling was that, in the face of a democratic vote to leave, there would arise a corresponding duty on the part of the rest of the country to at least negotiate that fact. That duty was grounded, in part, on recognizing the cultural uniqueness of Quebec in Canada. The Court noted, for example, that the whole point of federalism was the recognition of unity with diversity. In the case of Quebec, that diversity rested on the fact that it had a unique and distinct culture, which had to be acknowledged as the basic justification of the underlying principle of federalism:

> The principle of federalism facilitates the pursuit of collective goals by cultural and linguistic minorities which form the majority within a particular province. This is the case in Quebec, where the majority of the population is French-speaking, and which possesses a distinct culture. This is not merely the result of chance. The social and demographic reality of Quebec explains the existence of the province of Quebec as a political unit and indeed, was one of the essential reasons for establishing a federal structure

for the Canadian union in 1867. The experience of both Canada East and Canada West under the *Union Act, 1840* (UK), 3–4 Vict., c. 35, had not been satisfactory. The federal structure adopted at Confederation enabled French-speaking Canadians to form a numerical majority in the province of Quebec, and so exercise the considerable provincial powers conferred by the *Constitution Act, 1867* in such a way as to promote their language and culture. It also made provision for certain guaranteed representation within the federal Parliament itself. (Reference re Secession of Quebec 1998, at para. 39)

The Court took a more thoroughgoing and complete approach in *Reference re Sections 5 and 6 of the Supreme Court Act* (Reference re Supreme Court Act, ss. 5 and 6, 2014), or what is usually known as the *Nadon Reference*. In that case the Court was confronted with what was actually a very narrow question surrounding the eligibility of an appointment to the Court, Justice Marc Nadon, given that he was being elevated from the Federal Court of Appeal. The argument was that elevating Justice Nadon ran afoul of sections 5 and 6 of the Supreme Court Act which guaranteed Quebec three seats on the Court. Because he did not count as a "lawyer" (he was a judge), and since he was not a "Quebec judge" (he was on the federal court), the argument was that Nadon was not eligible. The decision was made to simply appoint him, a decision challenged by Toronto lawyer Rocco Galati. The Court ultimately decided that Nadon could not be appointed, citing the need to protect the integrity of the Quebec view of the Court and its respect for its distinct culture:

> The purpose of s. 6 is to ensure not only civil law training and experience on the Court, but also to ensure that Quebec's distinct legal traditions and social values are represented on the Court, thereby enhancing the confidence of the people of Quebec in the Supreme Court as the final arbiter of their rights. Put differently, s. 6 protects both the *functioning* and the *legitimacy* of the Supreme Court as a general court of appeal for Canada. This broader purpose was succinctly described by Professor Russell in terms that are well supported by the historical record:
> ... the antipathy to having the Civil Code of Lower Canada interpreted by judges from an alien legal tradition was not based merely on a concern for legal purity or accuracy. It stemmed more often from the more fundamental premise that Quebec's civil-law system was an essential ingredient of its distinctive culture and therefore it required, as a matter of *right*, judicial custodians imbued with the methods of jurisprudence and social values integral to that culture. (Reference re Supreme Court Act, ss. 5 and 6, 2014, at para. 48–9; italics in the original)

The political and juridical recognition of Quebec's distinct status falls short of an express recognition of the fact in the Constitution. Politically, this remains a central problem. But to the extent that the Meech Lake Accord promised Quebec a constitutional mechanism through which the Constitution would be *interpreted* in such a way that would recognize Quebec as a distinct society, political and judicial rulings over the last thirty years suggest that the threshold has now been reached.

Opting Out, with Compensation

Quebec's objective at Meech Lake was to constitutionalize the right to opt out of federal programs with monetary compensation for a program of the province's own design. This had been a concern for Quebec since the start of the era of "cooperative federalism" in the 1960s when the elements of the modern welfare state were being established. The problem arose out of a belief that Quebec needed more money to fund the programs in its jurisdiction, money that only Ottawa could provide. The basic fiscal problem in Canada's constitutional system was the failure of the founders to anticipate that the provinces would be the level of government responsible for the most expensive jurisdictions. This failure meant, on the one hand, that the provinces were left without the sufficient taxing capacity needed to fund the jurisdictions that emerged as the most expensive, such as health and education. On the other hand, Ottawa was given the unlimited power to tax, but with less costly jurisdictions. This tension has been central to the development of Canadian federalism and public policy.

Beginning in the 1960s, Ottawa and the provinces created shared-cost programs, like the provincial health insurance programs, which were run by the provinces with some conditional funding from Ottawa. In return, Ottawa would have some say over the content of the programs, usually through legislation that surrounded the conditional grants. The mechanism allowing the federal government to spend in the provincial area was the constitutionally murky "spending power" that derives at least in part from the principle that the Crown can spend the money it raises on anything it deems fit. Specifically, the spending power arises out of a couple of constitutional provisions, namely the foundations of the consolidated revenue fund (section 102 of the Constitution Act, 1867), the ability to raise taxes (section 91(3)), legislating in relation to "public property" (section 91(1a)), and the right to appropriate funds for constitutionally mandated charges (section 106) (Telford 2003, 25). Its limits and validity have never been directly tested by the courts, which have only gone so far as to rule that while the federal government can give money to a province for a program, it cannot set up a program of its own that falls under provincial jurisdiction.[4] Although the shared-cost programs worked well at first, the provinces (in particular Quebec, where opposition to the spending power predates the Quiet Revolution) have resented the conditions that Ottawa places on their programs. The problem was less acute in the early years of cooperative federalism when Ottawa matched the provincial contributions, leading to so-called fifty-cent dollars. But by the 1980s and 1990s, growing federal deficits and program budgets meant that Canada, like most Western countries, was forced into a period of retrenchment in which Ottawa backed out of matching funding agreements and downloaded costs to the provinces. The politics boiled over once Ottawa had decoupled the funding from previous agreements, leaving the provinces with the bill (and the blame) for programs that had originally been expected to be shared-cost programs.

Quebec had always been a less eager participant than other provinces in these shared-cost programs because of the role that social policy played as a defining feature of the Quiet Revolution. The province has been irritated by the use of the spending power in areas of its jurisdiction and the conditions that come with federal money. The Quiet Revolution was about the reconfiguration of society, as much as it was about the building of the provincial state, and so it took on a political meaning that was absent in the other provinces. To that end, the province had often sought to develop its own programs (such as the Quebec Pension Plan, which runs parallel to, but is distinct from, the Canada Pension Plan) or run its own programs while receiving financial compensation from Ottawa with no strings attached. Constitutionalizing these rights was something Quebec wanted out of the Meech Lake Accord. But all the provinces were involved to a degree, and a limited provincial right for opting out with compensation had already been constitutionalized during the patriation process. Specifically, section 40 of the Constitution Act, 1982, provided that any province could opt out of a transfer of its legislative jurisdiction with respect to education or cultural matters to Ottawa and would receive compensation in return. Quebec wanted more; it wanted compensation for opting out of any federal program that operated in the provincial sphere (Monahan 1991, 44–5). In the Meech Lake Accord, all the provinces were given the right to "reasonable financial compensation" if they chose to opt out of federal programs that spent money in areas of exclusive provincial jurisdiction.

The collapse of the Meech Lake Accord suggested that Ottawa would remain unbound in its use of the spending power and free to spend in provincial jurisdiction. In the years since the agreement's collapse, however, the management of the social union has given rise to new, constraining norms that have given Quebec a degree of control over social policy that it did not have in the 1980s. There have been relatively few overly controversial intrusions by Ottawa into Quebec's jurisdiction, and a growing acceptance by everyone at the federal level that to do so is inappropriate. To be fair, the last thirty years has seen its share of federal-provincial squabbling around social policy, as is to be expected in every federation, but there were a couple of very substantial wins for Quebec. The most important was the devolution of active labour-market policy to the provinces in 1996, a long-standing demand of Quebec. There have also been at least some intrusions, including the 1998 Canada Research Chairs Program that funds research at post-secondary institutions and the Millennium Scholarship Program (now the Canada Student Grants Program) that gives assistance to university students (R. Young 2006, 48). And, of course, equalization remains a universally contentious issue throughout the country. The overall approach since at least the government of Paul Martin, though, is that the federal government will not intrude unnecessarily into provincial jurisdiction and will accept a level of asymmetry in program development.

The first genuinely important shift in terms of norms began with the Calgary Declaration of 1997 (ratified through all provincial legislatures with the exception of Quebec in 1998). Among other things, the document recognized the "unique character" of Quebec while stressing the equality of the provinces. Though primarily symbolic, it set the stage for a new direction in Canadian federalism in which the country would be governed through broad program asymmetries developed within the bounds of broadly accepted national frameworks and norms. In essence, Quebec was free to deviate from the rest of the country in program development, but so was every other province (Courchene 2004b). In 1999 the first tangible acceptance of the need for limits on the spending power appeared when the federal government committed itself to the Social Union Framework Agreement (SUFA). Among other things, it specified that consent by a majority of the provinces and three months' notice were required before Ottawa could introduce new shared-cost programs. The agreement tried to set a new tone for intergovernmental cooperation. For example, it emphasized the need for a collaborative approach in social policy, it promised to give one year's notice of major changes to existing funding agreements, and, if a province had a program in which Ottawa was planning to spend, the province could keep the excess money if it were reinvested in the same or substantially the same policy area (Richards 2002, 2–3). SUFA is broadly considered to be a failure today, and there was a vigorous debate at the time as to whether it ever had potential (for two views see Lazar 2001 and Noël 2003). Seen in historical context, SUFA and the Calgary Declaration represented the launch of what have come to be enduring norms around collaboration, consultation, and asymmetrical federalism (see for example Schertzer, McDougall, and Skogstad 2018 on the importance of collaborative and asymmetric norms in Canadian federalism). The management of Canada's intergovernmental relations field is now defined in most areas as operating in a multilateral framework with substantial acceptance of bilateral agreements, allowing for local particularities (Schertzer, McDougall, and Skogstad 2018).

Quebec's demand for the right to opt out of shared-cost programs with compensation continued to gain broader acceptance in the first decade of the twenty-first century. For example, in 2004 the Council of the Federation suggested that Ottawa take over a national "pharmacare" program – which the federal government said it would consider – while recommending that Quebec be allowed to opt out with compensation for its own program (Courchene 2004a, 23–4). "It is understood that Québec will maintain its own program," the communiqué read, "and will receive a comparable compensation for the program put in place by the federal government" (Council of the Federation 2004, 2). The importance of this statement was not lost on observers: "This is a remarkable concession, one that builds upon the spirit and the letter of the 1998 Calgary Declaration (and also resurrects one of the principles of the Meech Lake Accord). Indeed, it fits squarely in the venerable tradition (pre-Charter) of 'opting out' facilitating a 'win-win solution' – Quebec is allowed to opt out and advance its 'nationhood' agenda, while the rest of the provinces can work with Ottawa to design a mutually acceptable national program which would not have been possible without Quebec's opting out" (Courchene 2004a, 23). Although the program went nowhere, the allowing of Quebec to run its programs with few hindrances was emblematic of the level of bilateralism to which Ottawa was open. In a memorandum from the First Minister's Meeting held on health care in September that year, Ottawa recognized the need for asymmetrical federalism for Quebec. While promising more money for health care, it did so by assuring Quebec that it would not interfere in the province's jurisdiction in the matter (Health Canada 2004). By assuring British Columbia and Alberta that it could have the same deal, Ottawa became consistent with the Calgary Declaration and set the mould for the coming years (Courchene 2004b).

The question of opting out with compensation has not been a significant issue over the past two decades as there have been no new programs to force the issue. But the overall shift in the field has meant that while there are tensions in fiscal federalism (e.g., equalization), there are rarely high-profile political fights that threaten the autonomy of Quebec. Despite the limitations of SUFA, it can still be contextualized as part of a wider shift of non-interference in provincial affairs by the federal government and the acceptance of provincial asymmetries in program development. SUFA was a Liberal creation, and although it was never embraced by the Conservative government that replaced the Liberals, it was superseded by their philosophy of "open federalism," which specified that each jurisdiction should refrain from infringing on the other's territory (Fox 2007; Harmes 2007; Gotz 2010). Health care and infrastructure were exceptions but managed with the same eye to provincial sensitivities. Rather than interfering with Quebec's jurisdiction, or introducing new shared-cost programs, Harper got to work to correct the "fiscal imbalance" between Quebec and Ottawa – the dubious idea that Ottawa had money that belonged to Quebec, given the jurisdictional burden. An agreement was reached to "correct" it (after which Premier Jean Charest promptly raised taxes), but otherwise Harper left Quebec alone. At no point were new shared-cost programs even considered.

The first term of the Justin Trudeau government did not explicitly endorse open federalism but largely practised it nonetheless. Otherwise occupied with the threat of the cancellation of NAFTA, the cannabis file, and Indigenous reconciliation, the Liberals did not introduce any new social programs – and certainly none that Quebec could not opt out of. In doing so, the Liberals may in fact have broken a campaign promise. In 2015 they ran on a pledge to introduce pharmacare, which never materialized or even evolved into a political issue. Although they ran on a similar promise in the 2019 election, pharmacare is now framed by a report they commissioned Eric Hoskins, former health minister of Ontario, to prepare, which suggests that it will be much more limited in scope, if it happens at all. Although the Liberals recommitted themselves to the project upon entering a confidence-and-supply agreement with the NDP in 2022, there is little evidence that it is advancing. Furthermore, all of the other federal parties are, if anything, more committed to allowing Quebec to opt out with compensation than are the Liberals or the Conservatives. It has been a long-standing plank of the NDP platform, for example (Bryden 2015). Thus, although the Meech Lake Accord would have put constitutional limits on the spending power and provided greater scope for opting out of federal shared-cost programs, this outcome has occurred in practice anyway and despite the failure of the Accord.

Expanded Veto over National Institutions

A veto over constitutional change is one of Quebec's oldest demands. It emerged in the 1920s, driven by the lack of a clear amending formula in the Constitution agreed to in 1867. One of the biggest myths about the Canadian constitution is that the fathers of Confederation drafted the document without thinking about how it might be changed, a problem that created much mischief during the patriation period. While a fiction, this story has been hard to shake. The reality is that, in 1867, the British North America Act could be amended upon a request from Ottawa to the Imperial Parliament, which would normally grant what the country wanted with little interference (Russell 2004, 48–52; Reference re: Resolution to Amend the Constitution 1981, 1:800; but see Fournier 1991, 19–20, for a competing view of the use of the veto in historical terms). This practice started to change with the emergence of modern Canadian federalism.

The evolution of Quebec's demands regarding a free-standing veto are well known (see Russell 2004; Dupras 1992; Stein 1984; Saywell 2002, among many others). The question arose with the provincial rights movement of the nineteenth century during which Canada evolved into a fully federal state, and it became conventional for Ottawa to ask the provinces about amendments that were relevant to them. The matter first took on urgency in the years after the First World War, when Canadians began to re-examine their previously unquestioned loyalty to the British Empire. By 1926, Canada and other dominions had insisted on and received recognition as coequals in the Empire, something that was entrenched in law in the Statute of Westminster, 1931. The first time that the question of formalizing provincial vetoes in the Constitution entered Canadian politics in a significant way was at a federal-provincial conference in 1927 (Stein 1984, 122). That year, right after the Balfour Declaration (the precursor to the Statute of Westminster), Prime Minister Mackenzie King sought advice from the provinces on the matter of constitutional amendment with a view towards possible patriation. The lack of agreement meant that the matter was dropped, but this showed how far the constitutional conventions had developed and how they could limit the federal government's room to manoeuvre.

The question remained central over the next half century, during which Quebec insisted it had a veto over constitutional change by convention. Quebec's position was essentially denied by the Supreme Court of Canada, first in the *Patriation Reference* and later in the essentially redundant *Quebec Veto Reference*, which found that the convention only amounted to the requirement that Ottawa needed "substantial provincial consent" rather than actual legal agreement for a change. In the end, Canada opted for a multi-tiered amending formula in 1982 with four branches: one requiring unanimous consent, for changes to institutions like the Queen; a bilateral formula for matters affecting one province and the federal government only; "a unilateral formula for matters solely in the discretion of one jurisdiction"; and everything else covered by a "general formula" requiring Parliament and two thirds of the provinces with 50 per cent of the population between them – the so-called seven/fifty formula. Still, the fact that Quebec had been cut out during the patriation process and had not agreed to this formulation was a political disaster and a major reason that Meech Lake happened at all. In the end, the Meech Lake settlement did not provide a free-standing veto for Quebec; rather, it simply extended the unanimous veto provisions to include the powers of the Senate and how members were selected, the appointment process of the Supreme Court, the regional basis of representation to the House of Commons, and the creation of new provinces (Fournier 1991, 20). However, with the collapse of the Accord, the impression that Quebec had once again failed to acquire the powers it sought was in the air. Subsequent legal and political developments have done much to secure for Quebec what the Meech Lake Accord had promised when it came to a veto over national institutions.

The most recent changes concern the Supreme Court. The Supreme Court of Canada has nine members, three of whom are appointed from Quebec by law under the Supreme Court Act. No other province has such a statutory allotment. The reason Quebec has this recognition is a reflection of the distinct civil law tradition in the province, something that predates Canada and which was initially abolished after the British conquest but then reinstated in the Quebec Act of 1774 as part of the British government's efforts to keep the colony from joining the American Revolution. At Confederation, section 101 of the Constitution Act, 1867, provided that Canada could create a general court of appeal for the country (i.e., the Supreme Court). When it did in 1875, Quebec was guaranteed three seats in order to recognize its distinctiveness. No mention was made of the other provinces, but a series of conventions emerged that gave three seats to Ontario, two to the West, and one to Atlantic Canada, with the seats generally rotating around a region. At Meech Lake, Quebec argued that a statutory guarantee was not enough and that additional constitutional protections were needed. In the final text of the Accord, it was agreed that the three statutory judges would be entrenched in the Constitution. There was a catch, however, when it came to the method of selection: it was no longer the sole responsibility of Ottawa to decide on an appointment. There was to be a "double veto" whereby Quebec drew up a list of candidates from which Ottawa selected, so long as there was one acceptable candidate (Fournier 1991, 20). The death of the Meech Lake and Charlottetown Accords seemed to kill the proposal for good.

Recent developments, however, have largely delivered what Quebec wanted. First, the *Nadon Reference*, discussed above, has effectively made the quasi-constitutional Supreme Court Act an entrenched constitutional document. Since the Court is only a "section 101" court, or one that has been created by statute, it has always been theoretically open to the federal government to change or, if it wished, to abolish the Court altogether. The Court ruled in the reference that constitutional developments had overtaken the circumstances of the Court's creation and that any change to the composition of the Court would require the unanimous consent of the provinces as well as the federal government (Reference re Supreme Court Act, ss. 5 and 6, 2014, at para 72). Other significant changes would be subject to the general amending formula, although it was still open to Ottawa to make more minor changes to the operation of the Court. The fact is, the ruling was almost exactly what Quebec sought and failed to achieve in Meech Lake.

More recently, Quebec has gained the right to become involved in the selection of judges as well. In early 2019, in a little noticed and complex announcement by Justin Trudeau and Quebec premier François Legault, a change was made in the way that Supreme Court judges from Quebec are selected (Prime Minister of Canada Justin Trudeau and Premier of Quebec François Legault 2019). Both men agreed on a new process to fill the newly vacant seat of Clement Gascon. Specifically, an independent advisory board was set up for Supreme Court appointments, which would be distinct from the board that had been set up to advise on all appointments. This board would have eight members selected by different parties. Two members (including the chair) would be appointed by the government of Canada, two by the attorney general for Quebec (one of whom would not be a lawyer); a retired judge would be nominated by the Canadian Judicial Council; a practising Quebec lawyer would be nominated by the Quebec law society, as would the Quebec branch of the Canadian Bar Association; and finally a legal scholar would be nominated by the deans of the Quebec law schools along with the Civil Law Section of the University of Ottawa (Prime Minister of Canada Justin Trudeau and Premier of Quebec François Legault 2019, s. 3). That group would then compile and submit a group of three to five names (s. 7). At this point the process becomes a little murky. In essence, the prime minister and the premier receive the list and consult – in the case of the prime minister with the Chief Justice of Canada, and the Quebec premier with the Quebec Justice Minister. The premier then sends a recommendation to the prime minister for final approval. However, all consultations must be confidential (Prime Minister of Canada Justin Trudeau and Premier of Quebec François Legault 2019 ss. 6–13). Nobody has connected this back to the Meech Lake Accord, but the new process effectively gives Quebec much of what it was seeking all along: a voice in the selection of the Quebec judges on the Supreme Court of Canada. This is not an opportunity that has been offered to the other provinces, and it remains to be seen if it will endure. For now, it marks a significant change to Quebec's role in the Supreme Court appointment process.

There have been fewer developments with regards to the Senate, but those that have taken place are noteworthy. In 1978 the Supreme Court ruled that the federal government was not entitled to reform Canada's senate unilaterally, something Pierre Trudeau sought as part of his makeover of Canadian federalism. In the 1978 *Senate Reference* (Reference re Authority of Parliament in Relation to the Upper House 1980) the Court found that the federal government was not entitled to simply turn it into a "House of the Federation," which the federal government had proposed in a document entitled *A Time for Action* (Canada 1978). As a result, the Senate was still on the table when the Meech Lake Accord came up for renewal. However, there was (and is) no agreement as to what the reform should look like. In anticipation of eventual reform efforts, a veto over Senate reform was a condition that Quebec demanded for signing the Accord. In the end, this was what Quebec got, but so did all the other provinces, which squared the circle of Quebec specificity with provincial equality. When the Accord failed, it looked like Quebec's position had been rejected once again. Quebec's position vis-à-vis the Senate has not changed substantially since then, and in fact reforms *have* been made to the Senate without Quebec's consent. Specifically, the Justin Trudeau government's decision to begin appointing senators on a non-partisan basis, and to expel the Liberal senators from the caucus, was championed by supporters as an overdue effort to shake things up in the upper chamber. At the time of writing, the provinces had not articulated a clear position, for or against, what the Trudeau government has done, but the reforms do not seem to have radically changed how Parliament functions. Quebec's hand, however, has been strengthened by the Supreme Court's decision in the 2014 *Reference re Senate Reform*, and in ways that are less superficial than the Trudeau amendments.

In 2014 the government of Canada had asked the Court to answer four questions on its powers of unilateral amendment to the Senate.

Specifically, the federal government asked (1) whether the federal government could change the selection criteria of senators to be based on consultative elections; (2) whether it could set term limits; (3) whether or not it could change the property requirement for senators; and (4) what level of consent was needed to abolish the Senate altogether (Reference re Senate Reform 2014, at para. 2). On the final question, the Court was the most unequivocal: abolishing the Senate would require the unanimous consent of all the provinces. This effectively gave Quebec a veto over the process and was in fact what the Meech Lake Accord had largely envisioned. The Court was quite clear that the Senate was an integral part of the Constitution and an important component of the country's federal structure. It was also necessary because the Senate is part of Parliament, which *also* must consent to any constitutional change. Thus, abolishing the Senate amounts to a change of the amending formula itself, which needs unanimous provincial consent. Quebec was also given a veto over any change to the property qualifications for one to be a senator from the province because those qualifications work slightly differently in Quebec than elsewhere. In Quebec the senators represent a geographical district, the point being to represent both anglophones and francophones. Any change to this scheme would also need the province's approval. On the other two points, however, Quebec's position was not as strong. Other changes to the Chamber can be done with the seven/fifty amending formula. Even though the formula is weighted so that Quebec (and Ontario) has a bigger say than the other provinces, this was not what was contemplated in Meech Lake.

Immigration

Greater control over immigration was one of Quebec's constitutional demands from early on. The area is of concurrent jurisdiction under the Constitution Act, 1867, but by the 1960s Quebec was no longer comfortable with Ottawa being the dominant player in the field (Paquet 2019, 6). This policy shift was tied directly to the emergence of Quebec's nationhood and the period of competitive nation building that the province took against Ottawa, and which can be differentiated from the related and overlapping process of province building in the literature (Linz 1993; Linz, Darviche, and Genieys 1997; Paquet 2019, 38). Contrary to the assumptions of many people in English Canada, the debate over immigration was not solely about the preservation of the French language (although that was perhaps the primary concern) but part of a general project of national construction that reflected the weakness of the state after the Quiet Revolution. The demands that Quebec made around immigration were not fundamentally about ethnocentrism, populist politics, or even anti-anglophone sentiment. Unlike the often poisonous politics around immigration that we see in many countries driven by the cultural insecurities of their publics, the demand for control was a top-down affair. At root, it reflected an *elite consensus* about the value of immigration.[5] This also means that the question of immigration was, like other demands that were made by the province, one that could be solved at the elite level.

Throughout the 1960s and 1970s, successive governments, both federalist and sovereigntist, began negotiating the process of devolution with Ottawa. For its part, Ottawa was not particularly resistant and was willing to work with the province to answer its demands. This culminated in a set of agreements throughout the 1970s that slowly gave Quebec more say over the immigration process. The first of these agreements, the Lang-Cloutier Agreement in 1971, allowed Quebec immigration officers to be posted to foreign posts. In 1975 the Andras-Bienvenue Agreement stipulated that Quebec-bound immigrants would be met by a Quebec immigration officer on arrival. Most importantly, however, was the Cullen-Couture Agreement of 1979, which gave Quebec a say in the selection of immigrants, an effective veto over refugees and economic immigrants, and control over the criteria for the sponsorship of new immigrants (Paquet 2019, 39). To be sure, there was some urgency in the signing of the latter agreement after the election of the PQ in 1976. But all of these agreements reflected the fact that negotiations had been underway long before the Meech Lake Accord was proposed. In fact, the demands on immigration were arguably among the *least* contentious in Meech Lake. The Accord promised an updated Cullen-Couture Agreement with Quebec and that it would receive constitutional recognition. While this might have created an unacceptable appearance of asymmetrical federalism, Ottawa made it clear that any province could also have the deal that Quebec achieved. It was another classic example of recognizing Quebec's uniqueness on the one hand while respecting the equality of the provinces on the other (Monahan 1991, 93).

The long history of pre-existing devolution negotiations in this area meant that when the Meech Lake Accord collapsed, the immigration file simply fell back out onto the separate track on which it had started. Within a year of the collapse of the Accord (and before Charlottetown), a new intergovernmental agreement on immigration emerged that, in a substantial sense, gave Quebec everything it wanted. The 1991

Gagnon-Tremblay–McDougall Agreement (the Canada-Québec Accord) gave Quebec the money it wanted to take over immigration and settlement services. Dollar amounts were agreed for the first four years, with a funding mechanism agreed for subsequent years that was very generous to the province and was largely divorced from the numbers of immigrants that the province would receive (Paquet 2019, 55). This agreement cemented the province's holistic and bipartisan approach to the immigration file and removed it as a political irritant between Quebec City and Ottawa. After 1991 the Quebec government had both the financial resources and the political power to develop an immigration policy that met its needs. At the heart of this model was a commitment to immigration that aimed to develop the *economy* of the province where language was an important, but not the sole, consideration. Following a period of consolidation in the late 1990s, the strategy that was adopted by the PQ governments of Lucien Bouchard and Bernard Landry was essentially continued by Jean Charest and later by Pauline Marois and Philippe Couillard.

The decision by Ottawa to yield so much to Quebec in the area of settlement and integration services might be seen by some as an abdication of the federal government's responsibilities over immigration. But it also had the effect, probably unanticipated at the time, of extricating the federal government (and the federal system) from what was to become the dominant political conversation in the province after the mega-constitutional era: reasonable accommodations. Indeed, more than anything else, it might have been the devolution of immigration that saved the country in the 1990s. Once Quebec took control of the field, the debate shifted to the question of *integration*, an issue over which the province had sole control. Immigration and integration became a fundamentally intra-Quebec debate rather than a Canada-Quebec debate about the protection of identity. If that had not happened, the history of Canadian federalism would surely be very different today.

Conclusion

Although the question "What does Quebec want?" has notoriously haunted Canadian politics since the 1960s, this chapter has argued that the question found a clear answer in the Meech Lake Accord, the failure of which triggered one of the most dangerous periods in Canadian federalism. The shock of that experience led directly into the Charlottetown Accord and, from there, the referendum of 1995. Although the Meech Lake Accord was (and is) considered a failure, subsequent developments in Canadian politics and public law have in fact provided Quebec with much that it had sought in that failed Accord – to the point that the grievances expressed by Quebec towards Canada during the Meech Lake era no longer have the same foundation today.

Understanding this process and theorizing this kind of change helps us understand why Quebec separatism has died down while Quebec nationalism has not. There are many things that Quebec could still ask Ottawa for. The fact that it has not become conflictual reflects a new style of non-constitutional renewal and accommodation that is done on the sidelines and less visibly than it was in the past. Although the constitutional recognition that Quebec wanted has not been achieved in the formal sense, the substantive gains that the province has made have taken much of the force out of the argument that there is a pressing need for separation, as well as demonstrating that there are many ways for Quebec to achieve its objectives inside of Canada, whatever those might be.

5 Quebec's Changing Identity Politics

In the last chapter we looked at how the incremental accommodation of Quebec's demands has left far less for federalists with conflicting views about the Constitution to argue about. In this chapter we will look at an explanation rooted more firmly inside Quebec: the evolution of the Quebec identity debate. In this we are particularly interested in how provincial elites have shifted their focus on identity politics from one rooted in a discussion about Quebec's place in Canada to one about how minorities are accommodated inside Quebec, in order to protect the French language and culture through exercises like the Bouchard-Taylor Commission on interculturalism and the resulting laws like Bill 21. Thus, this chapter argues that the turn has been a largely top-down development; in other words, it can be hard to find out whether or not the "person on the street" has really changed their identity. Furthermore, it is an open question as to whether the shift to identity politics reflected the decline in the salience of the sovereignty movement or if the shift was itself responsible for displacing it, or a combination of the two. Identity politics might just be filling the vacuum left by the constitutional question. Without any doubt, however, on identity questions, all major parties in Quebec have been happy to move the conversation to one that focuses on reasonable accommodations rather than on how Quebecers fit into the Canadian framework. Although it has appalled English Canadians and many inside Quebec, and also required the CAQ to use the notwithstanding clause to enact its program, this shift has suited the federal and provincial governments well because it left no need to address constitutional issues. And electorally this turn appears to have paid off for parties like the CAQ and the BQ, each of which have gained in popularity by promising to put separatism on the back burner, while playing up issues at the heart of reasonable accommodations.

This chapter will focus on several themes. First, it will take stock of the "new nationalism" of the CAQ, BQ, and Québec solidaire (QS), to argue that Quebecers are not less *nationalist* but that the nationalism no longer insists on being *secessionist*. This is a major change from the past. In particular, the chapter will examine the growing discussion that Quebec's elites have had about immigration and minority accommodation, the environment, the politics of energy, and the social economy, which are now the hallmarks of Quebec politics. The change in Quebec politics is being driven by many of the same forces that have been allegedly driving English Canada over the last several decades, in particular a shift to post-material values. But perhaps at the most basic level, the transition is the opposite of what happened to Quebec nationalism in the 1960s. During the Quiet Revolution, Quebec nationalism became more closely associated with the state, essentially moving from being French Canadian to being Québécois. Today the opposite is true: nationalism is less focused on the state, is more questioning of its leaders, and more sceptical of the unqualified benefits of a government-driven, state-building exercise (though it remains far more open on this front than elsewhere). More than anything, the identity debate is focused on who can be "reasonably accommodated" in the public sphere in order to protect the French language and culture. And this debate can be explosive. Whereas many in Quebec and Canada see the current debate on reasonable accommodations as rooted in Islamophobia, others see such criticisms as an example of prejudice against Quebecers ("Quebec-bashing") who are otherwise simply trying to defend their culture and language in their own way.[1] The subject is perhaps the most fraught in contemporary Quebec-Canada relations.

Examining Quebec Nationalism's Alleged Civic and Ethnic Basis

The different attachments that Quebecers have, as compared to those in the rest of Canada, and the importance of identity politics in general, have long been at the heart of scholarship on nationalism in this field and in contributing to the study of and theories of secession generally (e.g., Mendelsohn 2003; Beaulieu 2003; Maclure 2003; G. Hamilton 2004; Daniel 2012; Perrella and Bélanger 2009; Bélanger and Perrella 2008; K. Gagnon 2014a, 2014b; Rocher 2023). An enduring theme in Quebec nationalism is the extent to which it is rooted in the people of Quebec, either in the form of a soft ethnic nationalism or basically civic in nature, defined by one's citizenship as a member of the provincial state.[2] The tension between ethnic and civic nationalism is never far from the surface, and in this, Quebec nationalism is not fundamentally different from other nationalisms in the West that are struggling with economic globalization or the realities that come with existing in a multinational democracy. The tension informs both federalist and separatist thought in the province to varying degrees, and the emphasis on ethnic versus civic nationalism shifts over time. How Quebec nationalism has changed since the mega-constitutional era, and in particular how it has refocused on accommodating alleged outsiders, has been the subject of much recent work. For example, François Rocher (2023) has observed that since 1995 there appears to have been a shift in Quebec nationalism's cultural anxieties from being most concerned about the relationship with the rest of Canada to accommodating groups traditionally not seen as sharing common Western values.

The Quebec nationalism of the 1960s was defined in particular by its move from the ethnically derived concept of the *French Canadian* to that of the *Québécois*, which saw the state of Quebec as the basis for its new identity. That it still had an ethnic overtone was undeniable, but it was far more positive about the potential for state action to improve the life of its citizens, and represented a step towards a more open and tolerant twentieth-century modernity. More than anything, the nationalism of the Quiet Revolution was hostile to what preceded it, usually described as being rooted in the philosophy of *la survivance* that was religious (specifically Catholic), traditional, conservative on social issues, valued the agrarian and rural as opposed to the urban, was deferential to authority, and was ethnonationalistic in outlook (Zubrzycki 2016, 3–15; A.-G. Gagnon 1990).[3] It broadly believed that French Canadians were best served through the structures of the Catholic Church, which, in conjunction with the Quebec state, could provide the kind of education that was needed to preserve the unique culture and heritage of the French Canadian people, and which served to safeguard the institutions that made the community whole. To that extent, it saw very little need for the secular state except as the adjunct to the Church and its social mission. The provincial state, while necessary, was useful mostly as a vehicle for the propagation of these more basic, essential values of community life. French Canada needed to defend itself against the rest of the country, and the Quebec state was seen as a vehicle for safeguarding the heritage of the Quebec people even as it remained part of Canada. The writing most associated with this strain of thought had its roots in the nineteenth century. By the early twentieth century, however, it was best articulated by thinkers such as the cleric Lionel Groulx, who never pursued separatism but nevertheless believed that French Canada should defend itself against those who would erode its ancient heritage. Groulx's belief that the British conquest was a disaster for French Canada, and an event that necessitated an ambivalence about Quebec's place in Canada, won a large following and influenced many thinkers, in particular those connected to the "Montreal school" such as Guy Frégault, Michel Brunet, and Maurice Séguin. Later writers such as Ferdinand Dumont in the 1960s or Serge Cantin in the late twentieth century took the view that, prior to the Quiet Revolution, Quebec society had never overcome the disaster of the conquest and was held in thrall by an elite that saw little reason to expose the rest of the population to the wider forces of modernity.

To a degree, this was a throwback to earlier debates about Quebec's culture, in particular the debate over the legacy of the conquest and the alleged erosion of the core French Canadian identity in North America. How immigration played into it overlaid what were in fact quite traditional discussions about who counted as a Quebecer. In line with thinkers such as Fernand Dumont and others associated with the Montreal school, much of Quebec's past has been defined by the British conquest, from which Quebec never escaped and which has prevented it from reaching its full potential (Maclure 2003, 22–3). The tragedy of that event has touched every aspect of political life in Quebec, and although there have been empowering moves towards independence and ultimately nationhood for the province, Quebecers have never truly been able to escape their status as a conquered people. Guy Frégault, Maurice Séguin, and Michel Brunet made up a constellation of thinkers who argued that Quebec had been on a trajectory to prosperity like any other society in North America until that future was crushed by a British invasion from which it never recovered (Maclure 2003, 23). Others concentrated more heavily on conditions inside of Quebec and the conservativism of the Church, and less on the conquest. This strain found cultural expression in the manifesto *Le refus global* of Paul-Émile Bourduas and his compatriots, the iconoclastic artists of the 1940s and 1950s who argued that the culture of Quebec was too backward to save and who called for the people to shake off the oppression under which they lived and take control of their future (Maclure 2003, 23). It was of a piece with similar works such as Paul DeBiens's 1960 work *Les insolences du Frère Untel* and the attack it launched on the clergy in particular and the state of Quebec society generally. Later the themes of cultural fatigue and economic exploitation would be taken up by writers like Hubert Aquin (1962) and Pierre Vallières (1971).

Other thinkers, however, have supported a more open civic nationalism and tend not to see federalism as a problem for Quebecers. This group also has deep historical antecedents in Quebec. If the Montreal school was the home of the declinist literature about Quebec, the "Laval school" embodied a more outwardly focused nationalism (see Behiels,

1998, 94–7, for an excellent review of the origins and authors connected with this group). These historians, such as Fernand Ouellet, Claude Galarneau, Marcel Trudel, Jean Hamelin, and many others, took the view that Quebec's problems could be traced to the population itself. Quebec was a society *comme les autres* in North America; the differences of culture or religion were only important on the margins. There was nothing *special* about Quebec or its history; responsibility for its evolution rested squarely on its own people. For these scholars, the British conquest had no real impact on the population of Quebec at the time (which was too rural and agrarian to really notice the change in the empires governing them), and it may have even had some benefits, like the introduction of parliamentary democracy (Momryk 1999, 1–3). For many, the real cleavage in Quebec was not culture or religion but class – economic domination by the anglophone elite. This group had the financial sophistication to dominate Quebec and the merchant and urban classes with whom they were in conflict (3). These later writers, like Paul André-Linteau, René Durocher, and Jean-Claude Robert (the latter associated in particular with Marxist thought), argued that structural and economic forces produced the Quebec of their day. One could argue that, like all North Americans, Quebecers were propagators of a capitalist system in which they themselves were caught up (Behiels, 1998, 95–6). Adherents to the Laval school suggested, as a solution, a special status for Quebec and a reformed federalism, rather than the Montreal school's cultural nationalism, which was more likely to demand separatism. It was this agenda that deeply informed thinkers like Pierre Trudeau, Jean Marchand, and André Laurendeau, and intellectually one can trace the influence to later federalist thinkers such as former Liberal leader Stéphane Dion or the former editor of *La Presse* and senator, André Pratte.

Both schools were reactions to the conservative nationalism that preceded them. The philosophy of *la survivance*, and the support it offered to the Church and anglophone business interests, had many adherents in government. This was particularly true of the Union nationale, whose leaders were closely affiliated with the Church and who ensured that the public knew it. The apotheosis of this link between Church and state came under Maurice Duplessis, premier of Quebec between 1944 and 1959. It was evident in the Liberal Party of Quebec as well under Lomer Gouin (1905–20) and Louis Alexander Tachereau (1920–36), who hung the now infamous crucifix in the National Assembly. Nevertheless, Duplessis represented the culmination of pre–Quiet Revolution Quebec. A deeply conservative figure, he was notably hostile to communism, Jehovah's Witnesses, separatist forces, and other groups he considered to be a threat to the social order. Duplessis is remembered for some of the most egregious abuses of civil rights ever seen in the country, in particular the anti-communist "padlock laws" and his attack on the freedoms of speech and religion, which gave rise to such famous civil rights cases as *Saumur v. Quebec (City)* [1953] 2 S.C.R. 299, *Switzman v. Elbing* [1957] S.C.R. 285, and *Roncarelli v. Duplessis* [1959] S.C.R. 121. His actions, alongside those in other provinces like Alberta under the Social Credit premier William "Bible Bill" Aberhart, led the courts to institute the so-called implied bill of rights to protect basic legal guarantees against state intervention. Duplessis also embraced capitalism and foreign investment and encouraged anglophone and American business to invest in the province. His views made him a friend of the forces that would come to be seen with scepticism by the nationalists of the 1960s, who were far more liberal and individualistic, sought more French Canadian leadership in the business sphere, and were open to feminism, separatism, and state intervention.

By the 1960s, however, this consensus had started to change. The reaction against Duplessis essentially split young French Canadians along two paths. The first, best espoused by Pierre Trudeau and many (although not all) connected with the journal *Cité Libre*, offered a vision of Quebec that was fundamentally liberal, individualistic, based on the protection of civil liberties and the defence of federalism, and more sceptical of nationalism in general. It sought to challenge the anglophone business interests through improved education and civic involvement, and to limit government through the robust protection of rights. The second was a different type of nationalism, one espoused by René Lévesque and eventually the PQ. This nationalism also shared a scepticism of the conservative nationalism of the Union nationale and was eager to challenge the ascendancy of anglophone power in Quebec society. It was far more sceptical of federalism, however, and its potential to promote French Canada's interests. The leaders of both strains came out of the Quebec Liberal Party, which had become the vehicle for change in Quebec under premiers Jean Lesage and Robert Bourassa. Still, by 1968, the PQ had begun to emerge and with it the two-party split that would come to dominate provincial politics across a federalist-separatist axis for the next fifty years.

For both parties, the priority was reforming Quebec itself. Within that project, though, the question of Quebec's place in Canada was a major point of difference. The federalist Liberals were not uncritical of federalism, but they did not see Canada as beyond saving or even necessarily a major obstacle to the development of French Canada. Throughout the 1960s, both the federal and the Quebec Liberal parties engaged in a process of soul searching to strike the right balance between federalism and Quebec nationalism, though it was not easy. The provincial and national branches of the party had disaffiliated by 1964. In 1963, Prime Minister Lester Pearson struck the Royal Commission on Bilingualism and Biculturalism. In its report one of its co-authors, André Laurendeau, warned that Canada was going through the deepest crisis in its history. Pearson tried, in the form of entrenched cultural dualism, to give voice to disaffected Quebecers, through new language and cultural guarantees and some limited decentralization (for the canonical take on this process, see McRoberts 1997). Trudeau would ultimately replace Pearson's binational-approach efforts with a more muscular view of federal power and a vision of Canada based on multiculturalism and individual rights (although he was happy to continue with a policy of state bilingualism). But Trudeau never questioned the value of the federal system and its potential for allowing different communities in Canada to achieve their goals (for the classic statement on the difference between the Pearson and the Trudeau approach to Quebec, see McRoberts 1997).

Arising out of a number of organizations in the late 1960s, many in the PQ had given up on Canada by the turn of the 1970s. Self-determination was only possible for Quebecers with a state of their own, and although it would only ever be voted upon as part of a plan for sovereignty association with the rest of Canada, the workability (or even honesty) of that claim was always suspicious. For Lévesque, who had been a member of the Parti Libéral du Québec (PLQ) and had even served in the US forces in the Second World War, Quebec was better off with a state of its own. To a degree, he felt that Canada would be better off without Quebec as well. Whereas in the past it might have made sense to remain in a federal union, the new cultural awareness in Quebec, and the need for cultural preservation and development, meant separation was necessary. Ironically, the success that the PQ may have had on this front may have undermined their overall project. Bill 101, or the Charter of the French Language, which was introduced in 1977, demonstrated to many Quebecers that the province had several tools at its disposal to pursue cultural projects inside of Canada (Rocher 2002, 74–7)

Still, a central tension that existed in this strain of nationalism was the relationship that it had to ethnonationalism. Others took the same path as Lévesque but found that the nation only made sense with some ethnic base to it. Lévesque's nationalism was essentially civic. While there was a clear linguistic and cultural basis to it, it was also fundamentally open to outsiders who wanted to participate in modern Quebec democracy. Many, notably Lucien Bouchard and Gilles Duceppe, shared this view of separatism. Others, such as former Quebec finance minister Yves Michaud or Mario Beaulieu of the Bloc Québécois, have been more willing to play to the idea of a core Quebec identity that had ethnic overtones. Both Yves-François Blanchet and Pauline Marois have run campaigns that made use of the *nous* concept, which raises eyebrows for the ethnic implications (e.g., Radio-Canada.ca and La Presse canadienne 2019). For them, the nation seems to be based on the original French and Catholic inhabitants, the so-called *pur lain Québécois*, descendants of the conquest and in constant cultural struggle with the rest of North America. This line of thought had a wide and cross-cutting following, which often skated around the intolerant. One of the fathers of modern Quebec nationalism, Lionel Groulx, was accused of anti-Semitism, which he denied. But many thinkers were accused of intolerance, although often only in the margins, and in some cases this was not concealed. Political movements engaged with separatist thinking. For example, the 1930s nationalist organization Jeune-Canada led by André Laurendeau was openly hostile to outsiders while harshly critical of the abuses and imperiousness of the conservative United Nations. The most famous example of the supposed articulation of a core Québécois identity that seemed to exclude outsiders was Jacques Parizeau's speech following the defeat of the 1995 referendum, in which he blamed the loss on "money and the ethnic vote." Reconciling the difference between civic and ethnic nationalism has remained a tension in the movement.

Whether it was Trudeau's liberal intellectual currents or the more culturally defined nationalism of Parizeau, both attributed the problem to a lack of leadership and to federalism – more broadly, the structures of the Canadian constitution. Both varieties of nationalism recentred Quebec identity on the provincial state. Both were unhappy with federalism, and the difference came down to whether or not it could be reformed sufficiently to meet the needs of Quebec. For separatists, the answer was no; federalism was, at best, an outmoded method of governing and one that held back the potential of the newly awakened Quebec people. At worst, it was a strait jacket on the province, one that hampered the legal powers the province should have, drained needed tax revenue, and burdened the province with unnecessary duplication in the form of the federal government. For Lévesque, the separation of Quebec was the end-point of history, similar to the arguments made by Thomas Paine during the American Revolution. For others, it was more a story of national liberation, which at the extremes could take the form of the Front de libération du Québec (FLQ) program in 1970 and those programs of other movements that have existed on the margins.

For federalists, federalism was salvageable but needed a new foundation in Canada, one that secured both language groups in linguistic and cultural equality. The patriation process and the constitutional wrangling that followed were attempts to do just that. Federalists could be quite varied in their reasons for supporting this constitutional arrangement. Pierre Trudeau himself was the ultimate opponent of ethnic Quebec nationalism (or any nationalism) and saw in federalism an important guarantee of civil rights and protection against a local parochialism. Like those in the PQ, though, federalists could have ethnic as well as civic overtones when it came to the need to protect Quebec's culture and community, and there was sometimes little agreement on precisely why Quebec should stay in Canada. Occasionally the reasons could be quite instrumental. Robert Bourassa, for example, often saw federalism in transactional terms, as captured in his idea of *fédéralism rentable*, or profitable federalism. Still others, like Stéphane Dion, saw federalism as a product of history, one that had a role to play in forestalling an infinite regression into smaller, more separated worlds. For most, federalism had to be reformed and then had to be defended against those who would lead Quebec towards a narrow-minded isolationism. Much of the mega-constitutional era was designed to do exactly that.

More-recent thinkers about Quebec nationalism have tended to return to the original dualist idea to search for ways that it can be expressed in an enhanced partnership between Canada and Quebec, often against the backdrop of Indigenous reconciliation and multiculturalism. Most of these thinkers now accept that Quebec will remain in Canada for the foreseeable future, and although often ambivalent about that outcome, this work tries to examine how Quebec is best accommodated in Canada. Thinkers like André Lecours, Éric Montpetit, and Alain Noël have focused in particular on institutional mechanisms and public policy for a better understanding of the accommodation and expression of Quebec's views in Canada, while those like Guy Laforest, François Rocher, and Alain-G. Gagnon have deeply explored the need for mutual recognition of each other as partners in the country and the ways in which the Constitution and federalism might gain legitimacy in respecting the often radically different views of culture and community (Laforest 1995, 2010; Graefe and Laforest 2013; Laforest and Mesa 2014; É. Montpetit 2007a, 2008; Rocher, Gagnon, and Guibernau 2003; Rocher 2002, 2007; A.-G. Gagnon 2010, 2021; Lecours 2021; Noël 2000, 2003).

The work of this generation of scholars is clearly informed by the debates in the comparative literature around substate nationalism and is conscious that Quebec is hardly alone as a minority nation in a globalizing world. Much more comfortable with diversity but often sceptical of majority Canadian narratives about the national identity, recent writing is often about the practice of Canadian federalism with an eye to how process and results generate support for the overall political framework. It is often highly developed methodologically and offers sophisticated approaches to the study of Canada, while continuing to insist on Canada as a fundamentally binational country working alongside the valid claims of Indigenous Peoples.

Quebec's Identity Politics after 1995

At some point after 1995 the fight over Quebec's identity politics became severed from the legal and constitutional context of federalism. Elites have instead engaged in a debate around reasonable accommodations of minorities and what is permissible in the public sphere in order to protect the French language and culture. The debate began in earnest after 2003 and culminated in the Bouchard-Taylor Report in 2008 which introduced interculturalism as a method of reconciling identities in a pluralistic society. Following the report and the interculturalist shift, the debate moved on to what would be permitted in the so-called public sphere in a province that had adopted a position of state religious neutrality. Alongside this was a broader shift to a discussion about Quebec as a people in the world; it concentrated on questions about the economy, the environment, and social justice.

The move to *laïcité* (laicity) had deep roots in Quebec. The idea itself is French and has guided French policy on accommodation since the beginning of the twentieth century. Calls for *laïcité* in Quebec have been long-standing, but the modern incarnation dates from the early 1990s when much of the control over immigration was devolved to Quebec. In 1990 the government of Quebec published a document that articulated the conceptual basis for integrating outsiders: *Let's Build Quebec Together: A Policy Statement on Immigration and Integration* (Quebec, Minister of Community Culture and Immigration 1990). The document prioritized three principles for establishing Quebec's immigration policy: French was the language of the society; the society would be democratic and open to everyone; and society was open to cultural difference within the limits required to promote democracy and intercultural exchanges (16). The last point makes a subtle move, both denying that there is an exclusive cultural basis to being Québécois and moving to preserve a public, francophone sphere that could be regulated to promote bigger democratic ideals (McAndrew 2009, 209).

The move to a more direct form of state secularism became particularly notable after 2003, when a series of controversies arose on the proper accommodation of cultural minorities. Some were high-profile fights played out in major state institutions, such as the case of *Multani v. Commission scolaire Marguerite Bourgeoys* [2006] in which the Supreme

Court found that a Sikh child had the right to bring a razor-sharp cere-monial knife, or kirpan, to school under strict safety conditions. Others were more media-generated sensations that, for some Quebecers, repre-sented the way in which cultural minorities were putting Quebec's cul-ture under threat (for an excellent discussion of these events, and a long list of examples, consult Zubrzycki 2016, 150–1). These perceived threats included a request by Orthodox Jews that a local YMCA frost the glass around a swimming pool to avoid tempting young men who might see the female swimmers; the widely publicized accommodations made for Muslim prayers at a maple-syrup sugar shack; and the provision of halal meals in hospitals and other public institutions. The culmination of these events was the widely ridiculed "code of conduct" for new immigrants introduced by Hérouxville city council in 2007. It banned stoning and genital cutting in a city with no history of these practices (see Zubrzycki 2016, 151). That the small city was nearly entirely white and Christian was lost on no one. Regardless, the rising media coverage suggesting a crisis in accommodations had adherents among the political leadership. The leader of the ADQ, Mario Dumont, was particularly vocal in crit-icizing the alleged failure of new immigrants to successfully integrate into Quebec society, and in an open letter he criticized Quebecers for be-ing excessively tolerant of what he saw as unreasonable accommodation requests (Zubrzycki 2016, 151; see also Boily 2018, 108–22).

Alarmed by what appeared to be a backlash against multicultural-ism, in 2007 the Liberal government of Jean Charest called the Que-bec Consultation Commission on Accommodation Practices Related to Cultural Differences, led by sociologist and historian Gérard Bouchard and philosopher Charles Taylor (the Bouchard-Taylor Commission). Reporting a year later, the commission was tasked with exploring the roots of the cultural crisis and advising on what policies should be adopted going forward. The report itself goes into some detail on the origins of the crisis, arguing that there were distinct eras, starting in the mid-1980s that began with the "antecedents" (December 1985 to April 2002), followed by "the intensification of controversy" (May 2002 to February 2006), which snowballed into a "time of turmoil" (March 2006 to June 2007). This escalation eventually gave way to "a time of calm" (July 2007 to April 2008), around the time that the report was submitted (G. Bouchard and Taylor 2008, 47). Overall, the report chronicles some seventy-three examples of what led to the "crisis of accommodation," with forty-three of them occurring in the most serious period of 2006–7 (47–60). It made thirty-seven recommendations on how best to recon-cile the diversity of Quebec with its traditional heritage and to integrate newcomers (CBC News 2008).

Conceptually, the biggest shift that the commission recommended was that the base of accommodation move from multiculturalism to interculturalism, which for many seemed like a distinction without a difference (e.g., Tremblay 2009). Whereas multiculturalism took a relaxed view of religion in society and relied only on a benign toleration of outsiders, interculturalism was more demanding. Interculturalism relies on a clear distinction between a public and a private sphere, with clear limits on what is acceptable between the two (Laxer 2019, 4–5). Whereas the private sphere is reserved for self-regarding matters of belief, behaviour, language, and faith (within the limits of more general rules of application like the Criminal Code), the public sphere restricts individual conduct with the aim of guaranteeing substantive equality between citizens *qua* citizens. What flows from this is a wider justification for limiting overt personal conduct in order to ensure that there is no privileging of any one faith or creed, among other things, and total equality between the sexes. Additionally, interculturalism prescribed that French was the only truly valid language of communication in the public sphere because it is the definitional characteristic of Quebec's historic culture, heritage, and identity.

The significance of the shift to interculturalism was not fully recognized at the time; indeed, the CBC reported that the headline takeaway from the authors was "let's move on" from the whole debate (CBC News 2008). Neither Bouchard nor Taylor thought that the foundations of Quebec society were in crisis; what was needed was a broader willingness to adapt to the realities of immigration. However, they were soon to find that this was not the trajectory on which Quebec was headed, and viewing the cultural flashpoints that they had identified as isolated incidents or based on media-driven hysteria was not in line with public opinion. Several of their suggestions for better minority accommodation were rejected out of hand by the government, like their suggestion that the crucifix that had been hanging in the National Assembly since 1936 be removed (CBC News 2008). Furthermore, the conversation that they had started around interculturalism and state secularism moved in directions they had not anticipated, with an even more vigorous public fixation on the kinds of restrictions that could be justifiably imposed on newcomers to secure the public sphere. As the concept sank in, and grew increasingly popular among French Canadians in particular, it became more common to talk about the need for a "charter of values" that would establish appropriate conduct in public. It was not at all the direction in which Bouchard or Taylor had thought their ideas would go.

Although the Quebec Liberals did little to introduce substantive state secularism following the report, it became a central pillar of the

PQ platform. Campaigning in 2012, PQ leader Pauline Marois promised that, once elected, she would introduce a charter that would establish what was appropriate when one gave or received public services. Quite soon after her government was elected, it became clear that intercultur-alist policies were overwhelmingly focused on limiting the clothing and practices of specific religious minorities. Critics of the PQ interpretation of interculturalism charged that it did not seem to offer the promised sub-stantial equality because it asked far more of new immigrants than of the largely secular French Canadian population, which did not customarily don ostentatious displays of religiosity. The announcement of the char-ter by the responsible minister, Pierre Drainville, was accompanied by a poster illustrating both "acceptable" and "unacceptable" religious garb, which was widely mocked and, to many, signalled a clear turn by the PQ into religious ethnonationalism (Wells 2013). The charter appeared to vi-olate several provisions in the Canadian and Quebec Charters of Rights and Freedoms, leading to allegations that it could only be sustained with additional reforms to Quebec laws and the use of the notwithstanding clause in the Canadian constitution (Banerjee 2013; Fine 2013).

Bill 60 (Charter Affirming the Values of State Secularism and Reli-gious Neutrality and of Equality between Women and Men, and Pro-viding a Framework for Accommodation Requests) was introduced in 2013 (National Assembly of Quebec 2013), but with only a minority government the PQ was forced into an election before it could pass. The language of the PQ, in particular in the return of the notion of the *nous* (us) in the slogan *À nous de choisir* in the 2014 election campaign, seemed to many to be a dog whistle to an intolerant base. Although the PQ was defeated in that election, the overall project of a "charter of values" remained popular, especially among French Canadians, with one poll putting support for it at two-thirds of respondents (CTV News 2014a). Quite soon, a cross-party consensus began to emerge on inter-culturalism, one that no Quebec politician was able to resist. Even the Liberals, who had resisted legislating in the PQ vein, were not immune. Marois's Liberal successor, Phillip Couillard, eventually succumbed to public pressure and proposed a much weaker version of the charter in Bill 62 (an Act to Foster Adherence to State Religious Neutrality and, in Particular, to Provide a Framework for Requests for Accommodations on Religious Grounds in Certain Bodies) (Chouinard 2014; Macpherson n.d.; CTV News 2014b). Although it passed in 2017, it was seen by many as far too weak and did nothing to end the debate. Nor was it enough to stave off the electoral defeat of the Liberals in November 2018.

The successor to the Liberals, the government of François Legault and the CAQ, introduced Bill 21, which went much further than the

Liberals had and triggered a firestorm both inside and outside Canada. The law was almost certainly unconstitutional but was enacted pursuant to the notwithstanding clause, and appeared to put the jobs of many teachers, doctors, nurses, and other state employees at risk. There were questions about whether university students would be allowed to attend classes or even ride public transit while wearing religious clothing. Even so, it passed with broad support from Quebecers (Leger Marketing and *Journal de Montréal* 2019). That the bill was full of holes and inconsistencies did not seem to matter. In the National Assembly there were questions such as whether or not a religious tattoo would count as a symbol under the law, or if employees would have to be strip-searched before coming to work to find any offending items on their person (the answer to both questions appeared to be no). But the magnitude of the questions said a lot about the extent to which debate around Quebec's identity had shifted from a focus on Quebec's place and role within Canada to one that was primarily internal, concentrated on the dynamics of Quebec society itself and newcomers to it.

The fact that the politics of cultural nationalism had a wider audience was made clear in the federal election of 2019. In that year a moribund BQ experienced a strong revival under Yves-François Blanchet, who made the politics of cultural nationalism (but *not* separatism) central to his agenda. Borrowing a page from Legault, Blanchet agreed that it was not the right time to pursue separation, though as a long-term project it was not entirely off the table (J. Montpetit 2019). Instead, he portrayed the BQ as Quebec's best bet in Ottawa, one that would look out for its interests and be an advocate for its people. Pointedly, he made it clear that he supported the politics of cultural nationalism and shared the concerns of many voters about the boundaries of accommodation. This led to charges of intolerance from many quarters, especially after some BQ members made comments that were seen as Islamophobic and suspicious of minorities (Reynolds 2021). As of the date of writing, however, Blanchet remains a popular figure in Quebec, and the BQ's near-identical showing in Parliament after the 2022 federal election suggests that his political strategy remains a viable one.

Interculturalism and Broader Social Change

It would be wrong to push the interculturalist shift too far and ignore the other changes that have appeared in Quebec culture and of which interculturalism is a reflection. Indeed, there is empirical work that suggests the population is not particularly anti-immigrant. Luc Turgeon and Antoine Bilodeau have argued that francophones are far less intolerant of immigration than other Canadians are (Turgeon 2014). But the arc described earlier suggests that the Quebec nationalism of today has gone through changes that make it qualitatively different from the strains that emerged in the 1960s, 1970s, and 1980s. At the broadest level, the Quebec nationalism of the twenty-first century appears to have – at least to a degree – decoupled from the state. It is less dependent on the state and has shed its former fixation on how the state relates to the rest of Canada. In the 1960s the state was the basis of Quebec nationalism; retaking the levers of power was the first step towards national liberation. What followed was an enormous investment in education, infrastructure, cultural activities, and social programs. For many, independence was a logical next step. Today, in a global world, the belief that the province alone can answer the problems of modern Quebecers appears to be less obvious and receives less attention. This retreat of the state has extended well beyond questions of minority accommodation and mirrors changes seen in other Western countries in the rising importance of trade, social justice, and the economy. Politically, this has manifested itself in a rejection of the traditional mainline parties of the PQ and the PLQ and in a willingness to embrace other politicians who are harder to place on a federalist-separatist spectrum. Among them, the CAQ is the most successful, but the rise of the socialist Québec solidaire is emblematic of how the politics of class and equality have overshadowed those of federalism and separatism.

Alongside the debate over religious accommodation, there has been a shift (particularly on the left) in the perceived priorities of politics in a global world. Rather than focusing on the structures of the Canadian constitution, national liberation, and federalism, the 2000s in Quebec were notable for a new fixation on the politics of trade, globalization, and the environment. The global nature of these problems has made Canadian federalism a less visible target than in the past because all countries are implicated. Quebecers perceive themselves as part of a wider, more interconnected world in which Canada is only a small part of the overall picture. The new focus on globalization became more visible around the turn of the century with riots at the World Trade Organization meeting in Quebec City in 2001. Clearly in dialogue with the anti-globalization forces responsible for the riots at the Asia-Pacific Economic Cooperation summit in Vancouver in 1997, the "Battle of Seattle" at another meeting of the WTO in 1999, and the anti-G7 riots in Toronto in 2010, many on the left focused on the institutions of global capital and governance as root causes of economic injustice and inequality. Protesting against federalism was a wasted effort given that both Canada and Quebec were staunch supporters of a global order that shielded the establishment at the cost of the poor and disenfranchised. Similarly, the 2012 student protests against tuition increases by the Charest government (nicknamed the *printemps érable*) stressed amorphous themes of equality and economic justice and were oddly disconnected from traditional narratives of separatism and independence.

This focus on reforming the economy and on social inequality went far beyond globalization and education, though, and cut across all of Quebec society. Nowhere has this been more evident than in the rise of Quebec's "social economy." Between 1995 and 1998, Lucien Bouchard shifted attention to other concerns while waiting for the winning conditions for a referendum to manifest themselves. The decision to refocus was at least partly strategic given that there could not be another referendum on the same question in the same mandate. But the social-economy turn underscored the importance of the welfare state to Quebec's identity and was driven by the PQ as much as any party. It sought to show a unique social model in Canada, one aimed at ameliorating inequalities in society by offering better investments in higher education, childcare, and other family-friendly policies, including more generous employment leave and allowances; and labour-friendly reforms, often provided through social-economy enterprises, which are heavily subsidized non-profit or cooperative organizations that provide the goods (Arsenault 2016, 2–3; Noël 2019, 83–4). With roots in a major conference, the Economy and Employment Summit of 1996 (Arsenault 2016, 5), a shift was taken by Quebec's welfare state that was distinct from that found in other provinces, or other so-called liberal market states that are familiar to students of the Varieties of Capitalism literature (Esping-Andersen 1989). There are competing hypotheses as to why Quebec has taken this turn on social policy, but the timing was likely related to the fact that the left was highly mobilized after the 1995 referendum and had pushed hard for a yes win on the promise that it would lead to a more interventionist state (Arsenault 2016, 86). The momentum of that event was easy to capture for a PQ that needed direction on what to do next and which had to maintain some of the core supporters of the movement, such as unions, community groups, and the intellectual community. Still, although the development of the social economy has been lopsidedly accomplished by the PQ, the PLQ has not been overly hostile to it, and it has remained a basic premise of economic policy (Arsenault 2016, 96–7).

A similar, global shift in Quebec's identity politics can be seen in the politics of energy and the environment. The last twenty years have witnessed a growing appreciation of the problems posed by climate change and Canada's role as a major producer of oil and gas. While this might have left Canadian federalism vulnerable to attacks because most oil and gas comes out of the West, it has not panned out that way.[4] Instead, environmentalism has taken the form of a global conversation in which all of Canada takes part, one that largely transcends the state and calls for international action. As a developed society in the Global North, Quebec is deeply complicit in the environmentally destructive globalized capitalism that it views as ruining the planet. For believers, it is "thinking globally and acting locally" that counts. Although Alberta may be the epicentre of the tar sands, the focus of Quebec environmentalists has been to link up with global actors to effect change at the level of individuals or businesses and to leave the question of federalism more or less on the sidelines. Pipelines and environmental questions are also deeply implicated in the relations that the country has with its Indigenous Peoples, and in whether or not they consent to the projects. Here again, Quebec, like Canada, is viewed as a colonizing force, thus shifting the discussion away from constitutional problems to a wider discussion about reconciliation, Indigeneity, and environmental justice.

The reason for the salience of these other issues may be simply that Quebec's values are subject to the same forces that have brought about value change in the rest of the country. Beyond the question of accommodation, and that of who counts in the public sphere, the priorities of Quebecers are not broadly different from those of the rest of Canada. This was perhaps always true. Even during the early days of the separatist movement, there was much debate around the extent to which separatism was a concern of ordinary people. Most of the evidence suggested that the concern was not significant (e.g., D. Smiley 1978). More recent polling has converged around the realization that the priorities of the electorate are not that different from those of everyone else in Canada; that is, the economy, education, and the environment (D. LeBlanc 2014).

The rest of Canada has itself seen a major shift in its values, something which has been well documented and which mirrors changes that have been found in other countries over the course of the last several decades. The value change is normally associated with the generation that came of age in the 1960s, which saw a move towards women's equality and sexual liberation, a more individualistic political culture, and an emphasis on new issues such as racial equality and the environment. Although the phenomenon is most associated with the United States, the shift has been tracked across the developed world in the literature on post-material values. At root, the post–Second World War world ushered in a time of unrivalled peace and economic security, with important implications for the political cultures of Western democracies.

Ronald Inglehart's *Silent Revolution* (1977) in particular triggered a wave of literature on the way in which rising prosperity in the West shaped politics. It was rooted in two basic hypotheses. First, as material conditions improved, people's values would change, becoming less concerned with the problems of basic survival (the "security hypothesis"). Secondly, a socialization hypothesis held that people's values would reflect the conditions under which they grew up; in other words, one's values largely reflected the conditions that existed during one's childhood, and change at the society level was mostly driven by intergenerational replacement (Inglehart 2008, 131). In the rise of post-materialist values, people were less deferential to traditional institutions, more likely to care about issues disconnected from economic problems, and less likely to participate in traditional political activities such as joining a political party, signing a petition, or voting (Inglehart 2008). Post-materialists could be compared with those who were more traditional in outlook, who revered the Church, had more respect for authority, were more socially conservative, less open to globalization, and more attached to the nation state (139; see also Inglehart 1981, 1988, 1990).

This literature has been applied to the Canadian case in several instances. In the mid-1990s, Neil Nevitte offered such an application in his seminal work *The Decline of Deference* (1996). Working with the World Values Survey, Nevitte examined the 1980–91 period and argued that the politics of the time were exceptional for Canada but understandable when contextualized against the politics of similar countries. He argued that better economic security, along with structural changes in the economy resulting in people working less in the primary sectors and more in services, meant that Canadians had taken a strong post-material shift in their values. To some degree, this was a refutation (or at least a complication) of theories of Canadian political culture based on historical cultural fragments or formative events (Hartz 1955, 1964; Horowitz 1966; Lipset 1950; Wiseman 2007).

Implications of the Interculturalist Shift

Regardless, much of the identity debate in Quebec among political leaders in Quebec since 2000 has focused on accommodation. The shift to interculturalism has had two positive effects from the perspective of those interested in the stability of Canadian federalism. For one, it represented a return to an inward-looking Quebec, one that did not seek recognition from the rest of Canada or even the rest of the world. The debate over who counted in Quebec necessarily meant that the province was less interested in debating the constitutional structure, and to a degree reflected a return to the debates on melancholy nationalism of a piece with those of Hubert Aquin and the Montreal School. Some writing clearly dovetails with the affirmative nationalism and pro-federalism school, but it is in the minority (e.g., Watson and Pratte 2008; É. Montpetit 2008). Guy Laforest and Jean-Olivier Roy characterized Quebec as an "internal exile" in Canada: in it but not a full member of Confederation (2014). Some nationalists, like Alain-G. Gagnon, argue that Quebec now has an informal constitution based on its interculturalist outlook, language, and cultural laws and essentially has developed its own citizenship regime inside Canada (A.-G. Gagnon 2014). The Constitution lacks legitimacy, but Quebec society can survive inside of Canada even though more autonomy and respect for the province is necessary (É. Montpetit 2007a). In general, the theme of cultural exhaustion and frustration with multiculturalism and post-modernity is ascendant. Existing work often attacks multiculturalism as a corrosive force in society, one that erodes solidarity and has led to a cultural dissipation in Quebec. Perhaps the best examples are books by Mathieu Bock-Côté, a noted sociologist and public intellectual (2007, 2012; Bock-Côté et al. 2014). At the same time, there is no shortage of works that seek to express a more limited Quebec identity that must survive in a global world, often blaming members of the political class for abdicating their responsibility, or that sees Quebec as having failed to embrace the possibilities of existing as an independent state (e.g., Piotte and Couture 2012; Payette and Payette 2013; Marois and Sabourin 2014; Savard-Tremblay 2014, 2016; Beauchemin 2015; Mathieu 2017; Guénette and Mathieu 2018).

The second benefit of the shift to interculturalism has been to direct Quebec politics into an area where Quebecers *already* have control – culture. As discussed in the chapter on accommodations, perhaps one of the most salutary, and misunderstood, political moments of the early 1990s was the agreement between Ottawa and Quebec to devolve much of the control over immigration. Along with that control, and the unquestioned capacity of the province to manage questions of culture and language at the provincial level, the shift to interculturalism left Quebecers with a debate that only Quebec City could solve. Once all three parties had committed themselves to adopting some kind of state secularism, a confrontation with the rest of the country began to materialize. Whether one loves it or hates it, it was the moment for which section 33 of the Constitution was designed – a steam-release valve. Once Quebec had steered onto a collision course with the rest of the country, given the demands of state secularism, the triggering of the notwithstanding clause effectively served as a backstop that prevented a cultural crisis in Quebec from exploding into a constitutional one. The rest of the country was happy to take this for what it was, and although there was no support among federalist parties for what was happening in the province, there was no appetite for a conflict either. It was a classic example of an abeyance at the heart of the Constitution being allowed to persist; without a compelling reason to bring it into the open, the question has remained inside the province. That shift has had profound and arguably positive repercussions for the stability of Canadian federalism, even if its impact on minorities inside Quebec is debatable.

Conclusion

This chapter has argued that the shift in elite discourse to focus on the identity politics around reasonable accommodations for minorities has had a stabilizing effect on Canadian federalism because it has made Quebec's discussion about identity less reliant on Quebec's place in Canada. Some will see this discussion as drawing on a pre-existing ethnic strain in Quebec nationalism that has deep roots in the province. Quebec nationalism has evolved a great deal over the past century, moving from a conservative, agrarian, "French Canadian" nationalism to a liberal and progressive one in which the basic identification of Quebecers moved from Canada to that of the province. The last twenty years have seen ethnic nationalism, while containing both civic and ethnic strains within itself, become more popular among many leaders, and the role of the state diminish.

Whether or not this means ordinary Quebecers have become more attracted to the ethnic basis of their identity is an open question, but the discourse has moved in this direction. It is also possible that this was not an independent force causing the decline in the secessionist movement but one replacing a discussion that was receding anyway. Regardless, Quebecers' priorities appear to reflect a shift to post-materialism that is seen elsewhere in Canada. The concerns of Quebecers are now not particularly different from those of the rest of the country, which has made it easier for federalists to pursue a pan-Canadian agenda. This is especially so on the left, where adherents have come to see Quebec and Canada as interchangeable in the liberal order. Many of the policies that the old-line parties articulate are seen as ineffective against issues such as climate change, wealth inequality, and global consumerism. At the same time, voters on the right have been attracted by the politics of identity and have sought to define the problems faced by Quebec as less about its position in the constitutional order and more about how to properly accommodate minority groups in the public sphere. Fortunately for Canada, Quebec already has the tools – the notwithstanding clause is a glaring example – to resolve these questions on its own. This has meant that constitutional discussions are of less concern to Canada.

6 Generational Change

The oldest and by far the most common explanation for the decline of the sovereignty movement in Quebec is generational change. This argument holds that the sovereignty movement, and the national question generally, only ever really reflected the politics of one generation of Quebecers – those who came of age in the Quiet Revolution. It was this generation – broadly congruent with the baby boomers – that gave voice to the vigorous Québécois nationalism of the 1960s, rejected the power structures that underpinned Quebecers' relative exclusion, and succeeded in reshaping society to cater better to their needs. As that generation has been gradually replaced, the national question no longer holds the same allure as it did in the 1960s. This explanation seems to account for the fact that there is relatively little interest on the part of younger generations in constitutional questions; it is further explained by the older age of the members of the PQ, and the struggles that sovereigntist parties have had communicating their relevance to the electorate, who no longer live in the same world in which the parties were born.

The argument that the PQ itself might be the product of generational forces is not new; it was first proposed in the 1980s by Vincent Lemieux (2011). Subsequent research has confirmed that there is a strong generational divide among those who want sovereignty and those who do not, with the peak age for support of sovereignty being fixed firmly in middle age. This explanation for the decline in separatist sentiment has grown in popularity over the past few years (e.g., Langlois and Gangé 2002; J.-H. Guay 2004; Mendelsohn, Parkin, and Pinard 2007; Bélanger and Perrella 2008; Perrella and Bélanger 2009; Mahéo and Bélanger 2018; Dufresne, Tessier, and Montigny 2019). Even so, when it comes to young people, there is a debate about whether or not we see an *actual* decline in sovereignty support or whether younger people have simply stopped viewing it as a priority but would vote yes to independence if given a chance (Piroth 2004, 39). However, whether or not it is a decline in actual support or simply a shift in priorities among young people, the reality is that the leaders of the sovereignty movement are no longer connecting with young people in the way they once did, and this has helped the federalist leadership. Thus, the aim of the chapter is to review the evidence of generational effects and, more importantly, to contextualize them within the broader Canadian story of constitutional stabilization. In essence, the chapter argues that generational change contributed to the creation of conditions that allowed federalists to restore the question of Quebec's constitutional status to a taboo. This was especially so since the changes that the province was undergoing mimicked similar social changes in the rest of the country, with young people converging on similar political priorities everywhere. This meant that the political agenda could solidify around a common set of concerns on which national parties could focus that did not involve the compact-contract constitutional problem. This has also meant that Quebec looks less like an outlier in Canada on many important issues.

Generational Parties and Effects

In the 1980s, Vincent Lemieux of the University of Laval made a series of predictions about political parties in Quebec (1986). Consolidating these claims in 2011, he argued that all the historic parties in Quebec – the PQ, the PLQ, and the Union nationale – were the product of a single generation, each formed in response to a specific set of problems (2011). As those problems were solved, the reasons for the parties to exist would fade, and they would be replaced by new parties. While generational change has arguably affected the Quebec Liberals almost as much as the PQ, it is with the PQ (and the decline in youth interest in sovereignty) that generational effects have been the most visible.

The idea that a party might be connected to a single generation in time is an old one, deeply rooted in theories of political socialization. The main theory is that the political behaviours that people display as adults are those they learned in childhood and adolescence (Beck and Jennings 1982). The culture and events that people experience in their formative years have lasting effects on their political identity (Johnston 1985; Jennings 2002; Mahéo and Bélanger 2018, 338–9). Parents are crucial in political socialization, of course, so it can lead to ideas and values crossing generations (Jennings, Stoker, and Bowers 2009; Anja Neundorf, Smets, and García-Albacete 2013). Political scientists often categorize different groups of people according to the time period in which they grew up (generational change), the impacts of the era on a single group (cohort effect), or some specific event shared by all (period effects). Studying these different drivers of social change is a large part of what many political scientists do. Generational effects were first studied by Karl Mannheim in his 1928 book *The Problem of Generations: Essays on the Sociology of Knowledge* (M.T. Grasso et al. 2019; Mannheim 1996). Since then the profound effects of periodic events on generations have been found to influence many different aspects of political and social behaviour (Tilly 2001, 2002; A. Neundorf and Niemi 2014; M.T. Grasso 2014; Tilly and Evans 2014; M. Grasso 2016; M. Grasso et al. 2017; M.T. Grasso et al. 2019). The value of this kind of research is easy to understand; people experience similar problems at certain points in their lives that no other generation will experience in quite the same way. Parties can become associated with issues that voters care about, and that will carry through over time. Research has shown that one's political preferences are often formed early in life and that once one has started to vote for a party, one becomes wedded to it (Butler and Stokes 1983; Tilly 2002). But there is still considerable volatility that can occur over a person's lifetime.

If the party is the product of a single generation, this can have wider implications about the voter behaviour of that generation, sometimes known as the life-cycle effect (Goerres 2008, 286–7). The argument is that as a person ages, their politics change to reflect their changing circumstances. The study of the effects of aging on party affiliation began in earnest in the 1960s and 1970s (Crittenden 1962; Glenn 1974). Older people are classically thought to be more conservative across social and economic indicators because they are more established and have more to lose (occasionally captured by the old joke "Anyone under thirty who is not a liberal has no heart; anyone over thirty who is not a conservative has no brain") (Binstock and George 2001). There is a widespread belief that older people become more conservative on law and order issues and/or more authoritarian in their outlook (Danigelis and Cutler 1991; Goerres 2008, 286–7). Another argument connected to aging and partisanship holds that older people are more likely to support established parties that they know and trust. Younger people are more open to new parties because they do not have as long a memory of voting (e.g., Barnes et al. 1988). Still, most of these hypotheses remain just that, and the literature is not always consistent when it comes to finding the generational or age effects. It does appear, though, that the politics of the PQ have more recently come to resemble many of the predictions made in the literature on generational support for parties.

It is certainly true that Quebec is experiencing the same long-term demographic shift as is the rest of Canada and the Western world as a whole. Under any growth scenario, the percentage of the population above the age of sixty-five will rise above 20.0 per cent by 2043, from 17.2 per cent today. The median age has also been rising steadily, from 23.9 years old a century ago to just over forty years today (Statistics Canada 2019a). The situation in Quebec does not differ in outline, where if anything the population is a little older. The province has a median age of just over forty-two years old, and 18.8 per cent of the population was over sixty-five in 2018. This percentage is projected to grow to between 22.9 per cent and 28.0 per cent of the overall population by 2043 (Statistics Canada 2019b). The aging population has important political and economic consequences, in particular for a country where so many programs and pensions are funded on a "pay as you go" basis, largely on the backs of working people who fund current retirees.

It is important to understand how generational change, and in particular the parties that are connected with it, are implicated in the story. Since the 1980s there has been a growing literature studying the PQ as a generational party, and the separatist cause as being particularly subject to generational change. The literature has increased over the last decade or so, although it had been clearer previously. By the early 1980s, it became apparent that it was the baby boomers, more than any other generation, that supported the sovereigntist cause (Blais and Nadeau 1984). From this, a number of reasons were identified to explain the spike in support for sovereignty. The fact that the baby boomers were the product of a particularly wealthy time was identified as a relevant factor in the run-up to the second referendum. Other generations, in particular older generations, were much less open to the idea of sovereignty. This "silent generation" (as it is now called) had in the mid-1990s by far the lowest level of support for the project (Martin 1994, 351). For this generation, political stability mattered more than anything, and the idea of breaking up the country had much less appeal.

The Generational Impact of the Quiet Revolution

It is difficult to overestimate the importance of the Quiet Revolution to Quebecers who came of age in the 1960s. The political exclusion of French Canadians from positions of power in both Canada and Quebec gave rise to the social transformation in Quebec in which a largely deferential Catholic and agrarian society repudiated many of the culturally conservative touchstones on which it had been based, in favour of a vastly different and more activist political culture. Out of this process arose a strong nationalist movement that has dominated provincial politics to the present day. The process began in the 1950s, when the PLQ moved towards a more interventionist program that had as its objective the displacement of the anglophone elites in favour of a new francophone professional class, encapsulated in its motto *Maîtres chez nous* (Masters in our own house). The PLQ, under its leader Jean Lesage, gained power by linking organized labour, the francophone business class, and the middle-class intelligentsia into a single party (Behiels 1985, 220–1; generally, see Coleman 1984). Very quickly the party began the social and cultural transformation of Quebec, nationalizing critical industries (e.g., electricity), making major investments in the educational system, creating new social programs (such as the Quebec Pension Plan in 1964), and creating new vehicles through which investments in the province could be made (of which the Caisse de dépôt et placement du Québec is the best example). Furthermore, the government introduced the first protections for the French language in the form of new laws for commercial signs and related enforcement mechanisms. The precursor to the Office québécois de la langue française was established in 1961, for example.

Although the PLQ would ultimately remain federalist, many groups and individuals within this early coalition turned towards secessionism and eventually broke away from the PLQ in 1968 to form what became the dominant separatist provincial party, the Parti Québécois under former Liberal cabinet minister René Lévesque. The PQ emerged from several different political streams, many of which did not agree with one another on questions such as independence, language policy, or the role of the Church in society. Of these the Ralliement national (RN) and Rassemblement pour l'indépendance nationale (RIN) were the most important. In 1967, Lévesque broke from the Liberals to form the Mouvement souveraineté-association (MSA), which promised economic growth and a relationship with Canada of "associated states," or what would later be called "sovereignty association" (Behiels 1985, 220–1). The MSA would eventually absorb the RN, and most of the RIN membership joined the PQ in 1968 after it folded.

The PQ became the political vehicle of choice for those segments most alienated from Quebec society, in particular Quebec's "new professionals," organized labour, the working class, students, and artists (Behiels 1985, 220–1). Many of the movement's supporters, both inside and outside the PQ, were ideologically rooted in narratives of socialism and decolonization. A common theme was that Quebec represented little more than a colonial possession of a domineering and uncaring Anglo-Canadian elite. Another was that the Canadian state itself was little more than a projection of an unjust global capitalist political and economic order. Particularly pronounced was a sense of outrage against the rest of the country, which had not included Quebec and neither took it seriously nor saw it as an equal. While these narratives did not go without challenge, it was clear there was at least some truth to them. Both Quebec and Canada were generally dominated by Anglo-Canadian elites who had little time for most of French Canadian society and were utterly British in their outlook. There was no national state bilingualism in Canada until the introduction of the Official Languages Act of 1969. There was no separate Canadian citizenship from the United Kingdom until the 1940s, the current flag only replaced the British-inspired Red Ensign in 1965, and the national anthem only officially replaced "God Save the Queen" in 1980. Similarly, the first of July, the date of Canadian confederation, was celebrated as Dominion Day until 1982. Many constitutional guarantees for minority languages were entrenched that same year in the Canadian Charter of Rights and Freedoms, itself hugely controversial in Quebec where it was seen as having been adopted without the province's consent (Russell 2004, 124–6).

One of the defining features of this movement was that it was so *young*. Even before the PQ had won its first election, the growth of support for separatism among the young was identified by the scholar Léon Dion as the product of generational forces. Dion, along with many others, felt that it was easy to be a separatist when one was in one's twenties, given that younger people often had a lot less to lose than their parents had. He suspected it would become more difficult to remain a separatist later on in life, after its adherents became more established (L. Dion 1975, 89, cited in Martin, 1994, 351; Bélanger and Perrella 2008; Perrella and Bélanger 2009; Piroth 2004). That the independence movement slanted younger also seemed to be in keeping with other nationalist movements around the world. Nationalists tend to rely on the enthusiasm of young cohorts, who are more liberal, experimental, and less invested in the status quo (although traditionally also less likely to become involved in politics). A recent recognition of this fact in the United Kingdom was the effort to lower the voting age to sixteen before the 2014 Scottish referendum on independence (Black 2013). A similar idea was suggested in Quebec before 1995.

In 1970 and 1973 the PQ contested its first two elections and, while it fared poorly in the seat count (winning seven and six seats respectively), this outcome only masked its meteoric rise in popularity. The first three elections saw its popularity rise from 23 per cent, to 30 per cent, to 41 per cent in the breakthrough election of 1976 (Mahéo and Bélanger 2018, 338). Importantly, in all of these elections, it was clear that the PQ saw a disproportionate share of its vote coming from young people (R. Hamilton and Pinard 1976, 9). This was true even when controlling for education (closely correlated with age) as well as for class. Conversely, the Liberals did far better among older generations. The connection was evident in both the 1970 election and the 1973 election, despite the PQ's otherwise poor showing. In their study of the 1973 election Hamilton and Pinard found that the PQ had the support of 69 per cent of voters aged eighteen to twenty, and 57 per cent of those aged twenty-one to twenty-four (11). These authors also noted that it was not simply age; while youth was critical, education and class were also key, with the most support for the PQ coming from young, educated, urban, and affluent francophone Quebecers.[1] This startling success caught the rest of the country off guard, but Canadian politicians did nothing to challenge the PQ's right to govern or carry out its agenda. Following the initial shock, it became clear that the victorious PQ would not instantaneously attempt to secede but would assume power as any party would.[2] It was increasingly clear, though, that a referendum was inevitable. That the PQ seemed unstoppable among young people gave separatism an air of invincibility. This belief was not limited to Quebec. It was widely reflected in the English-language press of the time (e.g., Art 1970).

In the event, the PQ did not win the referendum, but neither the party nor the movement seemed to slow down throughout the late 1970s and early 1980s. During this period the PQ continued its generation-defining reforms in earnest. The party created or transformed many of the political institutions in the province, bringing in dramatic new cultural and linguistic protections as well as new social and educational programs. In the late 1970s, Bill 101 (or the Charter of the French Language) was introduced along with increased powers for the Office québécois de la langue française (Quebec Board of the French Language, OQLF). Although contentious, the charter was effective in bringing real cultural security to Quebecers and changing the language of life and business in the province. By the late 1970s, Quebec society had changed enormously and political power was now firmly grounded in an educated, secular francophone middle class. There were some who thought that as the middle classes of Quebec became more capitalist, like those in English Canada, it might reduce the differences between them (e.g., Coleman 1984). But this was not the story of the 1980s; throughout, the PQ's strength and appeal to young people remained. The PQ successfully played on a sense of outrage against the rest of the country and presented itself as the only effective voice for Quebec, either inside or outside of Canada. This was especially so after the Constitution was patriated over Quebec's objections, leading to enormous public outrage. Electorally, the PQ achieved its all-time high of 49.3 per cent of support in the 1981 provincial poll that took place in the middle of the patriation crisis (Mahéo and Bélanger 2018, 338). The party had benefited disproportionately from the youth vote in the referendum of 1980, which gave an image of vitality to the national project (Nadeau 1992, 13–14).

The decade following the referendum saw the PQ lose power to the Liberals, but its appeal to sovereignty remained relevant and popular. The appeal received full expression from the PQ's being the official opposition in the National Assembly and was rooted in the educated, left-leaning elite. The PQ's ongoing role in the Quebec political space deeply shaped the politics of the 1980s, in which the rest of the country sought to develop a constitutional offer that would satisfy Quebec enough for it to sign the Constitution and arrest the progress of the sovereignty movement (see generally Russell 2004). The failure of the Meech Lake Accord in 1990 saw the movement reach its highest peak of popularity and drive even the federalist Liberals towards a referendum on secession. This too reflected the enormous sense of disrespect and outrage that people felt in the face of the Accord's collapse. It also catapulted the secessionist movement into the federal House of Commons when Lucien Bouchard, a Conservative minister, left the Conservative caucus with a group of Quebec Members of Parliament to form the Bloc Québécois (BQ). The subsequent Charlottetown Accord – meant to address the failings of the Meech Lake Accord – failed in 1992. Since it had been long dismissed by many in Quebec as "too little too late," its defeat did not have the same psychological impact as the failure of the Meech Lake Accord had had, doubly so because it was also rejected in a referendum by most other Canadians throughout the country. These combined failures contributed to the Conservative collapse in the elections of 1993 and enormously amplified the secessionist strength.

These failed deals led Quebecers to throw their support to the BQ at the federal level and to the PQ at the provincial level between 1993 and 1994. First, the Bloc took almost every seat in Quebec and returned as the official opposition in the federal election. This led to some initial fears about the workability of the House of Commons, given the BQ's sovereigntist agenda. However, it became clear that, once elected, the Bloc would not otherwise interrupt the ordinary functioning of the House and would play a traditional and constructive opposition role. In 1994 the provincial PQ returned to power under the leadership of the hard sovereigntist Jacques Parizeau, who moved to hold a second referendum in October 1995. Dramatic and much more closely fought, this referendum failed by a mere half percentage point, shocking the rest of the country and ordinary Quebecers who had not believed that the referendum result would be so close at the start of the campaign. The result drove home the point that the break-up of the country was very much a possibility.

Nevertheless, by the 1990s it was becoming clear that generational effects were at play, with ominous implications for the independence project. The generation most committed to sovereignty had peaked. In 1991 one survey found that those born between 1936 and 1956 had the highest level of support for sovereignty, at 61 per cent. The generation that followed it (defined as those under thirty-five) was also still clearly in favour of independence, at 57 per cent, although there were signs that it was less committed than the generation that preceded it (Martin 1994, 351). Still, with the close call of the 1995 referendum and the PQ winning another victory, in 1998, it was not immediately clear that the sovereigntist movement faced a generational crisis or that it would be unable to maintain its appeal to young voters. Commentary in the mid-1990s suggested a mood of panic in the rest of Canada and one of optimism among the PQ that the next referendum would come soon and that the break-up of the country was imminent (e.g., Cameron 1996, 293–8; Broadbent 1996, 271–80).

The Younger Generation

A slew of studies in the years after the 1995 referendum confirmed that the generational problem faced by the PQ was not going away; if anything, it was intensifying (e.g., J.-H. Guay 1997, 2004; Caldwell 2003; G. Hamilton 2004; Piroth 2004; Bélanger and Perrella 2008; Perrella and Bélanger 2009; Lemieux 2011; K. Gagnon 2014a; Mahéo and Bélanger 2018; Dufresne, Tessier, and Montigny 2019). Not all studies agreed, and levels of support differed depending on when a poll was taken. One study still found a majority of support for the independence cause among youth (18–34 years old) in 2006, for example, with support around 60 per cent among francophones (Bélanger and Perrella 2008, 22). Thus, it was not clear that younger people were less supportive of the national project in the abstract; it may have simply reflected shifting priorities. If they were given the chance to vote, perhaps they would still be as supportive of independence as their parents are (Piroth 2004, 39). Regardless, as time went on, it became clear that the issue was declining with young people, either absolutely or in relative importance, and the further away a generation was from the baby boomers, the less it seemed to matter (Mahéo and Bélanger 2018, 336). Today youth consistently report lower levels of engagement with the national question, more interest in globalization, and greater comfort with Quebec as a global society (Mahéo and Bélanger 2018, 336; K. Gagnon 2014a; *La Presse* 2014). The priorities of young people, much like those of their counterparts elsewhere, include the environment, education, and the economy rather than separatism. Disinterest in the national question did not equate to a lack of interest in politics, however. A poll taken in the run-up to the 2018 provincial election found that voters aged eighteen to twenty-five were highly engaged politically, and the vast majority planned to vote. At 40 per cent, education ranked as their top concern, followed by health (32 per cent), and the economy (20 per cent). Of the twelve topics on which they were polled, sovereignty ranked dead last (Lau 2018; see also Mahéo and Bélanger 2018, 345). Furthermore, there was less dissatisfaction with Canada than there had been in earlier years. That did not translate to strong attachment to the country – Quebec itself commanded far more allegiance – but there did not seem to be the same level of alienation from Canadian federalism (Mahéo and Bélanger 2018, 343). Put differently, young Quebecers did not exactly love Canada, but they did not hate it either.

Their lack of outrage at Canada is a big shift from that of earlier generations. The latter's outrage had been a foundation on which the PQ had built its success during the 1960s, 1970s, and 1980s. The lack of alienation may reflect the fact that the Canada in which younger Quebecers grew up was far more accommodating than it had been in years past, meaning that they were shaped by different forces and experiences. Many studies have shown how the events and political context of adolescence shape political opinions, and the Canada of the 1980s, 1990s, and 2000s was not the same as that of the 1960s (e.g., Johnston 1985; Jennings 2002) After 1995 the secessionist narrative of exclusion and disrespect was harder to sustain and came increasingly under attack. A pan-Canadian counter-narrative developed among powerful Quebec politicians, journalists, and academics like Stéphane Dion, André Pratte, Alain Dubuc, Jean Charest, and Jean Chrétien (e.g., Pratte 2008; Dubuc 2008). Following several decades of francophone control at the provincial level and of the clear security of the French language in the province, and decades of French Canadian prime ministers, the idea that Quebecers were oppressed was increasingly difficult to maintain. Furthermore, two referendums had made it clear that Quebec could negotiate some form of secession whenever a majority of people decided to leave.

As Lemieux suggested in his book on generational parties, we have also seen continuing effects on the party system, obviously for the PQ but also for the Liberals, who are struggling too. Nevertheless, the generational issue is a bigger problem for the PQ, not only in the image it projects but also in reconciling the competing agendas that different generations may have. In the aftermath of the 2018 election – a disaster for the PQ – the generational problems have spilled out into the open and now represent a real cleavage that the PQ has to manage. It does not help that the average age of PQ members is now sixty, leading to accusations that the party is out of touch with youth (Patriquin 2016). In advance of its annual meeting in 2019, the PQ lost its youngest member, Catherine Fournier, who claimed that the party had lost its way. A week later, an open letter signed by thirty members of the youth wing claimed the PQ was failing to attract new voters (Canadian Press 2019). At the meeting itself, the youth wing of the party, frustrated with the age and the direction of the PQ, brought forward a resolution that called on the party to guarantee that half of the delegates from individual riding associations sent to the upcoming convention were under the age of forty (Authier 2019). That failed, as did several more attempts, before the party decided to stick to the "more or less status quo" proposition that one in four delegates be under thirty (Authier 2019). This lack of support from younger people has undermined the notion that the PQ will lead Quebec out of Canada.

The PQ's inability to speak to their concerns may be responsible for young people's willingness to move their support to other parties, of which the biggest winner may be Québec solidaire (QS). In 2006, QS came out of a merger of social activist Françoise David's Option citoyenne and the political party Union des forces progressistes (UFP), which itself had united a number of smaller parties. As Pascale Dufour has argued, QS was the product of a number of forces present in Quebec society at the time, namely the growing interest in left-wing causes in Quebec such as environmentalism and social justice, the weakening of links between the PQ and some traditional supporters such as women's and labour groups, and newer forms of political action (2009, 72–6) The unification was a reaction to Quebec's neoliberal agenda and was bolstered following Lucien Bouchard's fiscally conservative manifesto *Pour un Québec lucide*, which called on the province to take a more conservative stance on tuition rates, cheap electricity, and other social commitments (L. Bouchard et al. 2005). The response, *Pour un Quebec solidaire* (2006), was signed by twenty-six progressive leaders and completely rejected the conclusions that Bouchard had reached. Rather, the authors claimed that more needed to be done to propel Quebec to an environmentally sustainable and durable form of economic development, which meant increased investment in education, more concern for the environment, and less concern for financial or economic matters. *Pour un Québec solidaire* included seven calls for action, including strengthened labour laws, action against tax evasion, greater investment in education, cheap electricity, public health care, and support for socially minded enterprises and for environmental laws (2006). Importantly, the independence of Quebec did not rank in the list of things to be achieved. The omission was telling. For QS, the independence of Quebec was less important than challenging the basic political and economic assumptions upon which the economy of Quebec, and that of the broader world, was premised. While later clarifying that it was in favour of Quebec independence, it still defined itself as more socialist and anti-globalist than anything else. It offered a new prescription for the problems affecting Quebec, one that clearly differentiated the party from the traditional divide between the PLQ and the PQ.

Québec solidaire has been popular with young people. Initially, the party had an odd structure, in that it eschewed a formal leader. Instead, it had spokespeople, in particular Amir Khadir and Françoise David. The party remained very much on the fringes of Quebec society but began to make inroads with university students and attracted a following in parts of Montreal. From this foundation it began to gather force as an electoral machine. QS contested its first election in 2006 when community organizer Manon Massé ran under the party's mantle in a by-election in a riding in the Montreal region. The party ran almost a full slate of candidates in the 2007 provincial election but failed to win a seat, securing only around 3.5 per cent of the popular vote. Still, the party continued to organize, and a victory finally came in a 2008 by-election in Mercier, where Amir Khadir won. QS had its first breakout election in 2012, winning two seats and over 6 per cent of the vote. It bettered this performance in 2014, winning a third seat and nearly 7 per cent of the vote, and a real break-out followed in 2018 (16 per cent of the vote, ten seats, and official party status). QS continues to be popular in urban areas, particularly the east end of the island of Montreal, but it has also won seats in Quebec City, Sherbrooke, and Rouyn-Noranda-Tésmiscamingue, a large riding on the border with Ontario. The base remains largely francophone, young, educated, and nominally separatist. It has managed to attract "star candidates," perhaps most significantly Gabriel Nadeau-Dubois, who was made co-spokesman in 2017 along with Manon Massé, and who was well known from the student protests of 2012 that came to be known as the *printemps érable*.

The most obvious shift has been in the rise of the Coalition avenir Québec (CAQ), which shocked Canada and Quebec with its breakthrough election of 2018. The connection with youth is more tenuous in this case; the CAQ appeals to a broader and more conservative audience. The party is the product of a 2011 merger with the ADQ and reflects the more conservative nationalism that was apparent in the manifesto *Pour un Québec lucide* signed by Lucien Bouchard and other intellectuals. Former PQ minister and Air Transat founder François Legault promised an end to the politics of separatism promoted by the PQ and an end to corruption (associated with the long-enduring Liberals) in favour of a new course based around the promotion of economic growth, limited government, and a commitment to identity politics based around the French nation. While it has tried to eschew labels, the CAQ falls within almost any definition of a centre-right party. Among other things, Legault has suggested a desire to discontinue the federal equalization program, which he sees as infantilizing, and to decentralize Ottawa's powers (although the party has been vague on this score); he has also articulated a commitment to reform or even abolish the school boards in favour of giving school principals more say. The most common descriptor of the party is that it is neither separatist nor federalist, but simply nationalist. While it has promised not to touch Bill 101, CAQ has worked to reach out to the anglophone minority in the province, suggesting they can vote for the party and be confident that the CAQ will never hold a referendum.

In hindsight, the decision of the ADQ and the CAQ to merge seems both inevitable and consistent with a clear shift in Quebec's identity. The CAQ's manifesto imagines a party not fundamentally different from the one the ADQ had been promising (Legault et al. 2011). In setting out its vision of the future, the CAQ argued that, above all, Quebec was suffering from a malaise, a cultural defeatism reminiscent of Jimmy Carter's alleged view of America in the 1970s. It argued that, whether or not Quebecers were sovereigntists or federalists, they were all nationalists. The new party sought to transcend that debate and rebuild a more vibrant and entrepreneurial society (2–3). It rooted its vision in four priorities: supporting education, protecting Quebecois culture, improving the quality of Quebec's public services, and promoting an economy of ownership and investment rooted in the province rather than being a "branch plant" economy run from elsewhere (3–7). Little was said about energy, the environment, Indigenous Peoples, or other issues, but the emphasis on economic and cultural issues and the downplaying of the Constitution was in step with a conservative nationalism that had been growing since the founding of the ADQ in 1994. The merger of the parties in 2012, and Legault's vigorous control of the party, allowed it to grow at the expense of both the Liberals and the PQ until the breakthrough election in 2018. It arguably represents the best example of the contemporary priorities of mainstream Quebec's francophone nationalism.

This nationalism has coat-tails, and it was from this base that another party, the Bloc Québécois, has successfully reinvented itself at the national level. Under the leadership of Yves-François Blanchet, the BQ has evolved from a federal protest party to an increasingly irrelevant, extremist, ethnonationalist party to the reconstituted force that it became after the federal election of 2019. The BQ has never been able to explain the reasons for its existence; even its founder, Lucien Bouchard, has described it as a "one-shot" party that was not supposed to survive after the referendum of 1995 (CBC News / Canadian Press 2014). The fortunes of the Bloc revived following the election of Yves-François Blanchet as leader. Blanchet was a former PQ minister who had been defeated by a CAQ candidate in the 2018 provincial election (CBC News 2019). Unlike Martine Ouellette or Mario Beaulieu, Blanchet had recognized that the base of the party had evolved away from the PC and towards the CAQ. Facing an election, he worked to rebuild the party and present it as the best voice to stand up for Quebec issues in Ottawa. The renegade Members of Parliament who had abandoned the party under Ouellette quickly returned, and Blanchet made progress in redefining the BQ.

In the election of 2019 the Bloc returned with vengeance, taking thirty-two seats and almost 33 per cent of the vote, returning it to official party status and eclipsing the NDP, which had high hopes in the province (J. Montpetit 2019). Performing well in the debates, Blanchet surprised many with a steady campaign. He also seemed to strike a chord with Quebecers. But sovereignty was on the back burner, a point that Blanchet acknowledged in his speech. "We understand the depth of our mandate, but we also understand its limitations. This time, for this time, the realization of sovereignty is not our mandate" (J. Montpetit 2019). Of particular resonance was the question of the environment, and his forceful rejection of a pipeline in the province won plaudits from many. Blanchet also decided that he would take the party further to the right on social issues, which had not been the case during the years that Duceppe led the party. Duceppe had been a labour organizer and a member of a number of left-wing, socialist organizations in his youth, and he steered the Bloc towards social democracy. None of this was true with Blanchet. The campaign was clearly nationalist, but, again, effort was made to put the fight over *laïcité* front and centre, to which many voters responded. All of this was very much in keeping with the platform of the CAQ and was a contrast to the PQ, with which the BQ has been historically associated.

Youth do not share the same connection with the CAQ as they do with QS, but these parties all share a desire to move past the federalist-separatist axis. While the disengagement of youth from the PQ has been the most visible, it would be wrong to suggest that the Liberals are not vulnerable to the same generational forces – as Lemieux himself argued in his book on generational parties. It is important to remember as well that the CAQ is resonating with the younger generation. A poll taken before the 2018 election in Quebec showed that, if it were left to those under the age of thirty-five, QS would win the election, and the CAQ would take second place (Lajoie 2018; Ethan 2018).

The federal elections of 2021 and the provincial elections of 2022 in Quebec appeared to represent a solidification and continuation of the trends. Legault returned to a second mandate with a much larger majority, increasing his seat count from seventy-six to ninety, albeit with only a few extra percentage points of the popular vote (CBC News 2022). Although they had widely divergent seat counts, the PQ, PLQ, QS, and the upstart Conservative Party of Quebec (unrelated to the Conservative Party of Canada) all finished with similar results in the 15 per cent range (CBC News 2022). For the BQ's part, Blanchet held to his strategy during and after the federal election of 2021 and returned to Parliament with the identical seat count and nearly the identical vote share as he had received in 2019 (Elections Canada 2021).

Conclusion

This chapter has considered the possibility that federalists have been able to restore abeyance around Quebec's place in Canada because young people are no longer interested in the topic. Since many studies have shown at least some kind of a generational effect at play, it cannot be ignored as an explanation. This is not to say that young people would not vote yes if given the opportunity, perhaps with the right leader or on the right issue. Or perhaps there is a genuine drop in support for sovereignty. Regardless, there does not seem to be the desire among young people to put the national question at the top of the political agenda. There is a lack of outrage among young cohorts, less of a sense that Quebec has been disrespected by the rest of Canada. This marks a change from the politics of the 1960s and 1970s. In the early years of its existence the PQ was mostly attractive to a younger, more alienated type of Quebec nationalist who was frustrated by the clerical and agrarian elite of the province that articulated a view of society that was not in keeping with the modern world. In general, the frustration took two paths: one federalist, following the example of Pierre Trudeau into the Quebec Liberals, and one separatist, following René Lévesque into the Parti Québécois. The remaining members of the Union nationale eventually faded from view and had gone by the middle of the 1970s.

The two camps created by the Quiet Revolution dominated the political arena for four decades, roughly from the 1976 election until the 2018 election. Both the PLQ and the PQ have found themselves subject to generational forces, but it is the PQ that appears to be suffering the most from them. The average age of party members is higher, the youth wing more discontented, and its support more divided along generational lines than any other party. And it no longer seems to be keeping pace with what Quebec nationalism has become, instead yielding that position to the new Coalition avenir Quebec, itself a product of earlier parties that were less concerned with separatism and more conservative in outlook on the economy and social issues. Whether or not the PQ can survive remains to be seen.

7 Economic Globalization

No examination of the ways in which Canadian elites have managed to stabilize Canadian federalism and bury the national question in Quebec can omit the possibility that the driving force is ultimately economic. Since 1995 there have been huge changes to the Canadian and Quebec economies and the extent to which both are integrated into the global economic environment. This, of course, has had wide-ranging social and political effects that have changed the priorities of the Quebec people as well as the types of projects their leaders pursue. This chapter examines the impact of economic globalization on the national movement. Economic globalization in this sense is not concerned so much with cultural evolution, which is addressed in the chapters on generational change and identity, as it is with how the integration of the economy would be affected by independence. Of course, changes to the economy overlap with many other explanations examined in this book. The economy can clearly have an effect on people's identity. It may spur cultural change and have an impact on generational politics. Generally, growing economic integration is usually seen as a barrier to those seeking independence. As the world becomes more global and integrated, the conventional wisdom is that secession is harder because it drives up barriers to capital and investment, hurting the well-being of ordinary people (Rocher 2002, 86–90). On the one hand, convincing voters that leaving a country is fundamentally in their economic and financial interest is normally perceived as being a central challenge for secessionists. On the other hand, there are examples of "deglobalization" being a winning narrative as well, in which the idea of economic liberation from red tape and other economic obstacles is important. We have seen these arguments often used in Scotland and Catalonia and over the course of the Brexit debate. Indeed, while pan-state nationalism may have experienced mixed fortunes in an era of globalization, some research suggests that many small, internal nations have experienced a notable lift by the process (e.g., Keating 1996; Guibernau 1999).

Between these views one finds another, more complicated take: that the forces of globalization create opportunities for *both* federalist and secessionist elites to pursue their agendas, and it is here that this chapter takes its departure point. In this view, globalization and nationalism react dynamically, and each shapes the other or even gives rise to the other, and depending on the time and place, globalization can benefit or harm either pan-state or substate nationalists (Kaldor 2004, 162; Hutchinson 2004; Mann 2012, 10). Thus economic globalization is not necessarily "good" or "bad" for sovereigntists or federalists; rather it can create openings for either to push their cause. For Canada this has meant that federalists and sovereigntists argue about whether Quebec is better off staying in or leaving the country, and this chapter argues that the federalists have simply been better at winning the debate.

How does this play out? Economic globalization in Canada really raises two questions: First, how important are the perceived economic costs and benefits in the calculation of voting for independence? Secondly, has economic globalization affected that economic calculation by raising or lowering the perceived costs of independence? If the feeling is that independence is risky, it will create more political space for federalist elites to drop the subject by arguing that they should spend time on creating jobs and growing the economy. If separation is seen as a path to prosperity, then it makes secession more likely by empowering secessionists. This chapter argues that federalist elites have been more successful in arguing that independence is economically risky, and the PQ has never succeeded in making a convincing case that Quebec is better outside of Canada. This in turn has allowed federalists to successfully resist arguing about constitutional issues by claiming they are focused on bread-and-butter economic issues rather than on constitutional problems. Whether or not the federalist argument is *empirically* true is beside the point; they have leveraged their success to shift the discussion away from constitutional problems by saying they are focused on taking care of the issues that matter, thus keeping the constitutional question in abeyance.

How Do Economic Factors Affect Support for Secessionism?

There is extensive research on what motivates people to vote for secession in Quebec, especially with regard to the impact of economic factors (Pinard and Hamilton 1977, 1984b, 1986; Pinard 1992, 2003, 2005; Howe 1998; Langlois and Gangé 2002; Blais, Martin, and Nadeau 1995; Mendelsohn 2003; Mendelsohn, Parkin, and Pinard 2007). An obvious area of focus is the extent to which a voter might decide to vote yes or no in a referendum simply as a matter of naked economic trade-offs through the logic of rational choice. This focus is particularly associated with the work of the Montreal School (Mendelsohn 2003, 515).[1] Even outside of polling or survey experiments, theoretical models have suggested that the fear of instability will always weigh heavier on voters when they are presented with the option to vote yes in a referendum. In fact, such a model was developed by Stéphane Dion, former Liberal leader and minister of intergovernmental affairs in the government of Jean Chrétien. Dion argued that for the electorate, fear, and in particular economic fear, was a greater motivator than the promised benefits (S. Dion 1996). This trade-off shapes how supporters of independence must look at the project, and it means that there is an inherent advantage for those who support maintaining the status quo.

Others scholars, like Maurice Pinard, have argued that people vote for or against sovereignty for many reasons, including as a way to protest or give Quebec bargaining power against the federal government (Pinard and Hamilton 1984a, 367, 384; quoted in Mendelsohn 2003, 514). In a similar vein, in the late 1990s, Paul Howe looked at the ways in which different factors feed into the decision to vote yes. He found that the economy was an important consideration, but that it was not necessarily the most important. As sovereignty is a hypothetical event, what might happen after independence is a matter of speculation. On the one hand, those who support sovereignty will be able to marshal arguments and evidence to convince others about the problems of the federal system and the chances that exist for the province outside of Canada. On the other hand, champions of the status quo will be able to marshal evidence that they think supports their opinion (Howe 1998, 47). How people respond to that evidence may be more a product of their views on other issues like national identity or a sense of grievance. Regardless, empirical research has shown that concern over the economy was always greater for those voting no (Pinard and Hamilton 1986, 236; Nadeau, Martin, and Blais 1999; see also Mendelsohn 2003). It has never been the leading factor for those voting yes. Yes voters have been motivated more out of a sense of rejection by the rest of Canada and grievances around the Constitution than out of a sense of impending economic benefit (Mendelsohn 2003, 527).

In Canada, exploiting voter fears around economic instability and independence has always been the strategy of federalists, who claim that breaking up the country would be economically devastating. There was good reason for taking this line of attack as even internal PQ polls showed that the party was unlikely to ever win a referendum outright without hope of an economic partnership (Pinard and Hamilton 1977, 230; D. Smiley 1978, 203). Ensuring voters that they would attempt to leave the country only after holding a referendum, and even then only after securing a deal with the rest of the country, the PQ formed the framework for sovereignty association that has shaped the debate since the 1970s. In the face of denial by the federal government, which insists that any such deal would be impossible without the support of the rest of the country, the PQ has assured supporters of independence that a deal would be easy because Ottawa would have no choice but to reach one. This is known as the "knife to the throat" strategy, and it worked, to some degree, to convince hard-line supporters that the PQ could force a deal after a yes vote. Even so, the strategy has never been totally successful in putting to rest Quebecers' fears about the project. Whenever the PQ has promised that independence would bring a bright economic future, it has been met with suspicion by the public – and even by former separatist leaders themselves (e.g., see G. Hamilton 2014a).

This story, in which federalists warn of the economic risks of secession and separatists play up the economic benefits of independence, is a familiar one. In the Scottish referendum of 2014, the Scottish National Party (SNP) claimed that leaving the country would unleash new opportunities and that there was almost no downside given that both Scotland and the United Kingdom would be members of the European Union (although the EU made it clear through both officials and member states that admission would not be automatic). It was not at all certain that the strategy worked, however, with polls suggesting that the public was sceptical of the promises (e.g., Hakim 2014). In the marquee economic document released by the Scottish government in the lead-up to the referendum, a continuing relationship with the United Kingdom was outlined (e.g., perhaps keeping a currency union), but independence was framed as allowing for differences where it was politically important and more advantageous for Scotland. Examples included a more globally oriented outlook on economic policy and the ability to invest more in social programs (Scottish Government 2013, 42). The echoes with Quebec are obvious. Similar assertions have been made in Catalonia where the European context is held up as a safety net that will insulate a minority nation from the collapse of the home state. Even in the Brexit referendum, the "Brexiteers" were happy to point out the unrealized possibilities of independence, and dismissed the warnings of economic carnage arising from independence as "Project Fear." Much like the PQ in Quebec, the Brexiteers also claimed that the rest of Europe needed the British too much to simply allow them to go without a deal. They argued that there would be opportunities for cooperation where the British wanted it, such as a more flexible free trade deal with the EU, while dropping what they did not want, such as membership in the European Court of Justice or free movement.

How Does Globalization Affect Secessionist Sentiment in Quebec?

The literature around the role that the economy and globalization played in suppressing the sovereignty movement began to shift after the Liberals succeeded the PQ in 2003, and even more so after 2010. Up to that point, much research focused on the topics discussed earlier, including the reasons that people vote yes or no and how the sovereignty movement in Quebec fit into the comparative picture. Later, as the 1995 referendum faded into the past, people started to look for other reasons for the decline in separatism, such as whether economic factors, and in particular globalization, were having an impact (Rocher 2023). In general, the view was that globalization was most important for changing the way people viewed the state and the need for sovereignty. In a globalizing world, Canada and Quebec are both bit players, and sovereignty is less important because countries and provinces generally cannot solve the big questions on their own. As issues like climate change, social injustice, and free trade rise to the surface, the state receives less attention and leads to a declining support for separatism (e.g., Dufour 2007; Salée 2001; Mendelsohn, Parkin, and Pinard 2007; Lammert and Vormann 2015, 47). This line of reasoning was also evident in the hard left, especially among those who wanted to challenge capitalism and who felt that the state itself was part of the problem. Perhaps the high point of this view came in early 2000 with the anti–World Trade Organization protests in Quebec City.

It is also not much of a secret that the business class has preferred a more stable political climate that is resistant to the threats of enormous political change that separatism might bring, and during the neoliberal era of the 1980s and 1990s this class also seemed to be suppressing support for independence. Its preference was sometimes connected to the idea that Quebec had outgrown the need for a strong state to promote economic growth and was now as integrated into the world economy as anywhere else, which in turn challenged a secessionist agenda (Rocher 2002, 87; Courchene 1986). In the years after the referendum perhaps Quebec nationalism moved on from an outlook that relied on the state for improving the economic conditions of French Canadians to an outlook that relied more on the private sector, which is often hostile to independence. Business is generally continentalist in outlook and sceptical of any break with Canada. It prefers to know the "rules of the game," and referendums put those rules in doubt (Rocher 2002, 87). To the extent that the business class had any interests during the mega-constitutional era, and certainly around events like the Meech Lake conference, the focus was to "get a deal" and return to the questions that were "really important," namely economic management (87). Although the PQ was in a position in the 1960s to offer a more statist economic philosophy that put francophones first, this is no longer the case, either in Quebec or for governments in a similar situation anywhere else in the world. The independence program therefore struggles with an important economic lobby that sees little upside in ushering in the program that would put many questions around the business environment.

It also may just be harder for a socially left party like the PQ to defend independence in a world subject to market forces, with or without the support of business. Nadine Changfoot and Blair Cullen argued that the coalescence of the elites around the neoliberal political agenda has made life particularly hard for parties on the left (Changfoot and Cullen 2011). In Quebec, where the PQ is to the left of the Liberals, neoliberalism made its policy agenda – which is focused on unions, social and national solidarity, and state education – harder to implement. The PQ was no longer in a position to raise the taxes needed to advance its agenda because such a raise would have an impact on the province's economic competitiveness. The Quiet Revolution was, again, a victim of its own success; after it had succeeded in economically empowering French Canadians in Quebec, the attitude towards the state was disengaged in favour of one that was more supportive of limited interventions and of the private sector, which was common in many other countries in the 1980s and 1990s (Rocher 2002, 85). Furthermore, directly following the Great Recession of 2008, parties were asked to make cutbacks and not to increase spending. As Quebec suffered from a heavy debt load compared to that of other provinces and a more sluggish economy, the PQ had a difficult time governing during this period. Taking it a step further, Cory Blad of Manhattan College argued that the effect of neoliberalism was to legitimate Quebec *inside* of Canada because the cultural challenges had meant there was more of a role for the state in the economy than elsewhere as it tried to demonstrate Quebec's distinctiveness (Blad 2012). Hence the popular success of the so-called Quebec model around the social economy, a philosophy that has allowed Quebec to manage globalization while still in Canada and illustrating a role for the Quebec state in providing cultural protection and distinctiveness (e.g., Arsenault 2016).

Others have argued that globalization poses a threat to the separatist movement not so much from the top-down as from the bottom-up.

Nowhere has this been truer than for unions and young people in Quebec, two constituencies upon which the separatist movement has historically relied. Both groups have softened in their support for independence over the past decades. Historically, unions and their working-class membership have been a core part of the nationalist cause, especially after the collapse of the Meech Lake Accord and the lead-up to the 1995 referendum (Güntzel 2011, 280). Unionization has normally been much higher in Quebec than in the other provinces and has tended to support the separatist cause – a direct result of the provincial government's economic development policies since the Quiet Revolution and of a union-friendly political climate in the province. Even today, the percentage of the workforce that is in a union remains very high compared to the other provinces, at 40 per cent or so (Haddow 2014, 43). This figure cannot cover the fact that all the major unions are less committed to supporting the cause of independence than they were in the past (Savage 2008). For one, since the Quiet Revolution there has been a fraying of the class connection that the unions had with the francophone working class in their attitude against the anglophone elite. Although this was an important characteristic of the politics of the Quiet Revolution, unions today are more cross-cutting on class issues. As with everywhere else in the world, the past few decades have been hard on organized labour. By the early 1990s, scholars such as Carla Lipsig-Mummé observed the toll that globalization was taking on unions in Quebec as workers were exposed to growing international competition (Lipsig-Mummé 1993, 404; quoted in Graefe 2003, 154–5). The unions have not been able to escape the fact that their members now work in industries that have become more exposed to the forces of globalization, and their jobs would be threatened by independence. The PQ has tried to maintain its connection with organized labour with mixed results. In the mid-1990s, as Peter Graefe has shown, the PQ and unions formed a pact around the idea of "progressive competitiveness" and "competitive nationalism." The philosophy that globalization needed more state intervention rather than less in order for a society to remain on top, solidified a link with organized labour in 1995 (156–60). More recently, the budgetary realities facing Quebec have weakened the connection. At a series of social and economic summits in 1996, the unions were forced to agree with a political agenda that was somewhat against the interests of their membership given the real problems Quebec was facing with the budget (163). With the PQ losing power in 2003 and firmly sidelined for most of the twenty-first century, unions have become more ambiguous in their stance on the national question in Quebec.

The unions were not the only part of the base affected by the forces of globalization. Support among the youth of the province was also affected. Generally speaking, young people are far less interested in separatism than their parents were, a real problem from the perspective of the PQ (G. Hamilton 2004, 2014b; K. Gagnon 2014a; Lemieux 2011). At least part of this seems to be economic, with the concerns of young people being rooted in questions related to economic inequality, environmentalism, and social justice. One work of note is the collection *Lettres à un souverainiste*, a group of essays by young sovereigntists from a variety of backgrounds who offer their thoughts on the movement, and for which economic justice is a priority (Michaud and Clermont-Dion 2014). Many of this ilk want a return to the sense of the possible that reigned during the student strikes of the 2012 *printemps érable*. They are deeply resistant to the strictures of globalization, reject its prescriptions in favour of a focus on the individual, and in particular, disavow its reduction in the state's role in the economy.

A more populist take has come from Simon-Pierre Savard-Tremblay, an economist and Bloc Québécois Member of Parliament who argued, in *L'État succursale: La démission politique du Québec*, that globalization has effectively led to a loss of control by local officials over the province's future. Savard-Tremblay argues that the forces of global capitalism have created a political class in Quebec that is no longer interested in the province's future or its place in the world. Rather, in this view, Quebec is now governed by a self-interested group of elites who have largely moved beyond constitutional politics (Savard-Tremblay 2016). In essence, Savard-Tremblay argues that Quebec has become a branch of global liberalism – being governed by outside experts who have no interest in the local issues of the population. It is a populist line of argument that echoes others about the "deep state" and international financial institutions, common all over the world: that the IMF has too much power, that shadowy bureaucrats govern in the place of elected officials, and so forth. In a similar vein, the historian Roger Payette and political scientist Jean-François Payette trace the cultural exhaustion of Quebec to the fact that it was never a sovereign country in the first place and that neoliberalism has undercut the province's culture (Payette and Payette 2013). The fact that Quebec has never had sovereignty has meant that there is no appetite for it and the population does not understand how to govern. Short of winning outright independence, Quebec should seek maximum control over its affairs and hope that the onerous responsibilities of self-determination will reawaken the political class. The latter sees Canada not just as a colonizer but also as a neoliberal one; the state is founded on capitalist ideas that are culturally suffocating and homogenizing. Quebec must have the autonomy to challenge not only those structures in Canada but also the broader project of Western neoliberalism in the world.

A Question of Framing?

However one looks at the global picture, or indeed the role of underlying economic forces, the simplest explanation of how globalization and economic factors have affected the sovereignty movement in Quebec is that its leaders simply were never able to convince the public that it was in their economic interest to vote yes.

One senses this admission in Parizeau's bitter comment that "money and the ethnic vote" caused his defeat in 1995. The wild swoons of the Canadian dollar throughout the campaign seemed to drive home the point that voting for independence would prove economically risky. There were external actors at work as well that put pressure on secessionist economic claims, including a press conference by President Bill Clinton on the eve of the 1995 vote in which he expressed his clear desire for a "strong and united" Canada (Giffin 2017). While other countries such as Jacques Chirac's France were more equivocal, the importance of the United States as a trading partner meant that Washington held disproportionate weight, and Quebec was left with the impression that it might not be so easy for the province to join a trade pact like NAFTA after the vote.

Ultimately in both referendums the PQ essentially left the economic argument to the federalists by making independence conditional on having an economic partnership with the rest of Canada. The fact that it was always conditional on the PQ's negotiating a deal for sovereignty association naturally led to the suggestion that true independence was not a good choice economically. As a result, the PQ has never been able to mount a truly compelling or popular economic argument along the lines of the claims by former United Kingdom Independence Party leader Nigel Farage that Brexit would bring billions of pounds sterling back to the National Health Service. This presumption that secession would be best done with some kind of a continuing economic relationship with Canada was baked into the referendum questions themselves. The 1980 question began by asking if the voter wanted political sovereignty for Quebec and "at the same time to maintain with Canada an economic association including a common currency"; and "any change in political status resulting from these negotiations will only be implemented with popular approval through another referendum." The 1995 question was similar: "Do you agree that Quebec should become sovereign, after having made a formal offer to Canada for a new economic and political partnership, within the scope of the bill respecting the future of Quebec and of the agreement signed on June 12, 1995?" (Rocher 2002, 90). These questions differ from similar referendum questions asked elsewhere, in which there is no promise of a continued economic partnership. The question that was posed in the failed 2014 Scottish referendum on independence was simply "Should Scotland be an independent country?"; and the Brexit question, which was successful, was just "Should the United Kingdom remain a member of the European Union or leave the European Union?" Furthermore, the fact that the Quebec government could not guarantee that such a relationship would happen after independence put the PQ in a dubious position and open to furious attack on the campaign trail. The attacks could sometimes strain credulity; Paul Martin notably claimed during the 1995 referendum that a yes vote would put over a million jobs at risk, which was a third of the workforce in Quebec, and lead to widespread derision (Feaver 1996, 55). But it did not detract from the fact that economic arguments were always at the heart of the "no" campaign.

Even outside of the campaign trail or during lulls in the national unity debate, selling Canada as good for Quebec economically is at the centre of federal policy on national unity. Significantly, the fact that Quebec has been a major beneficiary of equalization contributes to the impression that Canada is a good economic choice, and federalists have done what they can to promote this image. Robert Bourassa famously called it *federalism rentable*, arguing that Quebec received far more from the country than it brought in (Béland and Lecours 2008, 689). As Béland and Lecours have argued, equalization is a powerful symbol, whether or not Quebec technically wins under it: "[E]qualization payments represent tangible benefits that are difficult for sovereignist politicians to minimize," they note. "In sum, there are reasons to think that equalization has accommodated Quebeckers not only by providing fiscal incentives for the province to remain within Canada, but also by working to keep many Quebeckers feeling they are part of the Canadian political community" (689). This has come at huge political costs in the rest of the country, which often feels cheated by the program and that Quebec wins unfairly. This feeling partially gives rise to the many political cries for equalization's reform, ranging from the 2021 Alberta referendum on the program to the "fair shares federalism" philosophy of former Ontario premier Bob Rae in the early 1990s. Nevertheless, inside the province, equalization serves to undercut the idea that Quebec would do better outside of the country than inside of it.

Furthermore, the sense that the PQ is generally unable to address economic problems as effectively as the Liberals or CAQ has been a theme over the past two decades. The basis of the provincial Liberal strategy (and all federalist parties at both levels of government) is to try to attract voters to a government that cares about the "real" issues, and to forgo the distractions of endless constitutional politics. Federalist parties at the provincial and national levels have always suggested that constitutional politics and good economic stewardship are in tension – the former pulls attention away from the latter. This decision to focus on the economy goes a long way to keep the Constitution in abeyance because the issues are far less inflammatory. And the criticisms faced by the PQ on economic management have come not just from its opposition but also from supposed allies, often former leaders. This could not be truer of Jacques Parizeau, who delighted in criticizing the leadership of the party after he left office, especially around its economic management (G. Hamilton 2014a). Arguably, the most damage came from Lucien Bouchard, who was supposedly the saviour of the PQ when he took over in 1996. Bouchard eventually broke with the PQ and lost interest in politics thereafter. He became a prominent voice for the economic right, asserting that more needed to be done to promote prosperity, which undermined the PQ leadership. He became an important member of the *lucides*, a group of thinkers who wrote a letter arguing that separation was no longer as important as other things, in particular the economy (L. Bouchard et al. 2005). The letter faced backlash from the economic left but was influential in the development of subsequent ideas that emerged in the CAQ. As a final coup de grâce, Bouchard himself broke with the movement, telling its supporters that it was time to move on from independence (G. Hamilton 2012).

The PQ was out of power between 2003 and 2012, when Jean Charest was premier. Throughout that period the Liberal government staked much of its legitimacy on economic management and differentiated itself from the PQ on that basis. The Liberals had always argued that debating the benefits of separation was a distraction that kept Quebec from tackling issues that really mattered – namely, jobs, health care, and the economy. Making the Canada-Quebec relationship "work" for Quebec to bring about economic prosperity without getting bogged down in the sovereignty debate was a common theme. This was clear given the prominence Charest placed on fixing the so-called fiscal imbalance with the federal government, based on a belief that Ottawa had too much power to impose taxes and that this could be "corrected" by Ottawa transferring some of the missing funds to the province. Stephen Harper proved more than happy to support this initiative and came to an agreement with Charest that showed that both leaders were keen to demonstrate that Canada was a good economic choice. That Harper and Charest clearly came down on different sides of the constitutional question is notable: by focusing on the economy, they could keep their differences on the national question in abeyance among both themselves and their respective supporters. Of course, Charest's decision to offer a tax cut as soon as the issue was "resolved" was seen by many as evidence that the fiscal imbalance was a politically created myth all along (Y. Séguin 2002; Canada, Department of Finance 2006; Rabeau 2011). It was, however, illustrative of the Liberals' claim that they could "get things done" and focus on what really mattered. Charest also pushed hard for the Comprehensive Economic and Trade Agreement (CETA) with the EU and otherwise tried to bring some order to the public accounts. Not all of these efforts worked – as the attempt to raise tuition in 2012 showed, which led to weeks of protest. But the Liberals maintained that it was the economy that people were worried about, and this resonated even more strongly in the aftermath of the 2008 financial crisis. Despite the two-year PQ interregnum after 2012 under Pauline Marois, the strategy of focusing on the economy remained at the core of the PLQ's election strategy, captured in their slogan "Together, let's take care of what really matters."

While out of power, the PQ has continued to offer little to suggest that separation has nothing but economic upsides, and this may partially explain the drift to a focus on identity and culture that others have noted (e.g., Rocher 2023, 281). To be fair, as with Brexit or the SNP, there have always been arguments that Quebec will be freer outside of Canada to work with the world in a way that makes more sense for its people. And there is always the argument that considerable savings will be gained by eliminating one order of government (e.g., Gobeil 2012). Following the departure of Bouchard, however, and the turn to the social economy, no PQ leader has tried to make a convincing economic case for full separation from Canada with no partnership. André Boisclair's brief tenure left many with the impression that the PQ was out of touch with the problems of "ordinary" Quebecers, and Boisclair's successor, Pauline Marois, was committed far more to the question of cultural values than to the economic case for independence. Subsequent leaders have taken a similar tack, despite being arguably in a better position to advance a clear economic case for leaving Canada. Pierre-Karl Péladeau (2015–16), the head of Quebecor, arrived in the job seemingly well placed to translate his business experience into an economic case for independence; he could show why leaving Canada was good for the pocketbook. A year later, though, Péladeau was out, leaving behind him the impression that success in business did not mean success in government. Jean-François Lisée (2016–18) succeeded Péladeau but was focused on the question of culture over the economy. (He is also the author of the book *Nous*, which is an extended take on the limits of cultural accommodation; see Lisée 2007.) The most recent leader, Paul St-Pierre Plamondon, took over the leadership in 2020 and has worked to revive both the party and the idea of sovereignty in the contemporary era. He has met with only limited success, and in the elections of 2022 the party won only three seats, although its vote share essentially matched that of all the other opposition parties, at 14.6 per cent (CBC News 2022).

Other prominent leaders of the independence movement have either moved on or given up, and none is associated with offering a powerful, undeniable economic case for leaving Canada. This was true of Mario Dumont and the ADQ after 1995, which ultimately decided that it actually made more sense to stay in a reformed Canada, and drifted towards identity politics. The party eventually became part of the CAQ, under another former PQ politician and sovereigntist, François Legault, whose thinking has evolved to swearing off another referendum in order to focus on economic and social reforms – which, once again, would be best done *inside* Canada. Echoes of this approach are clear in the new BQ as well, as Yves-François Blanchet has successfully transitioned his party to one that sticks up for Quebec's culture and, for the moment at least, for getting the "best deal" in Canadian federalism. While the BQ remains committed to independence, it is clearly more focused on the question of identity and offers relatively little in terms of promoting an economic case for independence for Quebec.

Conclusion

This chapter has argued that the PQ could never effectively deal with the allegation that the success of Quebec's phenomenal development since the Quiet Revolution relied on the stability of the province's integration in Canada, and that breaking from Canada would damage the economy. Federalists have done a better job by suggesting that leaving Canada would be economically harmful. While the economy plays a key role in many people's calculations and support for separation, evidence suggests that it comes second to fundamental questions of citizenship, culture, belonging, and recognition by other Canadians. (It does, of course, seem to weigh more heavily for federalists.) The hypothetical nature of the economic future, the ability to marshal experts on one side or the other, and the willingness to see what one wants, mute the power of economic globalization. This may explain the PQ's early move to embrace the identity question with state secularism, on which it knew it was on much stronger ground.

It is not clear from the research that voting around the national question in Quebec was ever primarily driven by economic concerns, although they were a factor. This reflects the lack of clarity in the literature around nationalism and globalization: each constitutes the other, and nationalists of any variety can use the forces of globalization to justify their own idiosyncratic political projects. But that street runs both ways: federalists can also use economic arguments to their advantage. Critically, the ability of federalists to define good economic management as being something that is in tension with mega-constitutional politics helps them to keep constitutional questions in abeyance. They are free to focus on so-called issues that matter, allowing them to drop the Constitution as a central political issue.

8 Conclusion

The question of how and why the Quebec question stabilized in Canada after 1995 remains an open one in the country's politics. There are very few international examples to which one can point where a strong secessionist movement has fizzled out in quite the same way. One might look to the Basques in Spain, or perhaps the Fuerzas armadas revolucionarias de Colombia (FARC) in Colombia, or even Northern Ireland in the United Kingdom. In each of these cases, however, there was a level of violence that made the respective separatist movements qualitatively different than those that existed in Canada. Understanding what happened is of more than passing interest. The case of Quebec in Canada has international implications for the accommodation of national minorities, generational politics, globalization, and the other explanations that have been explored here. Although none of these represents a full explanation on its own, each appears to have played some role in the stabilization of the Constitution and the end of mega-constitutional politics in Canada.

At the same time, it would be wrong to declare the issue settled. Throughout Canadian history, the linguistic divide is one constant that has defined the country's politics and has often been one of its most volatile. In several instances, it has been *the* cleavage of the country, driving apart political parties, pitting the provinces against each other, and jeopardizing the nation's existence. On two occasions the country has been put to a vote in Quebec, and in 1995 the province very nearly decided to leave. Then, all of the sudden, the debate seemed to stop. While attempting to make some sense of the apparent cessation, this book takes it as a given that the fundamental demographic cleavage of the country still exists and that there is still unfinished business at the heart of the Canadian constitution.

The book has classified the contract-compact problem at the heart of the politics around Quebec's place in Canada as a "constitutional abeyance." Drawing on the work of Foley and Thomas, it has argued that we can view the pause in constitutional politics as an example of a type of behaviour in which two mutually exclusive visions of the Constitution can exist and be held by different actors at the same time, in tension but not direct conflict. The abeyance persists because of the overarching interest of all involved in otherwise maintaining the stability of the constitutional whole. Examples of this type of behaviour have been found in many constitutions going back for centuries, and in the 1980s this theory was first applied to Canada's constitution as a way of explaining how the many deep cracks and differences of opinion could be successfully managed. The mega-constitutional era of the late twentieth century was seen as a breakdown of these abeyances, when the communities who held different visions of the country were no longer content to hold them quietly and to make small concessions to other views in the interests of ensuring the stability of the whole. By the end of the Quiet Revolution there were many people in Quebec who had given up on the Constitution altogether and who formed the core of the Parti Québécois. Others remained federalists and stayed with the Quebec Liberal Party but were not content with the status quo. Real changes were needed if Quebec was to remain a part of the country.

Promises to reform federalism were made, but they were never defined in the referendum of 1980. As the country came to terms with the PQ's win in 1976, Pierre Trudeau (with the blessing of the other premiers) made a commitment to Quebec that a vote for no was not a vote for the status quo; it was a vote to enter into the discussions that would find a solution that would square the circle at the heart of the contract-compact dispute. No one knew what that would look like, but the commitment was enough to keep those who were undecided inside the federalist camp. Tragically, but perhaps inevitably, there were no solutions to be had that would satisfy everyone. The end of the patriation debate collapsed into acrimony, with Quebec being more alienated than ever. That a deal may never have been possible – given that the PQ was in power at the time – is beside the point. The Constitution had failed to fulfil the promise that the rest of the country had made to Quebec in May of 1980.

The subsequent efforts to find a solution were well meaning but likely did more harm than good. The collapse of the Meech Lake Accord was the absolute apogee of the sovereignty movement, with support for separation in a very clear majority. The Charlottetown Accord was undertaken out of panic, with even the federalist Quebec Liberals promising their own referendum if they did not get satisfaction from the rest of the country. Finally, in 1995, the country's long-running national-unity crisis reached its apogee, and Canada only escaped by the skin of its teeth and with accusations of cheating and dirty tricks hurled by each side at the other. It seemed to resolve nothing, except perhaps that the third referendum would come sooner than the second had.

It did not. To the surprise of all, the issue seemed to subside, and the politics of abeyances returned when solutions appeared to be out of reach. While the separatists did not and will not give up, the federalists in Quebec, and Canadians more broadly, appear to have come to the conclusion that this is not a problem to be solved; rather, it is a problem that is best left untouched.

A Multi-causal Phenomenon

This book has focused on federalist elites and how they could take advantage of improved political conditions to rebury the national question as a taboo. Abeyances are ultimately a matter of agenda setting, and they reflect an unwillingness of a political leader to prioritize a contentious issue. But the ability to choose this route is not always possible; it was only possible in Canada because, arguably, other forces worked in the federalists' favour to create an environment in which Quebec's place in Canada could be dropped as an issue. Since 1995, conditions have improved sufficiently to allow federalists to adopt such a strategy. There are many theories to explain why this happened, each with some degree of merit. Causality is a thorny question in the social sciences, and it can be hard to disentangle what is at work in this story. It is safe to say, though, that each of the explanations reviewed in this book has played at least some part in the overall story.

After 1995 the easiest explanation was constitutional fatigue arising out of political exhaustion. To be fair, there was almost no evidence that anyone in the country wanted another referendum or another pass at constitutional politics. Canada was mired in a recession, the dollar was near an all-time low, unemployment was high and widespread, and the national debt was out of control. To the extent there was an appetite for change, it was reflected in the Reform Party of western Canada and the Bloc Québécois, but they soon realized that the base wanted none of it after the experience of 1995. People were far more taken with the Liberal message to focus on bread-and-butter issues. Both the BQ and the Reform Party would struggle in subsequent years as their supporters' priorities focused on competence and more basic issues. This created ideal conditions for federalists to argue that it was time to move on.

As tempting as the fatigue explanation is, it is not a well-developed concept and it becomes less salient the further we go from the 1995 referendum. It is the persistent lack of public interest over the long term that points to more complicated forces at play. The fact that the PQ has had almost no ability to widen its base suggests there was limited interest in resurrecting the topic beyond its hard-core supporters. And as the thirtieth anniversary of the referendum of 1995 approaches, a growing percentage of the population has no memory of the entire mega-constitutional era at all. The fact that this younger group has been disinterested in pushing the sovereignty movement, or does not seek the same sort of recognition in the Constitution, means that the explanation of fatigue cannot be the entire story. It is also peculiar when looked at comparatively. Has any population, beyond that which has suffered actual violence, ever lost interest in the narrative of national liberation as it appears to have done in the province of Quebec?

If not fatigue, what else can we point to as an explanation? By far the most popular suggestion, and one of the oldest reasons for the decline of the sovereignty movement, is generational change. Here, there is a debate about whether federalists gained an advantage because there was a genuine drop in support for independence among young people or because young people stopped viewing independence as a priority. In either case, federalists could take advantage of the shift to change the political conversation. The generation that came of age during the Quiet Revolution had very different views of the Canadian federation, and of the politics of Quebec, than any that had come before it. Quebec was caught up in the 1960s, as so much of the rest of the world was, with the forces of modernity, progress, equality, and liberation. The alleged cultural backwardness of the French Canadian population was squarely confronted, first at home and then within Canada generally, and Quebec was transformed into a modern society. It is not surprising that many people saw in independence a new way to break free from the past and to leave behind the legacy of the conquest that many saw as the root event that had held Quebecers back. The subsequent mega-constitutional era forced a reconsideration of Canada's dualist history and brought new opportunities to Quebecers. Today, younger people appear to see less reason to leave Canada, due in no small part to the different world in which they live. The average age of PQ members is now around that of retirement, and there are many signs that the party has been struggling to connect successfully with young people. As with their counterparts all over the developed world, young people seem to be much more preoccupied with issues like the environment, social equality, education, and the economy than they are with independence. To a degree, this may reflect a sense that Quebec as a state is no different from Canada in the extent to which it is implicated as a cause of the problems they identify as important. For these voters, real change can only come through a rethinking of the wider social structure by voting for parties like Quebec solidaire rather than older parties like the PQ or the Liberals.

Economic globalization has a role to play too. Looked at comparatively, there is some evidence that when a society becomes enmeshed in the global economy, it can effectively put a damper on secessionist tendencies. The evidence here is very weak, though, and it remains an open question in political science. Rising wealth can lead to a revolution of rising expectations that can challenge traditional structures of power. One problem with economic forces as an explanation for vote choice is that it can be used effectively by both sides to promote their agendas to either remain within a country or leave it. Since projections are so speculative, secessionists can point to the globalized trade environment to suggest that independence would unleash previously hidden opportunities for wealth and growth. This line seems to have been very effective among those supporting the Brexit referendum in 2016, for example. At the same time, those who are against independence can equally play on the fears of the population that a vote to leave would bring about dire economic consequences and that there would be no guarantees of a solid relationship with the former state or with the rest of the world. On balance, the evidence suggests that the fear of economic instability has been the stronger argument in Quebec and led people to vote against sovereignty association.

The most significant impact of the economic forces, however, has been the bringing about of a value change for voters in Quebec in the same way that it seems to have occurred in the rest of Canada. In line with a post-materialist trend, the people of Quebec have become less trusting of the elites of both parties, less willing to engage in traditional political activity, and less likely to believe that their leaders reflect their concerns. Post-materialism follows a shift in which people become more concerned with the individual and the individual's rights than with the collective, leaving less room for nationalism. Furthermore, and especially for those on the left, the Quebec and Canadian states are equally to blame for neglecting people's real priorities, including health care, jobs, and the environment. Secession offers nothing on this score. From a tactical point of view, it also means that there is less of a difference between parties like the PQ and the Quebec Liberals, who are both constrained by the global context in the types of reforms they can pursue.

This global aspect has also likely contributed to a related but separate explanation for the decline of separatism – shifts in Quebec's identity politics. Quebec, far more than any other province, has embarked on a process of self-definition that is squarely concerned with who counts as a Quebecer in a globalized world. Born out of a frustration with multiculturalism, while simultaneously seeking to embrace an open and pluralistic society, the shift towards interculturalism, *laïcité*, and the focus on the public square has moved the political debate in Quebec away from constitutional topics, much to the relief of federalist politicians. Adherents of interculturalism tend to see in Canadian-style multiculturalism something that could jeopardize the core cultural values of Quebec – namely, the francophone basis of the society and its secular traditions that are informed by a Catholic cultural background and which cannot (and should not) be forgotten. For some, the allure of interculturalism is the way in which it preserves this cultural basis for public discourse while guaranteeing most of the basic liberal framework that Quebecers have universally accepted since the 1960s. For others, this program amounts to a covert form of Islamophobia or cultural intolerance. Nevertheless, this debate is internal to Quebec and does not directly implicate the question of independence. The shift in focus to this topic may have helped reduce the pressure on the constitutional file over the past fifteen years.

Our final explanation is non-constitutional accommodation. What if Canada has changed just enough to ease some of the tension between Quebec and Canada? For this, at least, one can point to deliberate actions that aimed to reassure Quebecers that change was possible and constitutional problems could be resolved. By offering concessions to the dualist model, it is easier for federalists to suggest that there is no pressing need to reopen the question of Quebec's place in Canada. This strategy has been accompanied by a different, less visible style of intergovernmental relations that has helped reduce political pressure around sensitive topics. Still, from a substantive perspective, Canada has now admitted to a certain level of asymmetry in federalism, devolved labour-market training and much of the immigration field to the provincial level, and, perhaps more importantly, tried to keep constitutional politics off the agenda. Looked at holistically, there is a case to be made that Quebec has effectively achieved what it wanted from Canada, if one uses the demands articulated in the Meech Lake Accord as the baseline. The Canada of the twenty-first century is a far cry from the Canada of the 1950s, and Quebecers could be said to have achieved much of what they felt they needed to participate fully in the country.

Beyond Federalist and Separatist

Even if the constitutional politics of the late twentieth century have subsided, Canada remains a deeply binational, or "plurinational" state (A.-G. Gagnon and Tully 2001; Lecours 2021; A.-G. Gagnon 2023). While the appeal of secessionism has waned to a degree, this does not remove the challenges that come from living in a society that struggles with deep diversity. And no country that is as deeply federal as Canada, or one with such clear linguistic divisions, can expect national unity issues not to crop up from time to time.

What are the challenges ahead? Several possibilities suggest themselves. Inside of Quebec the past half-decade has seen the emergence of new voices and perspectives on Quebec nationalism that could signal fresh lines of fracture in the province and between Quebec and Canada. The CAQ may eventually come to see a political opportunity in pushing the rest of Canada for better constitutional recognition of Quebec, triggering a new crisis and a new debate. The secessionist cause that was sustained by the events of the mega-constitutional era is in a period of dormancy, but it is unlikely to fully disappear; independence retains a strong allure in Quebec. At the same time, the Couillard era (2014–18) suggests that there may be political limits to dwelling on 1982 in Quebec, and there are some political leaders who are more willing to embrace Canada as it is today rather than relitigating the Meech Lake Accord. These newer federalists might argue that, decades after patriation, the time might be right for Quebec to finally put this question in the past and sign on to the 1982 agreement even if it requires demanding fewer changes than Quebec did in the past, if any are needed at all. That might lead to a political landscape combining the emergence of the modern assertive nationalism of Legault, the separatism of Marois, and the liberal federalism of Couillard, all competing to be recognized as the best vision for Quebec's future. There is no reason that a clash between them might not bring the Quebec question back to the heart of provincial politics and, from there, to the top of the Canadian political agenda.

For the rest of the country, the growth of state secularism in Quebec will likely remain the biggest challenge in the national unity file for the immediate future. Its popularity suggests that it will continue to be a dominant idea in Quebec no matter who is in power. Its potential to play a role as a wedge issue has long been recognized by the PQ, which made it central to its campaign in 2014, and there is no suggestion that it will be going away soon. The nationalism of Legault and those like him is not overtly secessionist, but it is in conflict with English Canadian liberal nationalism. The CAQ's identity projects, in particular Bill 21 (restricting religious symbols and declaring Quebec a lay state) and Bill 96 (restricting languages other than French in the public sphere), speak to the accommodative challenges. Legault is not alone in his view that these laws are necessary to protect Quebec's language and culture; all major political parties in Quebec have adopted some vision of state secularism and have made firm commitments to protect the centrality of French in public life. Both of these laws have been enacted pursuant to the notwithstanding clause, because there is little doubt that they would not survive a court challenge under the Charter. But the recent reforms have been unwelcome for Quebec's anglophones and have been criticized elsewhere in the country. Furthermore, Legault has come very close to the line of turning his nationalistic agenda into a wider fight with Canada. His announcement in the spring of 2021 that Quebec could declare itself a "nation" in the Constitution under the Constitution Act 1982's "unilateral" amending formula in section 45 had real potential to set his government on a collision course with the rest of the country. But his insistence that the province could do this on its own, his tacit willingness to let the question be eventually sorted out in the courts, and his refusal to demand a response from the rest of Canada have kept it from becoming a national unity crisis. But it need not stay that way; it would not require much for Legault or another Quebec premier to insist that Quebec's specificity be constitutionally recognized by the rest of the country, just as it did in the past, setting up the conditions for another round of mega-constitutional politics. For right now, leaders outside of Quebec have tried to play down the differences, but that might prove harder in the future.

The fact that the state secularism project has been sustained by the notwithstanding clause is also significant. Traditionally, the notwithstanding clause has focused on disagreements over specific rights, in particular the different interpretations of rights that legislatures and courts arrive at (Hiebert 1996, 2002). This has limited the contexts in which the notwithstanding clause has historically arisen, such as campaign-finance laws in Ontario, the limitation of English-language rights in Quebec, or debates around whether to deny court-ordered compensation to victims of a forced sterilization program. The current use of the clause in Quebec is arguably different in Bill 21 and Bill 96 given that it grounds a different political vision of minority accommodation from that in the Charter (and in light of Bill 96's provisions that give Quebec's language law primacy over even the Quebec Charter of Human Rights and Freedoms). This has generated some of the most fractious language politics inside of Quebec in years. It also has strong potential to spill over into broader Canadian politics. As the debate will be channelled through executive federalism, there is always a chance of a clash.

Whatever happens, Canada will continue to struggle with competing views of itself. The contract-compact dispute represents a deep disagreement over the question of whether Canada is a single political community on the Trudeau model, a binational country, or something else entirely. Many in English Canada are drawn to the idea of a single citizenship, expressed through equal provinces and a sense of individual equality captured by constitutional documents like the Charter. There will always be strong support for this in Canada, in particular outside of Quebec. Other thinkers, especially but not exclusively inside Quebec, continue to see Canada in fundamentally dualist terms. Guy Laforest has written movingly about the importance of this vision in Quebec and to the Quebec people. In his view, Quebec will never be happy in Canada until it has been liberated from Trudeau's constitutional settlement, conditions that he has argued require parallel judiciaries, different charters of rights, recognition of Quebec's separate national status, and even renaming the country "Canada-Quebec" (Laforest 1995, 188). His proposals may seem far-fetched, but he notably still believes that Quebec is better in a union with the rest of Canada than as a fully independent state, even with such drastic changes. Even so, both views must keep up with still other views of Canada, not the least of which has been the enormous growth in interest and political action around Indigenous Peoples. Indigenous Canadians have challenged the contract-compact dispute with yet another polar division: that of Indigenous-settler. What role does reconciliation play in this argument? If a dualist vision of Canada can go so far as Laforest suggests, what is owed to Indigenous Canada? This promises to be one of the more interesting constitutional discussions in the years ahead.

Maintaining the Abeyance: Let Sleeping Dogs Lie

At the end of the day, Quebec's proper relationship to the rest of Canada remains an open question that must be addressed with care whenever it arises. That requires political leaders to tread carefully and with sensitivity whenever disagreements emerge if they hope to maintain national unity. This returns us to a basic character of the abeyance idea: their maintenance relies to a great extent on the goodwill of the people involved – as well as the people who vote for them. There must be an overall desire to preserve an otherwise satisfactory constitutional arrangement even though there are deep disagreements on certain fundamentals.

Preserving abeyances will not work unless there are political leaders who are willing to see the bigger picture, and publics who are willing to follow their lead. That Canada is a country which has historically been able to do this most of the time makes it very fortunate. While there is always an element of calculation in politics, it would be wrong to forget that Canada's federalist leaders share a real patriotism and desire to see Canada succeed, as do the vast majority of the Canadian people. While there are always opportunities to try to whip up animosities between national groups for political advantage, the past twenty-five years have seen a surprising absence of that type of politics. It should also be recognized that even those who would like to see Quebec achieve independence (or perhaps some kind of partnership arrangement) have never questioned both the need to do so through democratic means and the basic ability of the country's democratic processes to channel the wishes of the Quebec and the Canadian people. That is necessary for the country to work at all. The election of a PQ government in Quebec, for example, does not mean the immediate end of Canada, or even that it will function any worse than it would otherwise. There is a collective agreement that so long as Quebec is in Canada, it is everyone's responsibility to make the system work as well as possible on questions like growing the economy, guaranteeing high-quality health care for citizens, or ensuring students have access to world-class education. This requires a level of cooperation between governments, no matter who is in charge, and all parties in Canada and Quebec have shown a real commitment to reach these goals regardless of the constitutional situation. The commitment that political leaders have to their communities, be they federalist or sovereigntist, is genuine.

The fact remains, however, that Canada's constitution never reached a point at which the underlying abeyance was resolved. Despite the fact that the politics of the mega-constitutional era appears to have passed, there remains, lurking at the heart of Canada's constitution, the open wound of 1982 and the fact that Quebec has never assented to the Constitution as it is written. Unless and until that changes, the Quebec-Canada story will never be complete, and there is always the potential for a crisis to erupt once again. If history is any guide, that time is coming; it is only a question of when. Whether Canada will be as lucky as it has been in the past is undetermined. An abeyance relies on the goodwill of constitutional actors to recognize and manage irresolvable differences. To a certain degree, even if the various explanations discussed in this book have all played a role in suppressing the appetite for sovereignty, perhaps the one that will always matter the most for federalists is the willingness to offer some accommodation to those with rival views to their own. But it also means being willing to live with the uncertainty in the Constitution and accepting that there may never come a time when everyone (or even most people) share the same views. If federalists find that they cannot live with the ambiguities in Canada's constitution, it does not bode well for the future of the country.

Looking ahead, the question is obvious: should we try to resolve the contract-compact problem again? Perhaps in the next few years the various calming forces that have been canvassed here will bring the politics about the question to the point where an acceptable resolution can be reached, signified by obtaining Quebec's signature on the Constitution. Perhaps the time will come when enough people will have no memory of 1982 that this becomes possible. Perhaps, in a globalized world, English Canadians will accept that it is possible to be only one half of a two-nation community, and put provincial identities aside. Perhaps Quebecers will say that the idea of French Canada as a country has gone, and Quebec as a province can sign the Constitution as one province of ten. Perhaps a future leader will put forth a novel idea and have the political popularity to rally the provinces, territories, Indigenous Peoples, and Parliament behind a new vision of the country that will put an end to this debate once and for all.

Perhaps. In the view of this author, and probably in the view of anyone with any recollection of the mega-constitutional era, these possibilities seem naïve. At the moment, we seem no closer to solving the basic ambiguity at the heart of the Canadian constitution – and that means learning to live with it. For anyone seeking success in managing Canadian federalism and navigating sensitive linguistic and ethnic tensions, the best advice seems clear: avoid getting into arguments if you can, try to muddle through if you cannot, and, above all, try to let the sleeping dogs lie.

Appendix: Interviewees

No.	Name	Title at Time of Interview	Date of Interview
1.	Mel Cappe	Professor, School of Public Policy and Governance Former Clerk of the Privy Council, Government of Canada	25 February 2014
2.	Jim Eldridge	Special Advisor, Government of Manitoba Former Manitoba Cabinet Secretary	2 April 2014
3.	Robert Schertzer	Former Senior Policy Advisor, Government of Canada Associate Professor, Political Science, University of Toronto, Scarborough	5 March 2014
4.	Don Stevenson	Former Deputy Minister, Intergovernmental Affairs for Ontario	29 June 2014
5.	Matthew Mendelsohn	Head of the Mowat Centre Former Deputy Minister, Intergovernmental Relations, Democratic Renewal Secretariat, and Office of International Relations and Protocol for the Province of Ontario Former Senior Policy Advisor, Privy Council Office, Government of Canada, 1996–8	14 March 2014

(Continued)

No.	Name	Title at Time of Interview	Date of Interview
6.	Josh Hjartarson	Vice President, Policy and Government Relations, Ontario Economic Council Former Policy Advisor, Ministry of Intergovernmental Relations, Government of Ontario	4 April 2014
7.	James McAllister	Former Manager, Federal Provincial Relations, Ministry of Finance, Government of Ontario	13 March 2014
8.	Anonymous	Government of Ontario	21 March 2014
9.	Anonymous	Government of Ontario	4 April 2014
10.	Anonymous	Requested withheld	–
11.	Anonymous	Requested withheld	–
12.	Peter Russell	Professor Emeritus, Faculty of Law and Department of Political Science, University of Toronto	24 March 2014
13.	Ian Clark	Professor, School of Public Policy and Governance, University of Toronto Former Secretary of the Treasury Board, Government of Canada Former Deputy Secretary, Privy Council Office, Government of Canada	24 March 2014
14.	Rodney Haddow	Professor, Political Science, University of Toronto	15 August 2014
15.	Roger Gibbins	Former Chair, Canada West Foundation	17 March 2014
16.	François Rocher	Professor, Political Science, University of Ottawa	3 September 2014
17.	André Juneau	Chair, Institute of Public Administration of Canada Former Federal Deputy Minister, Intergovernmental Relations, Ottawa	14 October 2014

No.	Name	Title at Time of Interview	Date of Interview
18.	Philip Resnick	Professor, Department of Political Science, University of British Columbia	24 October 2014
19.	Carolina de Miguel Moyer	Assistant Professor, Department of Political Science, University of Toronto	24 October 2014
20.	Alfred LeBlanc	Assistant Deputy Minister, Intergovernmental Relations, Government of Canada	27 October 2014
21.	André McArdle	Chair, Canadian Intergovernmental Conference Secretariat	29 October 2014
22.	Alain Nöel	Professor, Université de Montreal	29 October 2014
23.	Roger Tassé	Former Deputy Minister of Justice and Attorney General	4 November 2014
24.	Luc Turgeon	Professor, Political Science, University of Ottawa	6 November 2014
25.	George R.M. Anderson	Former Federal Deputy Minister of Intergovernmental Relations Chairman, Forum of Federation	11 November 2014
26.	Ian Brodie	Former Chief of Staff to Prime Minister Stephen Harper	12 November 2014
27.	Jean Charest	Former Premier of Quebec	17 November 2014
28.	Anonymous	Professor	21 November 2014
29.	Michael Burgess	Professor, University of Kent	21 November 2014
30.	Jacqueline Krikorian	Professor, York University	24 November 2014
31.	Gordon DiGiacomo	PhD, Instructor, Carleton University	27 November 2014

(Continued)

No.	Name	Title at Time of Interview	Date of Interview
32.	Stéphane Dion	Former Liberal Leader of Canada and Minister of Intergovernmental Affairs	27 November 2014
33.	Ron Watts	Professor Emeritus of Political Science, Queen's University Former Director, Institute of Intergovernmental Relations (IIGR)	29 November 2014
34.	Derek Burney	Chief of Staff to Brian Mulroney Head of Conservative Party Transition Team, 2006	22 December 2014
35.	Lowell Murray	Former Chief of Staff to Robert Stanfield Progressive Conservative Senator Minister of State for Federal-Provincial Relations under Brian Mulroney	12 January 2015
36.	Hugh Segal	Former Senator Chief of Staff to Brian Mulroney and Ontario Premier Bill Davis	14 January 2015
37.	Julien Gagnon	Former President, Youth Wing of the Quebec Liberal Party	6 February 2015
38.	Eddie Goldenberg	Former Chief of Staff to Jean Chrétien	6 February 2015

Notes

1. Introduction

1 Technically, the only people who ever signed the Constitution were Queen Elizabeth II, Prime Minister Pierre Trudeau, Minister of Justice Jean Chrétien, and Registrar General André Ouellette. Regardless, because Quebec never gave its political consent to patriating the Constitution, it is customary to say that the province never "signed" the agreement.

2 As these were not legally binding, all three "referendums" were, strictly speaking, plebiscites. Regardless, it is customary to refer to them as referendums.

3 The term *Quebecer* in this book is generally used to refer to the francophone Québécois national majority in the province. However, it would be wrong to ignore the fact that no nation or province is homogenous, and Quebec is no exception. It is enriched by Indigenous, anglophone, and other communities who also count as Quebecers. Similarly, the book often refers to *Canada* and *Canadians* generally with regard to the majority anglophone community outside of Quebec, even though Quebecers are of course also Canadians and there are many francophone, Indigenous, and other minority communities that live in Canada outside Quebec.

4 The Hérouxville debacle refers to the well-publicized "code of conduct" that the municipality of Hérouxville introduced in 2007, laying out immigrant's religious practices that were banned in the city. The code was widely criticized for playing on ethnic stereotypes and prohibiting conduct that was in no sense prevalent in Canada's ethnic communities. In particular, its prohibition against the stoning of women and female genital circumcision received international media attention and derision and was seen in Quebec as an example of the province's failure to adequately accommodate religious minorities.

5 There are those in the separatist camp who would disagree (Lisée 2001; Parizeau 2014; see Güntzel 2011 for the ongoing connections to organized labour, despite how frayed the links can be; see R. Séguin 2013 for reporting on the "de-canadianization" of Quebec often alleged by the PQ).

2. An Abeyance Restored: The "Quebec Question" as the New Taboo

1 It is important to distinguish the line of literature on constitutional abeyances being discussed here from social movement abeyance theory, which is associated mostly with the sociological literature. It too is concerned with the rise and fall of social movements, but that theory is more concentrated on how social movements tend to survive when they appear to have subsided, and what links one movement upswing to the next. Developed initially by Verta Taylor (1989), currently of the University of California, Santa Barbara, it has been particularly associated with the periodic rise and fall of the women's rights movement in the United States. Nevertheless, it has been applied to a variety of other contexts as well (Holland and Cable 2002; McAdam 1982 provides some overviews of the literature and some examples). This literature on social movement abeyance theory would be most helpful for understanding how the sovereignty movement is surviving during its current dry spell, but it is not the theoretical lens being applied here to study the elite behaviour contributing to its current difficulties, which is rooted more in law and political science than in sociology.

2 These ambiguities have been adopted and repeated elsewhere as recognized critical gaps in the Canadian constitution; see, for example, Gibbins (1999), 265–6.

3 Specifically, An Act to give effect to the requirement for clarity as set out in the opinion of the Supreme Court of Canada in the Quebec Secession Reference, S.C. 2000, c. 26, was the legislation passed by the federal government in the wake of the *Secession Reference* to specify how it would assess whether or not a yes vote in a Quebec secession referendum qualified as a "clear result to a clear question."

3. Constitutional Fatigue

1 Findings derive from a search for the term through Factiva (English sources) and on BanQ (French sources), after 1992 it declined steadily in both languages.

2 *Constitutional fatigue* should not be confused with a separate idea *cultural fatigue*, which is a widely studied and discussed term in Quebec and is reviewed elsewhere in this book. That concept, which goes back decades, is

connected to an alleged malaise affecting Quebec society and has its roots in the scholarship of the Quiet Revolution.

3 The following discussion is inspired and loosely structured around Kingdon's (1984) Multiple Streams Framework (MSF) on agenda setting, which identifies three "streams" (problems, policies, and politics) for the ways in which issues rise to the top of the political agenda. While the discussion is not a true application of MSF, I acknowledge the debt.

4. Non-constitutional Accommodation

1 The text of the Accord is not hard to find. See Monahan (1991) for an extensive set of materials, and also Gibbins (1990), appendix E, for a more basic copy of the Accord.

2 Cohen notes that, for the Liberals, the split was along linguistic lines, and at one point as much as a third of the federal caucus had signalled that it could not support the deal (1990, 146–7).

3 Earlier iterations have been discussed previously (see for example Simeon 2006; Institute of Public Administration of Canada 1979; D.V. Smiley 1979, 1980; Dupré 1988; Stevenson 1979).

4 This would not come until after the collapse of the Meech Lake Accord, namely in the *Reference re Canada Assistance Plan*, [1991] 2 S.C.R. 525. In that case the provinces challenged Ottawa's decision to refuse to stick to the original funding agreement and back out of the equal shared-cost-funding arrangements for the Canada Assistance Plan. They lost, despite arguing on a number of grounds, including the fundamental value of federalism which would later be recognized in the *Secession Reference*.

5 I am deeply reliant on Paquet's (2019) work for this excellent insight.

5. Quebec's Changing Identity Politics

1 This could be seen in the recent controversy surrounding Amira Elghawaby, the federal government's special representative to combat Islamophobia, in January 2023. Comments she made in a co-written 2019 editorial in the *Ottawa Citizen* criticizing Quebec's Bill 21 and the majority of Quebecers who support it as Islamophobic led to calls for her resignation by members of the Quebec government (Serebrin 2023).

2 The usefulness of this distinction is highly contested. Regardless, it has purchase in this context because the debate surrounding minorities in the state secularism model often focuses on the challenges it creates for those who are normally "outsiders" in Quebec and who claim that the project is fundamentally ethnonationalist in outlook.

3 This image of the Quiet Revolution remains the predominant one, but there is a lively debate about the extent to which it truly changed Quebec society. For more sceptical interpretations about the magnitude of the change brought about by the Quiet Revolution, or of alleged limitations of the period that preceded it, see Couture (1991), Rouillard (1997), Létourneau (2004 [2001]), 108–13, and Cuccioletta and Lublin (2011).

4 There have been efforts, however; see the discussion of the new nationalism as espoused by the BQ in 2019.

6. Generational Change

1 A clear working-class group was also identified, in particular one whose members had union affiliations. See R. Hamilton and Pinard (1976), 19–20.

2 The reality was so perfectly captured in the famous cartoon in the *Montreal Gazette* on the morning afterwards, in which a smoking Lévesque calmly tells the readers "OK, everybody take a valium."

7. Economic Globalization

1 This refers to a different Montreal School than the one discussed in the chapter on identity.

References

Ajzenstat, Janet. 1988. *The Political Thought of Lord Durham*. Montreal: McGill-Queen's University Press.

Amato, Sean. 2021. "'Stirring Up Sentiment': Trudeau Pours Cold Water on Kenney's Equalization Vote." CTV News Edmonton, 21 October 2021, sec. Edmonton. https://edmonton.ctvnews.ca.

Aquin, Hubert. 1962. "La fatigue culturelle du Canada français." *Liberté* 4, no. 23: 299–325.

Argyle, Ray. 2004. *Turning Points: The Campaigns That Changed Canada; 2004 and Before*. Toronto: White Knight Publications.

Arsenault, Gabriel. 2016. "The Social Investment State and the Social Economy: The Politics of Quebec's Social Economy Turn, 1996–2015." PhD diss., University of Toronto. http://search.proquest.com/docview/1819527212/abstract/236AE1305986416CPQ/1.

– 2019. *L'économie sociale au Québec: Une perspective politique*. Quebec City: Presses de l'Université du Québec.

Art, Walter Stew. 1970. "The New Quebec – Federalism and Sovereignty; The Conflict Comes of Age with the Bourassa Years." *Maclean's*. June 1970. https://archive.macleans.ca/article/1970/6/1/the-new-quebec.

Assemblée Nationale du Québec. 1990. *Journal des débats*. August 1990.

Augenblick, Ned, and Scott Nicholson. 2016. "Ballot Position, Choice Fatigue, and Voter Behaviour." *Review of Economic Studies* 83, no. 2 (295: 460–80. https://doi.org/10.1093/restud/rdv047.

Aunger, Edmund A. 2001. "Justifying the End of Official Bilingualism: Canada's North-West Assembly and the Dual-Language Question, 1889–1892." *Canadian Journal of Political Science / Revue Canadienne de Science Politique* 34, no. 3: 451–86. https://doi.org/10.1017/S0008423901777979.

Authier, Philip. 2019. "PQ Council: Youth Wing Rocks the Boat But Meet Opposition from Veterans." *Montreal Gazette*, 3 March 2019.

Bakvis, Herman, and Grace Skogstad, eds. 2012. *Canadian Federalism: Performance, Effectiveness, and Legitimacy*. Don Mills, ON: OUP Canada.

Banerjee, Sidhartha. 2013. "Quebec's Human Rights Commission Says Values Charter Won't Pass Legal Challenges." CTV News, 17 January 2013.

Banting, Keith, and Richard Simeon, eds. 1983. *And No One Cheered: Federalism, Democracy and the Constitution Act*. Toronto: Methuen.

Barnes, Samuel H., M. Kent Jennings, Ronald Inglehart, and Barbara Farah. 1988. "Party Identification and Party Closeness in Comparative Perspective." *Political Behavior* 10, no. 3: 215–31. https://doi.org/10.1007/BF00990552.

Basta, Karlo. 2021. *The Symbolic State: Minority Recognition, Majority Backlash, and Secession in Multinational Countries*. Democracy, Diversity, and Citizen Engagement Series 7. Montreal: McGill-Queen's University Press.

Bateman, Thomas Michael Joseph. 2000. "Charter Rights Application Doctrine and the Clash of Constitutionalisms in Canada." PhD diss., University of Alberta. http://search.proquest.com.myaccess.library.utoronto.ca/pqdtft/docview/304647299/abstract/7F7B607864864ABBPQ/4?accountid=14771.

Baumgartner, Frank R., and Bryan D. Jones. 2009. *Agendas and Instability in American Politics*. London: University of Chicago Press.

Bayefsky, Anne F., ed. 1989. *Canada's Constitution Act 1982 & Amendments: A Documentary History*. Toronto: McGraw-Hill Ryerson.

Beauchemin, Jacques. 2015. *La souveraineté en héritage*. Montreal: Boréal.

Beaulieu, Isabelle. 2003. "Le premier portrait des enfants de la Loi 101." In *L'annuaire du Québec 2004*, edited by Michel Venne, 260–5. Les Editions Fides.

Beck, Paul Allen, and M. Kent Jennings. 1982. "Pathways to Participation." *American Political Science Review* 76, no. 1: 94–108. https://doi.org/10.2307/1960445.

Behiels, Michael, ed. 1985. *Prelude to Quebec's Quiet Revolution: Liberalism Versus Neo-Nationalism, 1945–1960*. Toronto: Gibson Publishing.

– 1992. "Review of *A Meech Lake Post-Mortem: Is Quebec Sovereignty Inevitable?*, by Pierre Fournier, trans. Sheila Fischman; *Toward a Canada-Quebec Union*, by Philip Resnick." *Canadian Journal of Political Science / Revue Canadienne de Science Politique* 25, no. 1: 156–8. https://doi.org/10.1017/S0008423900001979.

– 1998. "'Normalizing' the Writing of Quebec History." *Left History* 6, no. 1: 91–9.

– 2007. "Mulroney and Nationalist Quebec." In *Transforming the Nation: Canada and Brian Mulroney*, edited by Raymond Benjamin Blake, 250–93. Montreal: McGill-Queen's University Press.

Béland, Daniel. 2012. "Les partis générationnels au Québec: Passé, présent, avenir, par Vincent Lemieux." *Canadian Journal of Political Science / Revue Canadienne de Science Politique* 45, no. 2: 475–7.

Béland, Daniel, and André Lecours. 2008. *Nationalism and Social Policy: The Politics of Territorial Solidarity*. Oxford: Oxford University Press. https://doi.org/10.1093/acprof:oso/9780199546848.003.0002.

Bélanger, Éric, and Andrea Perrella. 2008. "Facteurs d'appui à la souveraineté du Québec chez les jeunes: Une comparaison entre francophones, anglophones et allophones." *Politique et Sociétés* 27, no. 3: 13–40. https://doi.org/10.7202/029846ar.

Binstock, Robert H., and Linda K. George, eds. 2001. "Aging and Politics." In *Handbook of Aging and the Social Sciences*, 5th ed., 333–51. Handbooks of Aging. San Diego, CA: Academic Press.

Birkland, Thomas A. 1998. "Focusing Events, Mobilization, and Agenda Setting." *Journal of Public Policy* 18, no. 1: 53–74. https://doi.org/10.1017/S0143814X98000038.

Black, Andrew. 2013. "Bill to Lower Referendum Voting Age." *BBC News*, 12 March 2013, sec. Scotland politics.

Blad, Cory. 2012. *Neoliberalism and National Culture: State-Building and Legitimacy in Canada and Quebec*. Studies in Critical Social Sciences, v. 38. Leiden and Boston: Brill.

Blais, André, Pierre Martin, and Richard Nadeau. 1995. "Attentes économiques et linguistiques et appui à la souveraineté du Québec: Une analyse prospective et comparative." *Canadian Journal of Political Science / Revue Canadienne de Science Politique* 28, no. 4: 637–57. https://doi.org/10.1017/S0008423900019338.

Blais, André, and Richard Nadeau. 1984. "L'appui au Parti Québécois: Évolution de la clientèle de 1970 à 1981." In *Comportement Électoral Au Québec*, edited by Jean Crête, 279–318. Chicoutimi, QC: Gaétan Morin.

Bock-Côté, Mathieu. 2007. *La dénationalisation tranquille: Mémoire, identité et multiculturalisme dans le Québec postréférendaire*. Montreal: Boréal.

– 2012. *Fin de Cycle*. Montreal: Boréal.

Bock-Côté, Mathieu, Guillaume Marois, Guillaume Rousseau, Charles-Philippe Courtois, and Patrick Sabourin. 2014. *Indépendance: Les conditions du renouveau*. Montreal: VLB.

Boily, Frederic. 2018. *La Coalition Avenir Québec: Une idéologie à la recherche du pouvoir*. Quebec, QC: Presses de l'Universite Laval.

Bouchard, Gérard, and Charles Taylor. 2008. *Building the Future: A Time for Reconciliation*. Quebec, QC: Commission de consultation sur les pratiques d'accomodement reliées aux différences culturelles.

Bouchard, Lucien, Joseph Facal, Pierre Fortin, Robert Lacroix, Sylvie Lalande, Claude Montmarquette, André Pratte, et al. 2005. *Pour un Québec lucide*. http://classiques.uqac.ca/contemporains/finances_publiques_qc/manifeste_qc_lucide.pdf.

Bourassa, Robert. 1992. Conférences de presse (1989–1994): | La Société du patrimoine politique du Québec. https://www.archivespolitiquesduquebec.com/discours/p-m-du-quebec/robert-bourassa/conferences-de-presse-1989-1994/.

Bourgault-Côté, Guillaume. 2013. "Sondage Léger Marketing – Constitution: Vive le statu quo!" *Le Devoir*, 30 March 2013.

Broadbent, Ed. 1996. "Post-Referendum Canada." In *Québec-Canada: What Is the Path Ahead? = Nouveaux Sentiers Vers l'avenir*, 271–80. Ottawa: University of Ottawa Press.

Broschek, Jörg. 2014. "Pathways of Federal Reform: Australia, Canada, Germany, and Switzerland." *Publius* 45, no. 1: 51–76. https://doi.org /10.1093/publius/pju030.

Bryden, Joan. 2015. "NDP Offers Quebec Alone Right to Opt Out of Federally-Funded Programs." CBC / Canadian Press, 2 October 2015.

Butler, David, and Donald Stokes. 1983. *Political Change in Britain: The Evolution of Electoral Choice*. London: Macmillan.

Cairns, Alan C. 1971. "The Judicial Committee and Its Critics." *Canadian Journal of Political Science / Revue Canadienne de Science Politique* 4, no. 3: 301–45. https://doi.org/10.1017/S0008423900026809.

– 1977. "The Governments and Societies of Canadian Federalism." *Canadian Journal of Political Science / Revue Canadienne de Science Politique* 10, no. 4: 695–725. https://doi.org/10.1017/S0008423900050861.

– 1988. "Citizens (Outsiders) and Governments (Insiders) in Constitution-Making: The Case of Meech Lake." *Canadian Public Policy / Analyse de Politiques* 14 (September): S121–45. https://doi.org/10.2307/3551222.

Caldwell, Gary. 2003. "Is the ADQ Quebec's Next Generational Party?" *Inroads*, Montreal, Summer 2003.

"Calgary Declaration." 1997. https://www.solon.org/Constitutions/Canada /English/Proposals/calgary-framework.html.

Cameron, David. 1974. *Nationalism, Self-Determination and the Quebec Question*. Toronto: Macmillan.

– 1990. "Lord Durham Then and Now." *Journal of Canadian Studies / Revue d'Études Canadiennes* 25, no. 1: 5–23. https://doi.org/10.3138/jcs.25.1.5.

– 1996. "Does Ottawa Know It Is Part of the Problem?" In *Québec-Canada: What Is the Path Ahead? = Nouveaux sentiers vers l'avenir*, edited by John E. Trent, Robert Young, and Guy Lachapelle, 293–8. Ottawa: University of Ottawa Press.

– 2009. "Ultimately, the System Worked." In *Parliamentary Democracy in Crisis*, edited by Peter H. Russell and Lorne Sossin, 189–94. Toronto: University of Toronto Press.

– 2015. "Canada's Constitutional Legitimacy Deficit: Learning to Live with It." In *Thinking Outside the Box: Innovation in Policy Ideas*, edited by Keith G. Banting, Richard P. Chaykowski, and Steven F. Lehrer, 277–94. Montreal: McGill-Queen's Press.

Cameron, David, and Jacqueline D. Krikorian. 2008. "Recognizing Quebec in the Constitution of Canada: Using the Bilateral Constitutional Amendment

Process." *University of Toronto Law Journal* 58, no. 4: 389–420. https://doi.org/10.1353/tlj.0.0010.

Cameron, David, and Richard Simeon. 2002. "Intergovernmental Relations in Canada: The Emergence of Collaborative Federalism." *Publius* 32, no. 2: 49–72. https://doi.org/10.1093/oxfordjournals.pubjof.a004947.

Canada. 1967. *Royal Commission on Bilingualism and Biculturalism.* https://epe.lac-bac.gc.ca/100/200/301/pco-bcp/commissions-ef/dunton1967-1970-eng/dunton1967-70-eng.html.

– 1978. *A Time for Action: Toward the Renewal of the Canadian Federation.* Ottawa: Government of Canada.

– 1982. *Constitution Act, 1982.* http://laws-lois.justice.gc.ca/eng/Const/page-1.html.

– 2012. *Constitution Act, 1867.* http://laws-lois.justice.gc.ca/eng/Const/page-1.html.

Canada. Department of Finance. 2006. *Restoring Fiscal Balance in Canada: Focusing on Priorities.* Ottawa, ON.

Canadian Press. 2012. "Citizen Referendums Were PQ's 'Time Bomb.'" CBC, 24 August 2012.

– 2014. "Couillard Reiterates Wish for Quebec to Sign Constitution at Event with Harper." *Globe and Mail*, 7 September 2014.

– 2019. "PQ May Have No Future, Youth Wing Members Say in Open Letter." CTV News, 3 March 2019.

Cantin, Serge. 2005. "L'urgence de réfléchir." In *Redonner sens à l'indépendance*, edited by Jocelyne. Couture, 55–64. Montreal: VLB.

CBC News. 2008. "Let's Move on, Says Quebec Accommodation Commission." 5 May 2008.

– 2019. "Yves-François Blanchet Becomes Bloc Québécois Leader." 17 January 2019.

– 2022. "Quebec Votes 2022." https://newsinteractives.cbc.ca/elections/quebec/2022/results/.

CBC News / Canadian Press. 2014. "Lucien Bouchard Says 'Wounds' Remain with Brian Mulroney." CBC News, 21 August 2014.

Changfoot, Nadine, and Blair Cullen. 2011. "Why Is Quebec Separatism off the Agenda? Reducing National Unity Crisis in the Neoliberal Era." *Canadian Journal of Political Science / Revue Canadienne de Science Politique* 44, no. 4: 769–87. https://doi.org/10.1017/S0008423911000746.

Chouinard, Tommy. 2014. "Philippe Couillard Releases Liberals' Secular Charter Position." *La Presse*, 31 March 2014.

Cloutier, Édouard, Jean H. Guay, and Daniel Latouche. 1992. *Le virage: L'évolution de l'opinion publique au Québec depuis 1960, Ou comment le Québec est devenu Souverainiste.* Dossiers Documents. Montreal: Québec/Amérique.

Cohen, Andrew. 1990. *A Deal Undone: The Making and Breaking of the Meech Lake Accord*. Vancouver, BC: Douglas & McIntyre.

Coleman, William D. 1984. *The Independence Movement in Quebec, 1945–1980*. Toronto: University of Toronto Press.

Contenta, Sandro. 1990. "'If They Don't Want Us … It's Goodbye.'" *Toronto Star*, 7 June 1990, fin. edition, sec. Insight.

Corbett, Anne. 2003. "Ideas, Institutions and Policy Entrepreneurs: Towards a New History of Higher Education in the European Community." *European Journal of Education* 38, no. 3: 315–30. https://doi.org/10.1111/1467 -3435.00150.

Council of the Federation. 2004. *Communique – Premiers' Action Plan for Better Health Care: Resolving Issues in the Spirit of True Federalism*. https:// canadaspremiers.ca/wp-content/uploads/2017/09/healtheng.pdf.

Courchene, Thomas. 1986. "Market Nationalism: Quebec's Disquieting Revolution." Policy Options (Fall 1986): 7–12.

– 2004a. "The Changing Nature of Quebec-Canada Relations: From the 1980 Referendum to the Summit of the Canadas." Report 2. Montreal: Institute for Research on Public Policy. https://irpp.org/wp-content/uploads/assets /research/canadian-federalism/new-research-article/wp2004-08.pdf.

– 2004b. "Pan-Canadian Provincialism: The New Federalism and the Old Constitution." *Policy Options*, 1 November 2004.

Couture, Claude. 1991. *Le mythe de la modernisation du Québec: Des années 1930 à la révolution tranquille*. Montreal: Méridien.

Crittenden, John. 1962. "Aging and Party Affiliation." *Public Opinion Quarterly* 26, no. 4: 648–57. https://doi.org/10.1086/267134.

CTV News. 2014a. "New Online Poll Claims 66% Support in Quebec for Values Charter." CTV News, 10 September 2014.

– 2014b. "Quebec Liberals Working on 'Moderate' Charter of Values." CTV News, 17 September 2014.

Cuccioletta, Donald, and Martin Lubin. 2011. "Quebec's Quiet Revolution: A Noisy Evolution." In *Contemporary Quebec: Selected Readings and Commentaries*, edited by Michael Behiels and Matthew Hayday, 182–96. Montreal and Kingston: McGill-Queen's University Press.

Daniel, Béland. 2012. "Les partis générationnels au Québec: Passé, présent, avenir, par Vincent Lemieux." *Canadian Journal of Political Science / Revue Canadienne de Science Politique* 45, no. 2: 475–77.

Danigelis, Nicholas L., and Stephen J. Cutler. 1991. "Cohort Trends in Attitudes about Law and Order: Who's Leading the Conservative Wave?" *Public Opinion Quarterly* 55, no. 1: 24–49. https://doi.org/10.1086/269240.

Dennison, James. 2019. "A Review of Public Issue Salience: Concepts, Determinants and Effects on Voting." *Political Studies Review* 17, no. 4: 436–46. https://doi.org/10.1177/1478929918819264.

DiGiacomo, Gordon. 2010. "The Impact of Constitutional Abeyance on the Assertiveness of the Federal Government." PhD diss., Carleton University, Ottawa. http://search.proquest.com.myaccess.library.utoronto.ca/pqdtft /docview/816190974/abstract?accountid=14771.

Dion, Léon. 1975. *Nationalismes et politique Au Québec*. Sciences de l'homme et Humanisme 7. Montreal: Hurtubise HMH.

Dion, Stéphane. 1996. "Why Is Secession Difficult in Well-Established Democracies? Lessons from Quebec." *British Journal of Political Science* 26, no. 2: 269–83. https://doi.org/10.1017/S0007123400000466.

Doyle, Kevin. 1990. "Constitutional Fatigue." *Maclean's*, 2 April 1990.

Dubuc, Alain. 2008. *À mes amis souverainistes*. Montreal: Éditions Voix parallèles.

Dufour, Pascale. 2007. "Globalization as a New Political Space: The End of the Quebec-Quebec Debate?" In *Quebec and Canada in the New Century: New Dynamics, New Opportunities*, edited by Michael Murphy, 130–52. Canada: The State of the Federation 2005. Kingston, ON: McGill-Queen's University Press.

– 2009. "From Protest to Partisan Politics: When and How Collective Actors Cross the Line? Sociological Perspective on Québec Solidaire." *Canadian Journal of Sociology* 34, no. 1: 55–82. https://doi.org/10.29173/cjs591.

Dufresne, Yannick, Charles Tessier, and Eric Montigny. 2019. "Generational and Life-Cycle Effects on Support for Quebec Independence." *French Politics* 17, no. 1: 50–63. https://doi.org/10.1057/s41253-019-00083-9.

Dunn, Christopher. 2008. "Canada's 'Open Federalism': Past, Present, and Future." In *The Federal Nation: Perspectives on American Federalism*, edited by Iwan W. Morgan and Philip J. Davies, 39–60. Studies of the Americas. New York: Palgrave Macmillan. https://doi.org/10.1057/9780230617254_4.

Dupras, Daniel. 1992. *The Constitution of Canada: A Brief History of Amending Procedure Discussions*. Ottawa: Law and Government Division, Department of Justice, Government of Canada.

Dupré, J. Stefan. 1988. "Reflections on the Workability of Executive Federalism." In *Perspectives on Canadian Federalism*, edited by R.D. Olling and M.W. Westmacott, 233–56. Scarborough, ON: Prentice-Hall.

Elections Canada. 2019. "Election Night Results – National." Elections Canada, 21 October 2019. https://enr.elections.ca/National.aspx?lang=e.

– 2021. "Election Results – National Validated Results." 2021. https:// www.elections.ca/enr/help/national_e.htm.

Erk, Jan. 2008. *Explaining Federalism*. Routledge Series in Federalism Studies 17. London and New York: Routledge.

Erk, Jan, and Alain-G. Gagnon. 2000. "Constitutional Ambiguity and Federal Trust: Codification of Federalism in Canada, Spain and Belgium." *Regional & Federal Studies* 10, no. 1: 92–111. https://doi.org/10.1080/13597560008421110.

Esping-Andersen, Gosta. 1989. *The Three Worlds of Welfare Capitalism*. Oxford: Polity Press.

Ethan, Cox. 2018. "Is This the End of the Parti Québécois?" Ricochet, 30 September 2018. https://ricochet.media/en/2362.

Feaver, George. 1996. "Canadian Political Miscalculation? Quebec's Referendum 95." *Government and Opposition* 31, no. 1: 45–61. https://doi.org/10.1111/j.1477-7053.1996.tb00148.x.

Figley, Charles R., ed. 1995. "Compassion Fatigue as a Secondary Traumatic Stress Disorder: An Overview." In *Compassion Fatigue: Coping with Secondary Traumatic Stress Disorder in Those Who Treat the Traumatized*. Brunner/Mazel Psychosocial Stress Series, no. 23. New York: Brunner/Mazel.

Fine, Sean. 2013. "Is Quebec's Secular Charter Constitutional? Nine Legal Experts Weigh In." *Globe and Mail*, 14 September 2013.

Foley, Michael. 2013. *The Silence of Constitutions (Routledge Revivals): Gaps, "Abeyances" and Political Temperament in the Maintenance of Government*. Routledge.

Font, Nuria, and Joan Subirats. 2010. "Water Management in Spain: The Role of Policy Entrepreneurs in Shaping Change." *Ecology and Society* 15, no. 2: 25. https://doi.org/10.5751/ES-03344-150225.

Fournier, Pierre. 1991. *A Meech Lake Post-Mortem: Is Quebec Sovereignty Inevitable?* Montreal: McGill-Queen's University Press.

Fox, Graham. 2007. "Harper's 'Open Federalism': From the Fiscal Imbalance to 'Effective Collaborative Management' of the Federation." *Policy Options*, 1 March 2007.

Franks, C.E.S. 2009. "To Prorogue or Not to Prorogue: Did the Governor General Make the Right Decision?" In *Parliamentary Democracy in Crisis*, edited by Peter H. Russell and Lorne Sossin, 33–46. Toronto: University of Toronto Press.

Gagnon, Alain-G. 1990. *Quebec: Beyond the Quiet Revolution*. Scarborough, ON: Nelson Canada.

– 2010. *The Case for Multinational Federalism*. Routledge Series in Federal Studies 18. London and New York: Routledge.

– 2014. *Minority Nations in the Age of Uncertainty: New Paths to National Emancipation and Empowerment*. Toronto: University of Toronto Press.

– 2021. *Le choc des légitimités*. Montreal: Presses de l'Université Laval.

– 2023. *The Legitimacy Clash: Challenges to Democracy in Multinational States – Chaire de recherche du Canada en études québécoises et canadiennes CRÉQC – UQAM*. Toronto: University of Toronto Press.

Gagnon, Alain-G., and James Tully. 2001. *Multinational Democracies*. Cambridge University Press.

Gagnon, Bernard. 2015. "Charles Taylor: Écrits sur la nation et le nationalisme au Québec." *Bulletin d'histoire politique* 23, no. 3: 105–30. https://doi.org/10.7202/1030760ar.

Gagnon, Katia. 2014a. "Les jeunes et la souveraineté: La generation 'non.'" *La Presse*, 2 June 2014.

– 2014b. "Portrait de génération: Quatre archétypes." *La Presse*, June 2014. http://www.lapresse.ca.

Garmann, Sebastian. 2017. "Election Frequency, Choice Fatigue, and Voter Turnout." *European Journal of Political Economy* 47 (March): 19–35. https://doi.org/10.1016/j.ejpoleco.2016.12.003.

Gibbins, Roger. 1990. *Conflict and Unity: An Introduction to Canadian Political Life*. Scarborough, ON: Nelson Canada.

– 1999. "Constitutional Politics." In *Canadian Politics*, edited by James Bickerton and Alain-G. Gagnon, 3rd ed., 263–77. Peterborough, ON: Broadview Press.

Gibson, James L., Gregory A. Caldeira, and Vanessa A. Baird. 1998. "On the Legitimacy of National High Courts." *American Political Science Review* 92, no. 2: 343–58. https://doi.org/10.2307/2585668.

Giffin, Gordon. 2017. "Opinion: Bill Clinton, Jean Chrétien and the Canada-US Relationship." *Montreal Gazette*, 4 October 2017.

Glenn, Norval D. 1974. "Aging and Conservatism." *Annals of the American Academy of Political and Social Science* 415, no. 1: 176–86. https://doi.org/10.1177/000271627441500113.

Gobeil, Stéphane. 2012. *Un gouvernement de trop*. Montreal: VLB éditeur.

Goerres, A. 2008. "The Grey Vote: Determinants of Older Voters' Party Choice in Britain and West Germany." *Electoral Studies* 27, no. 2: 285–304. https://doi.org/10.1016/j.electstud.2007.12.007.

Gomery, John H. 2005. "Who Is Responsible? Phase 1 Report of the Commission of Inquiry into the Sponsorship Program and Advertising Activities." Ottawa: Government of Canada.

Gotz, Adela. 2010. "Open Federalism and the 2006 Federal Election in Quebec: Did Quebecers Accept the Olive Branch?" Master's thesis, McGill University, Montreal. http://search.proquest.com.myaccess.library.utoronto.ca/pqdtft/docview/807621164/abstract/13E70ABA4D7699AE87F/1?accountid=14771.

Graefe, Peter. 2003. "State Restructuring and the Failure of Competitive Nationalism: Trying Times for Quebec Labour." In *Quebec and Canada in the New Century: New Dynamics, New Opportunities*, edited by Michael Murphy, 153–76. Kingston, ON: Institute of Intergovernmental Relations.

Graefe, Peter, and Rachel Laforest. 2013. "Federalism and Governance." Paper presented at the annual meeting of the Canadian Political Science Association, Victoria, BC, June. https://www.cpsa-acsp.ca/papers-2013/Graefe.pdf.

Grasso, Maria. 2016. *Grasso: Generations, Political Participation and Social Change in Western Europe*. London and New York: Routledge.

Grasso, Maria Teresa. 2014. "Age, Period and Cohort Analysis in a Comparative Context: Political Generations and Political Participation Repertoires in Western Europe." *Electoral Studies* 33 (March): 63–76. https://doi.org/10.1016/j.electstud.2013.06.003.

Grasso, Maria, Stephen Farrall, Emily Gray, Colin Hay, and Will Jennings. 2017. "Thatcher's Children, Blair's Babies, Political Socialization and Trickle-Down Value Change: An Age, Period and Cohort Analysis." *British Journal of Political Science* 49, no. 1: 17–36. https://doi.org/10.1017/S0007123416000375.

– 2019. "Socialization and Generational Political Trajectories: An Age, Period and Cohort Analysis of Political Participation in Britain." *Journal of Elections, Public Opinion and Parties* 29, no. 2: 199–221. https://doi.org/10.1080/17457289.2018.1476359.

Guay, Jean-Herman. 1997. *Avant, pendant et après le boom: Portrait de la culture politique de trois générations de Québécois*. Sherbrooke, QC: Éditions les Fous du roi.

– 2004. "Le Parti Québécois: Au-delà du conflit des ambitions." *Policy Options*, 1 December 2004.

Guénette, Par Dave, and Félix Mathieu. 2018. "Nations et nations fragiles." *Canadian Journal of Political Science / Revue Canadienne de Science Politique*, July, 1–25. https://doi.org/10.1017/S0008423918000355.

Guibernau, Montserrat. 1999. *Nations without States: Political Communities in a Global Age*. Cambridge: Polity Press / Blackwell Publishers.

Guindon, Hubert. 1978. "The Modernization of Quebec and the Legitimacy of the Canadian State." *Canadian Review of Sociology / Revue Canadienne de Sociologie* 15, no. 2: 227–45. https://doi.org/10.1111/j.1755-618X.1978.tb00995.x.

Güntzel, Ralph P. 2011. "'Rapprocher les lieux du pouvoir': The Quebec Labour Movement and Quebec Sovereigntism." In *Contemporary Quebec: Selected Readings and Commentaries*, edited by Michael Behiels and Matthew Hayday, 280–307. Montreal: McGill-Queen's University Press.

Haddow, Rodney. 2014. *Comparing Quebec and Ontario: Political Economy and Public Policy at the Turn of the Millennium*. Buffalo, NY: University of Toronto Press.

Hakim, Danny. 2014. "Scots Are Divided Over Independence, and Its Economic Costs." *New York Times*, 1 June 2014.

Hamilton, Graeme. 2004. "PQ's 'Young' All Have Grey Hair." *National Post*, 24 September 2004.

– 2012. "Graeme Hamilton: Lucien Bouchard Tells Parti Québécois to Move on from Sovereignty." *National Post*, 12 September 2012.

– 2014a. "Graeme Hamilton: Pauline Marois' Empty Prosperity Promises Trashed by Former PQ Premier Jacques Parizeau." *National Post*, 10 February 2014.

– 2014b. "Graeme Hamilton: Young Quebecers Quick to Adopt Nationalist Vision of Province's History, Survey Finds." *National Post*, 18 February 2014.

Hamilton, Richard, and Maurice Pinard. 1976. "The Bases of Parti Québécois Support in Recent Quebec Elections." *Canadian Journal of Political Science / Revue Canadienne de Science Politique* 9, no. 1: 3–26. https://doi.org/10.1017/S0008423900043158.

Harmes, Adam. 2007. "The Political Economy of Open Federalism." *Canadian Journal of Political Science/Revue Canadienne de Science Politique* 40, no. 2: 417–37. https://doi.org/10.1017/S0008423907070114.

Hartz, Louis. 1955. *The Liberal Tradition in America: An Interpretation of American Political Thought since the Revolution.* 1st ed. New York: Harcourt, Brace.

– 1964. *The Founding of New Societies: Studies in the History of the United States, Latin America, South Africa, Canada, and Australia.* 1st ed. New York: Harcourt, Brace & World.

Health Canada. 2004. "Asymmetrical Federalism That Respects Quebec's Jurisdiction." Government of Canada. 15 September 2004.

Hiebert, Janet. 1996. *Limiting Rights: The Dilemma of Judicial Review.* Montreal: McGill-Queen's University Press.

– 2002. *Charter Conflicts: What Is Parliament's Role?* Montreal: McGill-Queen's University Press.

Hogg, Peter W. 1988. *Meech Lake Constitutional Accord Annotated.* Toronto: Carswell.

Holland, Laurel L., and Sherry Cable. 2002. "Reconceptualizing Social Movement Abeyance: The Role of Internal Processes and Culture in Cycles of Movement Abeyance and Resurgence." *Sociological Focus* 35, no. 3: 297–314. https://doi.org/10.1080/00380237.2002.10570705.

Horowitz, G. 1966. "Conservatism, Liberalism and Socialism in Canada: An Interpretation." *Canadian Journal of Economics and Political Science* 32, no. 2: 143–71. https://doi.org/10.2307/139794.

Howe, Paul. 1998. "Rationality and Sovereignty Support in Quebec." *Canadian Journal of Political Science / Revue Canadienne de Science Politique* 31, no. 1: 31–59. https://doi.org/10.1017/S0008423900008672.

Howse, Robert. 1998. "Searching for Plan A: National Unity and the Chrétien Government's New Federalism." In *Non-constitutional Renewal*, edited by Harvey Lazar, 311–31. Canada: The State of the Federation 1997. Kingston, ON: Institute of Intergovernmental Relations.

Hutchinson, John. 2004. "Cultural Wars." In *Nations as Zones of Conflict*, 77–114. London: Sage. https://doi.org/10.4135/9781446217979.

Inglehart, Ronald. 1977. *The Silent Revolution: Changing Values and Political Styles among Western Publics.* Princeton, NJ: Princeton University Press.

– 1981. "Post-Materialism in an Environment of Insecurity." *American Political Science Review* 75, no. 4: 880–900. https://doi.org/10.2307/1962290.

– 1988. "Cultural Change in Advanced Industrial Societies: Postmaterialist Values and Their Consequences." *International Review of Sociology Series 1* 2, no. 3: 77–99. https://doi.org/10.1080/03906701.1988.9971376.

– 1990. *Culture Shift in Advanced Industrial Society.* Princeton, NJ: Princeton University Press.

– 2008. "Changing Values among Western Publics from 1970 to 2006." *West European Politics* 31, no. 1–2: 130–46. https://doi.org/10.1080 /01402380701834747.

Institute of Public Administration of Canada. 1979. *Intergovernmental Canada: Government by Conference?* Edited by Donald W. Craik, J. Stefan Dupré, Kenneth Kernaghan, James J. Macdonell, James D. McNiven, Richard Simeon, Donald V. Smiley, Gérard Veilleux, and Kenneth W. Wiltshire. Toronto: Institute of Public Administration of Canada.

Inwood, Gregory J., Carolyn M. Johns, and Patricia L. O'Reilly. 2011. *Intergovernmental Policy Capacity in Canada: Inside the Worlds of Finance, Environment, Trade, and Health.* Montreal: McGill-Queen's University Press.

Jacques, Daniel. 2008. *La fatigue politique du Québec français.* Montreal: Boréal.

Jeffrey, Brooke. 2006. "From Collaborative Federalism to the New Unilateralism: Implications for the Welfare State." In *Continuity and Change in Canadian Politics: Essays in Honour of David E. Smith*, edited by Hans J. Michelmann, David E. Smith, and Cristine de Clercy. Toronto: University of Toronto Press.

Jennings, M. Kent. 2002. "Generation Units and the Student Protest Movement in the United States: An Intra- and Intergenerational Analysis." *Political Psychology* 23, no. 2: 303–24. https://doi.org/10.1111 /0162-895X.00283.

Jennings, M. Kent, Laura Stoker, and Jake Bowers. 2009. "Politics across Generations: Family Transmission Reexamined." *Journal of Politics* 71, no. 3: 782–99. https://doi.org/10.1017/s0022381609090719.

Johnston, Richard. 1985. "The Reproduction of the Religious Cleavage in Canadian Elections." *Canadian Journal of Political Science / Revue Canadienne de Science Politique* 18, no. 1: 99–113. https://doi.org/10.1017 /S000842390002922X.

Jones, Bryan D., and Frank R. Baumgartner. 2005. *The Politics of Attention: How Government Prioritizes Problems.* Chicago: University of Chicago Press.

Journal des débats de la Commission des institutions. 1990. Quebec City: Assemblée Nationale du Quebec. http://www.assnat.qc.ca/fr/travaux -parlementaires/commissions/ci-34-1/journal-debats/CI-900611.html.

Kaldor, Mary. 2004. "Nationalism and Globalisation." *Nations and Nationalism* 10, no. 1–2: 161–77. https://doi.org/10.1111/j.1354-5078.2004.00161.x.

Keating, Michael. 1996. *Nations against the State: The New Politics of Nationalism in Quebec, Catalonia, and Scotland.* New York: St Martins Press.

Kelemen, R. Daniel. 2004. *The Rules of Federalism: Institutions and Regulatory Politics in the EU and Beyond*. Cambridge, MA: Harvard University Press.

Kelly, James B., and Michael Murphy. 2005. "Shaping the Constitutional Dialogue on Federalism: Canada's Supreme Court as Meta-political Actor." *Publius* 35, no. 2: 217–43. https://doi.org/10.1093/publius/pji010.

Kingdon, John W. 1984. *Agendas, Alternatives, and Public Policies*. Boston: Little, Brown.

Knopf, Rainer, and Anthony Sayers. 2005. "Constitutional Politics in Canada." In *Dialogues on Constitutional Origins, Structure, and Change in Federal Countries*, edited by Raoul Blindenbacher and Abigail Ostien Karos, 16–18. A Global Dialogue on Federalism Booklet Series, v. 1. Montreal: McGill-Queen's University Press.

Krosnick, Jon A. 1990. "Government Policy and Citizen Passion: A Study of Issue Publics in Contemporary America." *Political Behavior* 12, no. 1: 59–92. https://doi.org/10.1007/BF00992332.

L'actualité. 1993. "Le referendum de ses pairs: Passera-t-il a l'histoire comme un grand premier ministre? (*L'actualité* a demande a une vingtaine de leaders et d'anciens collaborateurs leur bilan des annees Bourassa)." *L'actualité*, 15 November 1993.

Laforest, Guy. 1995. *Trudeau and the End of a Canadian Dream*. Buffalo, NY: McGill-Queen's University Press.

– 2010. "The Meaning of Canadian Federalism in Quebec: Critical Reflections." *REAF* 11: 10–55.

Laforest, Guy, and Oscar Mejia Mesa. 2014. *Interpreting Quebec's Exile within the Federation: Selected Political Essays*. Diversitas, vol. 20. Brussels: P.I.E. Lang.

Laforest, Guy, and Jean-Olivier Roy. 2014. *Un Québec exilé dans la fédération: Essai d'histoire intellectuelle et de pensée politique*. Débats. Montreal: Québec Amérique.

Lajoie, Geneviève. 2018. "Sondage Léger / Le Journal: La CAQ vers le pouvoir." *Journal de Québec*, 29 September 2018.

Lammert, Christian, and Christian Vormann. 2015. "Has Quebecois Separatism Run Its Course? New Chances for Cooperative Arrangements in Canada." *Zeitschrift Für Kanada-Studien* 35: 45–62. https://doi.org/10.3196/186429501562572.

Langlois, Simon, and Gilles Gangé. 2002. *Les raisons fortes: Nature et signification de l'appui et la souveraineté du Québec*. Montreal: Université de Montréal.

La Presse. 2014. "Les jeunes décrochent de la souveraineté." 19 March 2014.

Lau, Rachel. 2018. "Young Quebecers 'Highly Engaged' in Provincial Election: IPSOS Poll." *Global News*, 14 September 2018.

Laxer, Emily. 2019. *Unveiling the Nation: The Politics of Secularism in France and Quebec*. Montreal: McGill-Queen's University Press.

Lazar, Harvey., ed. 1998. "Non-constitutional Renewal: Toward a New Equilibrium in the Federation." In *Non-constitutional Renewal. Canada: The State of the Federation 1997*. Kingston, ON: Institute of Intergovernmental Relations.

– 2001. "The Social Union Framework Agreement: Lost Opportunity or New Beginning?" Kingston, ON: Institute of Intergovernmental Relations.

LeBlanc, Daniel. 2014. "PQ's Sovereignty Focus Is Errant, Poll Finds." *Globe and Mail*, 15 March 2014.

Lecours, Andre. 2021. *Nationalism, Secessionism, and Autonomy*. Oxford Scholarship Online. Oxford: Oxford University Press.

Legault, François, Charles Sirois, Bruno-Marie Béchard Marinier, Lionel Carmant, Jean Lamarre, Sylvie Lemaire, Michel Lemay, et al. 2011. "2011 Manifesto of the Coalition pour l'Avenir du Québec." https://www.bibliotheque.assnat.qc.ca /DepotNumerique_v2/AffichageNotice.aspx?idn=832.

Leger Marketing, and *Journal de Montréal*. 2019. "Debate on Secularism." Opinion poll. https://leger360.com/wp-content/uploads/2019/09/11679 -221-Secularism-Report.pdf.

Lemieux, Vincent. 1986. "L'état et les jeunes." In *Une société des jeunes?*, edited by F. Dumont, 325–35. Quebec City: Institute québécois de reserche sur la culture.

– 2011. *Les partis générationnels au Québec*. Quebec City: Presses de L'Université Laval.

LeRoy, Sylvia. 2004. "Supreme Disabeyance: Law, Politics and the 'Secession Reference.'" Master's thesis, University of Calgary. http://search.proquest .com.myaccess.library.utoronto.ca/pqdtft/docview/305208343/abstract /BF95800ECE8A4C72PQ/3?accountid=14771.

Létourneau, Jocelyn. 2004 [2001]. *A History for the Future: Rewriting Memory and Identity in Quebec*. Translated by Phyllis Aronoff and Howard Scott. Studies on the History of Quebec 16. Montreal: McGill-Queen's University Press.

Lijphart, Arend. 1977. *Democracy in Plural Societies: A Comparative Exploration*. New Haven, CT: Yale University Press.

Linz, Juan J. 1993. "State Building and Nation Building." *European Review* 1, no. 4: 355–69. https://doi.org/10.1017/S1062798700000776.

Linz, Juan J., Mohammad-Saïd Darviche, and William Genieys. 1997. "Construction étatique et construction nationale." *Pôle Sud* 7, no. 1: 5–26. https://doi.org/10.3406/pole.1997.977.

Lipset, Seymour Martin. 1950. *Agrarian Socialism: The Cooperative Commonwealth Federation in Saskatchewan; A Study in Political Sociology*. Berkeley: University of California Press.

Lipsig-Mummé, Carla. 1993. "Quebec Labour, Politics, and the Economic Crisis: Defensive Accommodation Faces the Future." In *The Challenge of*

Restructuring: North American Labor Movements Respond, edited by Jane Jenson and Rianne Mahon, 403–21. Philadelphia: Temple University Press.

Lisée, Jean-François. 2001. "Is Quebec a North American Region-State?" *Policy Options Politique*, December. https://policyoptions.irpp.org/magazines/university-tenure/is-quebec-a-north-american-region-state/.

– 2007. *Nous*. Montreal: Boreal.

Maclure, Jocelyn. 2003. *Quebec Identity: The Challenge of Pluralism*. Ithaca, NY: McGill-Queen's University Press.

Macpherson, Don. n.d. "Don Macpherson: The Couillard Government's 'One Language, One Culture' Idea of Quebec." *Montreal Gazette* (blog). Accessed 24 July 2015.

Mahéo, Valérie-Anne, and Éric Bélanger. 2018. "Is the Parti Québécois Bound to Disappear? A Study of the Current Generational Dynamics of Electoral Behaviour in Quebec." *Canadian Journal of Political Science / Revue Canadienne de Science Politique* 51, no. 02: 335–56. https://doi.org/10.1017/S0008423917001147.

Mahler, Gregory S. 1995. "Canadian Federalism and the 1995 Referendum: A Perspective from Outside of Quebec." *American Review of Canadian Studies* 25, no. 4: 449–76. https://doi.org/10.1080/02722019509481547.

Mann, Michael. 2012. *The Sources of Social Power*. Vol. 4, *Globalizations, 1945–2011*. New York: Cambridge University Press.

Mannheim, Karl. 1996. "The Problem of Generations (1928)." In *Theories of Ethnicity*, edited by Werner Sollors, 109–55. London: Palgrave Macmillan. https://doi.org/10.1007/978-1-349-24984-8_9.

Marois, Guillaume, and Patrick Sabourin. 2014. "Le project d'une génération? Regard démographique sur l'avenir de l'indépendance." In *Indépendance: Les conditions du renouveau*, edited by Mathieu Bock-Côté, 59–94. Montreal: VLB.

Marotte, Bertrand. 2013. "Quebec's 'Welfare State' on the Decline? On the Contrary, Says New Study." *Globe and Mail*, 3 April 2013.

Martin, Pierre. 1994. "Générations politiques, rationalité économique et appui à la souveraineté au Québec." *Canadian Journal of Political Science / Revue Canadienne de Science Politique* 27, no. 2: 345–59. https://doi.org/10.1017/S0008423900017388.

– 1995. "Association after Sovereignty? Canadian Views on Economic Association with a Sovereign Quebec." *Canadian Public Policy / Analyse de Politiques* 21, no. 1: 53–71. https://doi.org/10.2307/3552043.

Mathieu, Félix. 2017. *Les défis du pluralisme: À l'ère des sociétés complexes*. Politeia Collection 6. Quebec City: Presses de l'Université du Québec.

McAdam, Doug. 1982. *Political Process and the Development of Black Insurgency, 1930–1970*. Chicago: University of Chicago Press.

McAndrew, Marie. 2009. "Quebec Immigration, Integration and Intercultural Policy: A Critical Assessment." In *Multiculturalism: Public Policy and Problem*

Areas in Canada and India, edited by Christopher Rai and Marie McAndrew, 204–21. New Delhi, India: Manak Publications.

McGill Law Publications. 2016. "Regards neufs sur la Constitution." *Focus Online*, January 2016.

McGregor, Janyce. 2017. "'We Are Not Opening the Constitution': Trudeau Pans Quebec's Plans." CBC, 1 June 2017.

McRoberts, Kenneth. 1991. *English Canada and Quebec: Avoiding the Issue*. Robarts Centre for Canadian Studies Lecture Series 6. North York, ON: Robarts Centre for Canadian Studies, York University.

– 1997. *Misconceiving Canada: The Struggle for National Unity*. Toronto: Oxford University Press.

McRoberts, Kenneth, and Patrick Monahan, eds. 1993. *The Charlottetown Accord, the Referendum, and the Future of Canada*. Toronto: University of Toronto Press.

Meisel, John. 1991. "The Media and Constitutional Reform in Canada." In *After Meech Lake: Lessons for the Future*, edited by David E. Smith, Peter. MacKinnon, and John C. Courtney, 147–68. Saskatoon, SK: Fifth House.

Mendelsohn, Matthew. 2003. "Rational Choice and Socio-psychological Explanation for Opinion on Quebec Sovereignty." *Canadian Journal of Political Science / Revue Canadienne de Science Politique* 36, no. 3: 511–37. https://doi.org/10.2307/3233082.

Mendelsohn, Matthew, Andrew Parkin, and Maurice Pinard. 2007. "A New Chapter or the Same Old Story? Public Opinion in Quebec from 1996–2003." In *Quebec and Canada in the New Century: New Dynamics, New Opportunities*, edited by Michael Murphy, 25–52. Canada: The State of the Federation 2005. Kingston, ON: McGill-Queen's University Press.

Michaud, Félix-Antoine, and Léa Clermont-Dion, eds. 2014. *Lettres à un souverainiste*. Montreal: VLB Éditeur.

Miller, J.M, Jon A. Krosnick, and L.A. Fabrigar. 2017. "The Origins of Policy Issue Salience." In *Political Psychology: New Explorations*, edited by Jon A. Krosnick, I-C.A. Chiang, and T.H. Stark, 125–77. London: Routledge.

Mintrom, Michael. 1997. "Policy Entrepreneurs and the Diffusion of Innovation." *American Journal of Political Science* 41, no. 3: 738–70. https://doi.org/10.2307/2111674.

Moeller, Susan D. 2002. *Compassion Fatigue: How the Media Sell Disease, Famine, War and Death*. New York: Routledge.

Momryk, Myron. 1999. "Book Review: *Making History in Twentieth-Century Quebec*, by Ronald Rudin." *H-Net Reviews*, March. https://www.h-net.org/reviews/showpdf.php?id=2952.

Monahan, Patrick. 1991. *Meech Lake: The Inside Story*. Toronto: University of Toronto Press.

Montpetit, Éric. 2007a. *Le fédéralisme d'ouverture: La recherche d'une légitimité canadienne au Québec*. Sillery, QC: Septentrion.

– 2007b. "Une charte du fédéralisme: Une idée attrayante qu'il faut mieux défendre." *Policy Options Politique*, 1 October 2007.

– 2008. "Easing Dissatisfaction with Canadian Federalism? The Promise of the Strategy of Disjointed Incrementalism." *Canadian Political Science Review* 2, no. 3: 12–28.

– 2012. "Are Interprovincial Relations More Important Than Federal-Provincial Ones?" The Federal Idea. http://ideefederale.ca/wp/?p =2060&lang=ang.

Montpetit, Jonathan. 2018. "Health Most Important Issue for Quebec Voters, Vote Compass Survey Says." CBC News, 18 August 2018.

– 2019. "Big Gains for the Bloc Québécois, But What Did It Sacrifice in the Process?" CBC News, 22 October 2019.

Morgan, Edmund. 1988. *Inventing the People: The Rise of Popular Sovereignty in England and America*. New York: W.W. Norton.

Nadeau, Richard. 1992. "Le virage souverainiste des Québécois, 1980–1990." *Recherches sociographiques* 33, no. 1: 9–28. https://doi.org/10.7202/056659ar.

Nadeau, Richard, Pierre Martin, and André Blais. 1999. "Attitude Towards Risk-Taking and Individual Choice in the Quebec Referendum on Sovereignty." *British Journal of Political Science* 29, no. 3: 523–39. https:// doi.org/10.1017/S0007123499000241.

National Assembly of Quebec. 2013. *Bill 60, Charter Affirming the Values of State Secularism and Religious Neutrality and of Equality between Women and Men, and Providing a Framework for Accommodation Requests*. http://www.assnat .qc.ca/en/travaux-parlementaires/projets-loi/projet-loi-60-40-1.html.

Neundorf, Anja, and Richard G. Niemi. 2014. "Beyond Political Socialization: New Approaches to Age, Period, Cohort Analysis." *Electoral Studies* 33: 1–6. https://doi.org/10.1016/j.electstud.2013.06.012.

Neundorf, Anja, Kaat Smets, and Gema M. García-Albacete. 2013. "Homemade Citizens: The Development of Political Interest during Adolescence and Young Adulthood." *Acta Politica* 48, no. 1: 92–116. https:// doi.org/10.1057/ap.2012.23.

Nevitte, Neil. 1996. *The Decline of Deference: Canadian Value Change in Cross-National Perspective*. Peterborough, ON: Broadview Press.

Noël, Alain. 2000. "Without Quebec: Collaborative Federalism with a Footnote?" *Policy Matters* 1, no. 2. Montreal: Institute for Research on Public Policy.

– 2003. "Power and Purpose in Intergovernmental Relations." In *Forging the Canadian Social Union: SUFA and Beyond*, edited by Sarah Fortin, Alain Noël, France St-Hilaire, and Institute for Research on Public Policy, 47–68. Montreal: Institute for Research on Public Policy.

– 2018. "Quebec's New Politics of Redistribution Meets Austerity." In *Federalism and the Welfare State in a Multicultural World*, edited by Elizabeth Goodyear-Grant, Richard Johnston, Will Kymlicka, and John Myles, 73–100. Montreal: McGill-Queen's University Press.

Norquay, Geoff. 2012. "The Death of Executive Federalism and the Rise of the 'Harper Doctrine': Prospects for the Next Health Care Accord." *Policy Options*, 2012.

O'Neal, Brian. 1995. "Distinct Society: Origins, Interpretations, Implications." Background Paper BP-408E. Ottawa: Political and Social Affairs Division, Parliamentary Research Branch, Library of Parliament. https://publications.gc.ca/Collection-R/LoPBdP/BP/bp408-e.htm.

Papillon, Martin. 2012. "Adapting Federalism: Indigenous Multilevel Governance in Canada and the United States." *Publius* 42, no. 2: 289–312. https://doi.org/10.1093/publius/pjr032.

Paquet, Mireille. 2014. "The Federalization of Immigration and Integration in Canada." *Canadian Journal of Political Science / Revue Canadienne de Science Politique* 47, no. 3: 519–48. https://doi.org/10.1017/S0008423914000766.

– 2019. *Province-Building and the Federalization of Immigration in Canada*. Translated by Howard Scott. Toronto: University of Toronto Press.

Parizeau, Jacques. 2014. "Le Québec vit-il au-dessus de ses moyens?" *Journal de Montréal*, 10 February 2014.

Patriquin, Martin. 2015. "Jaques Parizeau: A Legacy Larger than That Speech." Macleans.ca, 2 June 2015.

– 2016. "To the New PQ Leader: Good Luck." *Macleans.ca* (blog). 9 October 2016. https://www.macleans.ca/news/canada/to-the-new-pq-leader -good-luck/.

Payette, Roger, and Jean-François Payette. 2013. *Ce peuple qui ne fut jamais souverain: La tentation du suicide politique des Québécois*. Anjou, QC: Fides.

Pelletier, Jacques. 2007. *Question nationale et lutte sociale, la nouvelle fracture: Écrits à contre-courant*. Quebec City: Éditions Nota Bene.

Pelletier, Réjean. 1998. "From Jacques Parizeau to Lucien Bouchard: A New Vision? Yes, But …" In *Non-constitutional Renewal*, edited by Harvey Lazar, 295–310. Canada: The State of the Federation 1997. Kingston, ON: Institute of Intergovernmental Relations.

Perrella, Andrea, and Éric Bélanger. 2007. "Young Sovereigntists and Attitudes about Federalism." Paper prepared for presentation at the 2007 annual meeting of the Canadian Political Science Association, Saskatoon, 30 May–1 June.

– 2009. "Young Sovereigntists and Attitudes about Federalism." *Quebec Studies* 47, no. 1: 95–118.

Pinard, Maurice. 1992. "The Dramatic Reemergence of the Quebec Independence Movement." *Journal of International Affairs* 45, no. 2: 471–97.

– 2003. *A Great Realignment of Political Parties in Quebec.* The CRIC Papers. Montreal: Centre for Research and Information on Canada.

– 2005. "Political Ambivalence towards the Parti Québécois and Its Electoral Consequences, 1970–2003." *Canadian Journal of Sociology* 30, no. 3: 281–314. https://doi.org/10.1353/cjs.2005.0053.

Pinard, Maurice, and Richard Hamilton. 1977. "The Independence Issue and the Polarization of the Electorate: The 1973 Quebec Election." *Canadian Journal of Political Science / Revue Canadienne de Science Politique* 10, no. 2: 215–59. https://doi.org/10.1017/S0008423900041457.

– 1984a. "Les québécois votent non: Le sens et la portée du vote." In *Le Comportement Électoral Au Québec*, edited by Jean Crête, 335–85. Chicoutimi, QC: Gaétan Morin.

– 1984b. "The Class Bases of the Quebec Independence Movement: Conjectures and Evidence." *Ethnic and Racial Studies* 7, no. 1: 19–54. https://doi.org/10.1080/01419870.1984.9993433.

– 1986. "Motivational Dimensions in the Quebec Independence Movement: A Test of a New Model." In *Research in Social Movements, Conflict and Change*, edited by K. Lang and G.E. Lang, 225–80. Greenwich, CT: JAI Press.

Piotte, Jean-Marc, and Jean-Pierre Couture. 2012. *Les nouveaux visages du nationalisme conservateur au Québec.* Débats. Montreal: Québec Amérique.

Piroth, Scott. 2004. "Generational Replacement, Value Shifts, and Support for a Sovereign Quebec (1)." *Quebec Studies* 37 (March): 23–43. https://doi.org/10.3828/qs.37.1.23.

Pollard, Bruce G. 1986. *Managing the Interface: Intergovernmental Affairs Agencies in Canada.* Kingston, ON: Institute of Intergovernmental Relations.

Pour un Québec solidaire. 2006. n.p. http://jmt-sociologue.uqac.ca/www/word/387_135_CH/lecon_3/pourunquebecsolidaire.pdf.

Pratte, André. 2008. "Wiping the Slate Clean: Reviewing Our Past to Build a Better Future." In *Reconquering Canada*, edited by André Pratte, translated by Patrick Watson, 217–46. Vancouver, BC: Douglas & McIntyre.

Prime Minister of Canada Justin Trudeau, and Premier of Quebec François Legault. 2019. "Memorandum of Understanding – Arrangement Concerning the Appointment Process to Fill the Seat That Will Be Left Vacant on the Supreme Court of Canada Following the Departure of Justice Clément Gascon." https://pm.gc.ca/en/news/backgrounders/2019/05/15/arrangement-concerning-appointment-process-fill-seat-will-be-left.

Quebec. 1985. "Draft Agreement on the Constitution: Proposals by the Government of Quebec." Quebec. https://www.sqrc.gouv.qc.ca/documents/positions-historiques/positions-du-qc/part3/Document20_en.pdf.

Quebec. Minister of Community Culture and Immigration. 1990. *Let's Build Quebec Together: Policy Statement on Immigration and Integration:* [Au Québec pour bâtir ensemble: Énoncé de politique en matière d'immigration et d'intégration]." Quebec City. https://numerique.banq.qc.ca/patrimoine/details/52327/44435.

Rabeau, Yves. 2011. "The Myth of Fiscal Imblance." Montreal: The Federal Idea.

Radio-Canada.ca, and La Presse canadienne. 2019. "'Le Québec, c'est nous': Le Bloc dévoile son slogan électoral." Radio-Canada.ca. 19 September 2019.

Radmilovic, Vuk. 2010. "Strategic Legitimacy Cultivation at the Supreme Court of Canada: Quebec Secession Reference and Beyond." *Canadian Journal of Political Science / Revue Canadienne de Science Politique* 43, no. 4: 843–69. https://doi.org/10.1017/S0008423910000764.

Ramazani, Vaheed. 2013. "War Fatigue? Selective Compassion and Questionable Ethics in Mainstream Reporting on Afghanistan and Iraq." *Middle East Critique* 22, no. 1: 5–24. https://doi.org/10.1080/19436149.2012.755297.

Reference re: Amendment to the Canadian Constitution. 1982, 2 S.C.R. 793. SCC.

Reference re: Authority of Parliament in Relation to the Upper House. 1980, 1 S.C.R. 54. SCC.

Reference re: Resolution to Amend the Constitution. 1981, 1 S.C.R. 753.

Reference re: Secession of Quebec. 1998, 2 S.C.R. 217.

Reference re: Senate Reform. 2014, 1 S.C.R. 32. SCC.

Reference re: Supreme Court Act, ss. 5 and 6. 2014, 1 S.C.R. 433. SCC.

Reynolds, Christopher. 2021. "New Cabinet Minister Omar Alghabra Slams 'Harmful Innuendo' by Bloc about His Past." CBC News. 14 January 2021.

Richards, John. 2002. *The Paradox of the Social Union Framework Agreement*. C.D. Howe Institute Backgrounder 59. C.D. Howe Institute.

Robitaille, Antoine. 2014. "Contre la fatigue." *Le Devoir*, 23 June 2014.

Rocher, François. 2002. "The Evolving Parameters of Quebec Nationalism." In "The Impact of Government Policies on Territorially Based Ethnic or Nationalist Movements." Special issue, *International Journal on Multicultural Societies* 4, no. 1: 74–96.

– 2007. "The End of the 'Two Solitudes'? The Presence (or Absence) of the Work of French-Speaking Scholars in Canadian Politics." *Canadian Journal of Political Science / Revue Canadienne de Science Politique* 40, no. 4: 833–57. https://doi.org/10.1017/S0008423907071132.

– 2014. "The Orange Wave: A (Re)Canadianiazation of the Quebec Electorate?" In *Canada: The State of the Federation, 2011; The Changing Federal Environment: Rebalancing Roles*, edited by Nadia Verrelli, 65–82. Queen's Policy Studies Series. Montreal: McGill-Queen's University Press.

– 2019. "The Life and Death of an Issue: Canadian Political Science and Quebec Politics." *Canadian Journal of Political Science* 52, no. 4: 631–55. https://doi.org/10.1017/S0008423919000672.

– 2022. "Transformations in Contemporary Quebec Nationalism, 1960–2020: A Shift in the Sources of Collective Animosities." *Nations and Nationalism* 29, no. 1: 280–94. https://doi.org/10.1111/nana.12902.

– 2023. "Transformations in Contemporary Quebec Nationalism, 1960–2020: A Shift in the Sources of Collective Animosities." *Nations and Nationalism* 29, no. 1: 280–94. https://doi.org/10.1111/nana.12902.

Rocher, François., Alain-G. Gagnon, and Montserrat Guibernau. 2003. "The Conditions of Diversity in Multinational Democracies." In *The Conditions of Diversity in Multinational Democracies,* edited by Alain-G. Gagnon, François Rocher, and Maria Montserrat Guibernau i Berdún, 1–10. Montreal: IRPP.

Rouillard, Jacques. 1997. "La révolution tranquille: Rupture ou tournant?" *Journal of Canadian Studies* 32, no. 4: 23–51.

Russell, Peter H. 1993. "The End of Mega Constitutional Politics in Canada?" *PS: Political Science & Politics* 26, no. 1: 33–7. https://doi.org/10.2307/419501.

– 2004. *Constitutional Odyssey: Can Canadians Become a Sovereign People?* 3rd. ed. Toronto: University of Toronto Press.

Salée, Daniel. 2001. "Quebec's Changing Political Culture and the Future of Federal-Provincial Relations in Canada." In *Canadian Political Culture(s) in Transition,* edited by Hamish Telford and Harvey Lazar, 163–97. Canada: The State of the Federation 2001. Montreal: Institute of Intergovernmental Relations and McGill-Queen's University Press.

Savage, Larry. 2008. "Quebec Labour and the Referendums." *Canadian Journal of Political Science / Revue Canadienne de Science Politique* 41, no. 4: 861–87. https://doi.org/10.1017/S0008423908081067.

Savard-Tremblay, Simon-Pierre. 2014. *Le souverainisme de province.* Montreal: Boréal.

– 2016. *L'État succursale: La démission politique du Québec.* Montreal: VLB.

Savoie, Donald J. 1999. *Governing from the Centre: The Concentration of Power in Canadian Politics.* Toronto: University of Toronto Press.

Saywell, John T. 2002. *The Lawmakers: Judicial Power and the Shaping of Canadian Federalism.* Osgoode Society for Canadian Legal History Series. Toronto: University of Toronto Press.

Schertzer, Robert. 2008. "Recognition or Imposition? Federalism, National Minorities, and the Supreme Court of Canada." *Nations and Nationalism* 14, no. 1: 105–26. https://doi.org/10.1111/j.1469-8129.2008.00324.x.

– 2012. "Judging the Nation: The Supreme Court of Canada, Federalism and Managing Diversity." PhD diss., London School of Economics and Political Science. http://etheses.lse.ac.uk/376/.

Schertzer, Robert, Andrew McDougall, and Grace Skogstad. 2018. "Multilateral Collaboration in Canadian Intergovernmental Relations: The Role of Procedural and Reciprocal Norms." *Publius* 48, no. 4: 636–63. https://doi.org/10.1093/publius/pjx066.

Schertzer, Robert, and Eric Taylor Woods. 2011. "Beyond Multinational Canada." *Commonwealth & Comparative Politics* 49, no. 2: 196–222. https://doi.org/10.1080/14662043.2011.564473.

Scottish Government. 2013. "Scotland's Economy: The Case for Independence." Edinburgh: The Scottish Government.

Séguin, Rhéal. 2013. "PQ Touts Quebec's 'Decanadianization,' Citing New Poll's Findings." *Globe and Mail*, 11 December 2013.

Séguin, Yves. 2002. *Speaking Notes for Yves Séguin, President of the Commission on Fiscal Imbalance*. Québec City, 7 March 2002. http://www.groupes.finances .gouv.qc.ca/desequilibrefiscal/en/presse/index.htm#8.

Serebrin, Jacob. 2023. "Quebec Calls for Resignation of Federal Government's Anti-Islamophobia Representative." *Global News*, 30 January 2023.

Simeon, Richard. 2002. *Political Scientists and the Study of Federalism in Canada: Seven Decades of Scholarly Engagement*. Kingston, ON: Institute of Intergovernmental Affairs.

– 2006. *Federal-Provincial Diplomacy: The Making of Recent Policy in Canada; With a New Preface and Postscript*. Toronto: University of Toronto Press.

Simeon, Richard, Ian Robinson, and Jennifer Wallner. 2014. "The Dynamics of Canadian Federalism." In *Canadian Politics*, 6th ed., edited by James Bickerton and Alain-G Gagnon, 101–26. Peterborough, ON: Broadview Press.

Skogstad, Grace. 1998. "Canadian Federalism, Internationalization and Quebec Agriculture: Dis-Engagement, Re-Integration?" *Canadian Public Policy / Analyse de Politiques* 24, no. 1: 27–48. https://doi.org/10.2307 /3551728.

Smiley, Donald. 1978. "The Canadian Federation and the Challenge of Quebec Independence." *Publius* 8, no. 1: 199–224. https://doi.org/10.2307/3329637.

Smiley, Donald V. 1979. "An Outsider's Observations of Federal-Provincial Relations among Consenting Adults." In *Confrontation and Collaboration: Intergovernmental Relations in Canada Today*, edited by Richard Simeon, 105–13. Toronto: Institute of Public Administration of Canada.

– 1980. *Canada in Question: Federalism in the Eighties*. Toronto: McGraw-Hill Ryerson.

Smith, David E. 2010. *Federalism and the Constitution of Canada*. Toronto: University of Toronto Press.

Sorens, Jason. 2012. *Secessionism: Identity, Interest, and Strategy*. Montreal: McGill-Queen's University Press.

Spiller, Pablo T., and Rafael Gely. 2008. "Strategic Judicial Decision-Making." In *The Oxford Handbook of Law and Politics*, edited by Gregory Caldeira, R. Daniel Kelemen, and Keith E. Whittington, 34–45. Oxford: Oxford University Press.

Statistics Canada. 2019a. "Section 2 – Results at the Canada Level, 2018 to 2068." Population Projections for Canada (2018 to 2068), Provinces and Territories (2018 to 2043). 14 August 2019. https://www150.statcan.gc.ca /n1/pub/91-520-x/2019001/sect02-eng.htm.

– 2019b. "Section 3 – Results at the Provincial and Territorial Levels, 2018 to 2043 – Quebec." Population Projections for Canada (2018 to 2068), Provinces and Territories (2018 to 2043). 14 August 2019. https://www150.statcan .gc.ca/n1/pub/91-520-x/2019001/sect03-qc-eng.htm.

Stein, Michael B. 1984. "Canadian Constitutional Reform, 1927–1982: A Comparative Case Analysis over Time." *Publius* 14, no. 1: 121–39. https:// doi.org/10.2307/3330146.

Stevenson, Don. 1979. "The Role of Intergovernmental Conferences in the Decision-Making Process." In *Confrontation and Collaboration: Intergovernmental Relations in Canada Today*, edited by Richard. Simeon, 89–98. Toronto: Institute of Public Administration of Canada.

Sunstein, Cass R. 1995. "Incompletely Theorized Agreements." *Harvard Law Review* 108, no. 7: 1733–72. https://doi.org/10.2307/1341816.

Supreme Court of Canada. 1981. Reference re: Resolution to Amend the Constitution, 1 S.C.R. 753. Supreme Court of Canada.

Tansey, Oisín. 2007. "Process Tracing and Elite Interviewing: A Case for Non-probability Sampling." *PS: Political Science & Politics* 40, no. 4: 765–72. https://doi.org/10.1017/S1049096507071211.

Taras, David. 1991. "How Television Transformed the Meech Lake Negotiations." In *After Meech Lake: Lessons for the Future*, edited by David E. Smith, Peter MacKinnon, and John C. Courtney, 169–80. Saskatoon, SK: Fifth House.

Taylor, Verta. 1989. "Social Movement Continuity: The Women's Movement in Abeyance." *American Sociological Review* 54, no. 5: 761–75. https://doi.org /10.2307/2117752.

Telford, Hamish. 2003. "The Federal Spending Power in Canada: Nation-Building or Nation-Destroying?" *Publius* 33, no. 1: 23–44. https://doi.org /10.1093/oxfordjournals.pubjof.a004976.

Thomas, David M. 1997. *Whistling Past the Graveyard: Constitutional Abeyances, Quebec and the Future of Canada*. Toronto: Oxford University Press.

Tilly, James. 2001. "Social and Political Generations in Contemporary Britain." PhD diss., University of Oxford. https://scholar.google.com /scholar?hl=en&q=Tilley%2C+J.+2001.+%E2%80%9CSocial+and+Political +Generations+in+Contemporary+Britain.%E2%80%9D+D.Phil.+thesis%2C +Nuffield+College%2C+University+of+Oxford.

– 2002. "Political Generations and Partisanship in the UK, 1964–1997." *Journal of the Royal Statistical Society* 165, no. 1: 121–35. https://doi.org/10.1111 /1467-985X.00628.

Tilly, James, and Geoffrey Evans. 2014. "Ageing and Generational Effects on Vote Choice: Combining Cross-Sectional and Panel Data to Estimate APC Effects." *Electoral Studies* 33 (March 2014): 19–27.

Tremblay, Luc B. 2009. "The Bouchard-Taylor Report on Cultural and Religious Accommodation: Multiculturalism by Any Other Name?" Working Paper, EUI Law. https://cadmus.eui.eu//handle/1814/12971.

Trudeau, Pierre. 1987. "P.E. Trudeau: 'Say Goodbye to the Dream' of One Canada." *Toronto Star / La Presse*, 27 May 1987.

Turgeon, Luc. 2014. "Minority Nations and Attitudes towards Immigration: The Case of Quebec." *Nations and Nationalism* 20, no. 2: 317–36. https://doi.org/10.1111/nana.12068.

Vachet, Benjamin. 2019. "Démarche judiciaire pour rendre la Constitution officiellement bilingue." *Le Droit*, 19 September 2019.

Vallières, Pierre. 1971. *White N******* of America*. Toronto: McClelland & Stewart.

Verney, Douglas V. 1986. *Three Civilizations, Two Cultures, One State: Canada's Political Traditions*. Durham, NC: Duke University Press.

Vipond, Robert C. 1993. "Seeing Canada through the Referendum: Still a House Divided." *Publius* 23, no. 3: 39–55. https://doi.org/10.2307/3330841.

Walters, Mark D. 2011. "The Law behind the Conventions of the Constitution: Reassessing the Prorogation Debate." *Journal of Parliamentary and Political Law* 5: 127–50.

– 2023. "Constitutive Power and the Nation(s) of Quebec." In *A Written Constitution for Quebec?*, edited by Richard Albert and Leonid Sirota, 162–187. Montreal: McGill-Queen's University Press.

Watson, Patrick, and André Pratte, eds. 2008. *Reconquering Canada: Quebec Federalists Speak Up for Change*. Vancouver, BC: Douglas & McIntyre.

Weaver, R. Kent. 1992. "Political Institutions and Canada's Constitutional Crisis." In *The Collapse of Canada?*, edited by R. Kent Weaver, 7–75. Washington, DC: Brookings Institution.

Webber, Jeremy H.A. 2021. *The Constitution of Canada: A Contextual Analysis*. Second edition. Constitutional Systems of the World. Oxford; Hart Publishing.

Well, Paul. 2013."The Charter of Values: Old Dogs, Nous Tricks." Macleans.ca (blog), 12 September 2013.

White, Graham. 2010. "Cabinets and First Ministers." In *Auditing Canadian Democracy*, edited by William Cross, 40–64. Canadian Democratic Audit. Vancouver: UBC Press.

Wiseman, Nelson. 2007. *In Search of Canadian Political Culture*. Vancouver: UBC Press.

Wood, Donna. 2018. *Federalism in Action: The Devolution of Canada's Public Employment Service, 1995–2015*. The Institute of Public Administration of Canada in Public Management and Governance. Toronto: University of Toronto Press.

Woods, Eric Taylor, Robert Schertzer, and Eric Kaufmann. 2011. "Ethno-national Conflict and Its Management." *Commonwealth & Comparative Politics* 49, no. 2: 153–61. https://doi.org/10.1080/14662043.2011.564469.

Young, Huguette. 2000. "Malgré les sondages, les libéraux ne changent pas leur stratégie au Québec." La Presse Canadienne, 4 November 2000.

Young, Robert. 2006. "Jean Chrétien's Québec Legacy: Coasting, Then Stickhandling Hard." In *The Chrétien Legacy: Politics and Public Policy in Canada*, edited by Lois Harder and Steve Patten, 37–61. Montreal: McGill-Queen's Press.

Zubrzycki, Geneviève. 2016. *Beheading the Saint: Nationalism, Religion, and Secularism in Quebec*. Chicago: University of Chicago Press.

Index

abeyances: overview, 17, 21–5, 47–8; vs. ambiguities, 29–30; Canadian, 31, 32, 37, 54, 125, 142, 158n2; and Canadian federalism crisis, 31–8; confronting, 24, 54, 142; and constitutional fictions and myths, 30; vs. conventions, 28–9; defined, 21–2, 24; effect of adding provinces, 37; as federalist strategy, 3, 4–5, 9–10, 16; and future challenges to national unity, 149–51; global examples, 24–5; maintaining, 35, 46, 47, 110, 142, 149–51; vs. omissions, 30; politicizing, 25–7; restoring, 27, 38, 39, 47, 125; social context, 26; sources of, 22–3; and state secularism, 110; Supreme Court's role, 37, 44–7; as taboos, 15–16, 37–9, 48, 112, 143; theories, 4, 17, 38–9, 158n1. *See also* agenda setting; contract-compact dispute; intergovernmental relations; non-constitutional accommodations
Action démocratique du Québec (ADQ), 61, 101, 123, 139
agenda setting: abeyance strategy, 22, 143; effect of issue salience on, 50, 55–8, 64; by political leaders,

4, 16, 50, 55–63, 159n3; and reluctance of federalists to reopen the question, 4, 5, 54; role of policy entrepreneurs, 4, 59, 63, 64
agnostic constitutionalism, 23, 45
agricultural policies, 41
Alberta, 39, 60, 81, 96, 136
Andras-Bienvenue Agreement, 87
anglophones: anti-anglophone sentiment, 88, 133; and dualist institutions, 36, 87; economic domination by, 95, 96, 115; included in term *Canadian*, 157n3; outlook of, 116, 148; support of political parties, 61–2, 123; and *la survivance*, 95. *See also* language rights
Aquin, Hubert, 94, 109
autonomy, dynamic vs. static, 8, 19

baby boomers. *See* generational change
Bayefsky, Anne, 18
Beaulieu, Mario, 97
Behiels, Michael, 72
Béland, Daniel, 13, 136
Bill 21 (Act Respecting the Laicity of the State), 62, 91, 103–4, 148, 159n1. See also *laïcité*

www.ingramcontent.com/pod-product-compliance
Lightning Source LLC
Chambersburg PA
CBHW020458030426

42337CB00011B/148